Maryland
in
Africa

CAMPBELL, Penelope. **Maryland in Africa; the Maryland State Colonization Society, 1831-1857.** Illinois, 1971. 264p tab bibl 75-131058. 7.95. ISBN 0-252-00133-8

CHOICE   OCT. '71
History, Geography & Travel

At odds with the parent American Colonization Society over operation of its Liberian settlement, the Maryland State Colonization Society decided in 1833 to found its own African colony, Maryland in Liberia, at Cape Palmas, 200 miles south of Monrovia. For the next 21 years the society wheedled funds, coaxed several hundred skeptical Negroes into resettlement, and struggled to keep internal conflicts and quarrels with neighboring tribes from destroying the colony. In 1854 the settlement achieved independence and three years later it was absorbed into the Republic of Liberia. Campbell has researched and described these developments with a competence that recommends *Maryland in Africa* to general readers and serious scholars alike. The study provides splendid insights into the problems of colonization and the ideology of border-state reformers pursuing a rather left-handed solution to the race problem. Weaknesses exist, to be sure: no maps of the Cape Palmas area, and its indigenous population is given short shrift. Little information is provided on Maryland Negroes to support the questionable claim that "their situation was reasor   tolerable." Despite these shortcomings, *Maryland in Africa* joi.   .'. J. Staudenraus' *The*

Continued

CAMPBELL

CHOICE   OCT. '71
History, Geography & Travel

African colonization movement, 1816-1865 (1961, o.p.) as required reading for students of the crusade to end racial injustice by deporting its victims.

MARYLAND IN AFRICA

The Maryland State Colonization Society
1831-1857

PENELOPE CAMPBELL

University of Illinois Press
Urbana Chicago London

© 1971 by The Board of Trustees of the University of Illinois
Manufactured in the United States of America
Library of Congress Catalog Card No. 75-131058
252 00133 8

Acknowledgments

In the preparation of this book I have had the good counsel and assistance of many. Lowell Ragatz, my mentor at The Ohio State University, deserves to head the list because it was he who introduced me to the subject of African colonization. His careful scrutiny of my graduate work and his personal interest in my career have been valuable.

Among those who helped me gather research material none deserves more praise than staff members at the Maryland Historical Society. They facilitated the use of manuscripts and cheerfully tolerated the months of daily visits. Mention should be made also of the staff at the Houghton Library, Harvard College, where the ABCFM Papers are housed.

Agnes Scott College contributed substantially to the project in the way of financial assistance and a lightened teaching load. My colleagues in the Department of History and Political Science gave advice and showed understanding throughout the venture.

A special friend who has taken pride in this project and assisted with publication details is Seaborn Phillips Jones. His good humor and "interested layman's" view have kept the final stages from being merely a chore.

Ultimately, the greatest allies one has are those at home. In my case, there are two homes: one in Decatur, Georgia, where my friend Llewellyn Willet Wilburn has sustained me through a gamut of experiences, and another, my family residence, in Baltimore, Maryland. For their early nurture and limitless confidence I dedicate this work to my parents, Marie Ewers and Welford Shepard Campbell.

Penelope Campbell

Decatur, Georgia
December, 1970

Contents

Maryland
in
Africa

Introduction

The presence of Negroes within a white American society has been viewed with alarm by some citizens since colonial days. The supposed incompatibility of the two races as neighbors on the North American continent has preoccupied both the lowly and the high-placed. From the beginning slavery was often condemned, but opponents never considered that bondsmen should be set free without provision for their removal. Originally, abolition went hand in hand with colonization. Free-born as well as manumitted blacks were universally considered nuisances, either for their presumed nefarious influence upon slaves or for their anomalous position in the community. Many Americans believed that they, too, should be relocated beyond the United States's borders.

The colonial legislature of Virginia was the first to concern itself with the free black problem. In 1691 it prohibited further emancipation of slaves unless the owner arranged for their transportation out of the colony within six months.[1] Early in the nine-

---

1 Henry Noble Sherwood, "Early Negro Deportation Projects," *Mississippi Valley Historical Review,* II, no. 4 (Mar., 1916), 485.

teenth century the Virginia state legislature renewed its interest in the problem of Negroes residing there. First, it considered the establishment of a penal colony for those convicted of conspiracy or rebellion. Thomas Jefferson, a native son personally favoring colonization, was asked, as president of the United States, to make arrangements for carrying out that project. The Chief Executive, who wanted blacks colonized both outside the territorial limits of the United States and apart from any prospective national possession, corresponded with Great Britain about the use of the newly established Sierra Leone colony.[2] Agreement was never reached, but Jefferson's estimate of colonization as wise from the viewpoint of both races was not diminished. He foresaw the eventual extermination of one race or the other unless separation were effected.[3] Later, the Virginia legislature solicited the services of President James Monroe in obtaining territory for a colony in Africa, or along the coast of the North Pacific, or at some other spot outside the United States.[4]

One of the first serious proposals from an individual for the establishment of an African colony was made about 1790 by Ferdinando Fairfax, a neighbor and friend of George Washington. A promoter by nature, Fairfax advocated obtaining territory for a colony in Africa because the climate there seemed best suited for Negroes. Even more important, the miles of ocean separating white Americans from the colonists would prevent any intermarriage. His plan called for the U.S. government to provide for the defense, support, and administration of the colony until it could stand on its own. Moreover, the emigrants were to come not merely from Virginia but from the whole nation. Fairfax's motives were both selfish and religious: he expected the United States to benefit from a profitable commerce with Africa and he considered the colonial establishment a means of spreading Christianity on the Dark Continent.

A New Englander stirred by the plight of Negroes in the

---

2 Thomas Jefferson, *Writings,* ed. Paul Leicester Ford, 10 vols. (New York: G. P. Putnam's Sons, 1892–1899), III, 243–44; VIII, 104–5.

3 *Ibid.,* III, 244.

4 Herman V. Ames, *State Documents on Federal Relations,* no. 96 (Philadelphia: University of Pennsylvania, 1911), pp. 195–96.

United States was Samuel D. Hopkins, Yale graduate and long-time pastor of the First Congregational Church in Newport, Rhode Island. He was bold enough not only to preach against the slave trade, in which some of his parishioners engaged, but he also devised a plan for the education of prospective Negro missionaries to Africa. In 1793 he spelled out a program for the establishment of a colony of American blacks which, he believed, would spread Christianity on that continent, lead to the end of slavery in America, and provide a home and new opportunities for the Negro. Nothing concrete came of Hopkins' idea before his death in 1803. However, at one time in the years during which he was pondering the colony idea, he consulted Granville Sharp, the English philanthropist and humanitarian, about the possibility of experimental groups of American Negro families emigrating to Sierra Leone. Indeed, Hopkins seems to have gotten some of his ideas from his dynamic correspondent.[5]

Sharp was prominent in securing the Mansfield judgment of 1772 which ruled that slavery was contrary to English law and that there could therefore be no bondsmen in that country. In 1786 Sharp was a leader, though not a formal member, of the London-based Committee for the Black Poor. Undertaking the task of settling destitute Negroes in Africa, Sharp made plans for establishing a colony near the Sierra Leone River. The British Treasury underwrote the operation, Sharp drew up a constitution which provided for self-government, and the committee rounded up willing and unwilling prospects wherever they could be found. After numerous delays, including outbreaks of fever and repairs to vessels in the small fleet, 411 passengers set sail from Plymouth, England, in April, 1787.

The story of this first settlement in the Province of Freedom, as Sharp liked to call it, is an unhappy one. In spite of careful planning, abundant stores, and painstaking devotion by the committee to the project, disaster struck with regularity. Within three months after landing, a third of the emigrants were dead of fever. Even industrious colonists found their agricultural efforts futile and had to depend heavily upon stores which had

---

5 Sherwood, "Early Negro Deportation Projects," pp. 490–91, 505.

been sent out. As these dwindled, the new settlers were reduced to working for neighboring slave traders or seeking employment on passing ships. Less than a year after having embarked from England, only 130 blacks were left in the colony. Sharp, directing operations from home, undertook to send out more emigrants and to provide the colony with livestock and supplies.

Meanwhile, another group, to which Sharp likewise belonged, set about to form a private concern to take over the faltering settlement. At length, in 1791 the Sierra Leone Company, having won abolitionist support throughout Britain, succeeded in getting parliamentary approval for its incorporation. However, Sharp, although a director of the new organization, was no longer its leader because he emphasized the philanthropic rather than the business nature of the company. The other directors passed over him to elect Henry Thornton, a wealthy banker, chairman in 1791 and thereafter the latter was the dominant force behind the settlement. Yet even a commercial concern with an eye on profits could not place it on a self-sufficient footing. The company was soon dependent upon parliamentary grants which, by 1806, totaled £67,000. The following year a bill which transferred the colony to the Crown passed Parliament and, on January 1, 1808, the Union Jack replaced the company's flag above the tiny settlement. Of the original settlers, only ten were listed as heads of families in 1802 and in 1808 the total number of inhabitants was just 2,000.[6]

Nonetheless, the existence, however tenuous, of a colony on the coast of Africa founded by voluntary means gave impetus to a concerted action in the United States. The spirit of colonization, already widely diffused throughout the nation, was to add a new movement to the numerous benevolent organizations springing up during the first decades of the nineteenth century. All that was necessary was someone to initiate it. The spark kindling the flame was provided by Robert Finley of Baskingridge, New Jersey, a prominent Presbyterian clergyman who

---

6 Christopher Fyfe, *A History of Sierra Leone* (London: Oxford University Press, 1962), pp. 14–28, 97–98.

counted theologians, educators, politicians, and wealthy businessmen among his intimates. Influenced by the British efforts in Sierra Leone, Finley envisioned a colony which would enable white Americans to right their forefathers' wrongs. He expected both Africa and America to benefit. The former would receive partially civilized and Christianized settlers; the latter would eliminate a servile class in its presence. Finley believed Negroes capable of improvement and self-government but he also argued that only in Africa, which God had designed as their home, could they achieve that equality necessary for their uplift. Well aware that such a project would require large sums of money and widespread public support, Finley determined to make Washington the movement's headquarters.

In December, 1816, after enlisting the aid of his brother-in-law Elias B. Caldwell, clerk of the Supreme Court, and of Francis Scott Key, then best known as a prominent Washington attorney, Finley called for an organizational meeting to be held at the Davis Hotel. A small group of distinguished men met there on December 21. Presided over by Henry Clay, it voted to establish a colonization society and a few days later it reconvened in the hall of the House of Representatives, adopted a constitution, and chose the name "American Society for Colonizing the Free People of Color in the United States." [7]

The subsequent effort to persuade Congress to provide funds for an African colony was less successful. In 1817 the congressional Committee on the Slave Trade rejected a proposal that Congress back such an undertaking. Two years later President Monroe, who had himself favored the colonization idea ever since his governorship in Virginia when the legislature commanded him to communicate with President Jefferson about an overseas settlement for black insurrectionists, was unable to persuade the Cabinet to endorse his interpretation of the new Slave Trade Act. By that law the president was authorized to make arrangements for the care and removal of rescued Africans

[7] Philip J. Staudenraus, *The African Colonization Movement, 1816–1865* (New York: Columbia University Press, 1961), pp. 17–30.

stranded in this country, to send a naval squadron to African waters, and to resettle in Africa those Negroes retrieved from slave traders. Under its authority he sought to apply the $100,-000 appropriation to purchasing African lands and establishing a colony there. To this, his official family was distinctly cool.

Nonetheless, colonizationists won the battle when they badgered Attorney General William Wirt into approving a broad interpretation. President Monroe was consequently able to appoint two agents to travel to Africa with a group of laborers and mechanics to prepare a station for westward-bound Africans rescued from the slave traders. The two agents were men nominated by the American Colonization Society, and the expedition of eighty-six, sailing aboard the *Elizabeth* early in 1820, was clearly a colonizing venture. This initial group settled at Sherbro Island, off the West African coast south of Sierra Leone. Within a few weeks both agents were dead of fever and the remaining settlers fled to British protection at Freetown in Sierra Leone. A second expedition in 1821 fared no better.

Finally, late in 1821 Lieutenant Robert F. Stockton, a naval officer, and Doctor Eli Ayres, a Baltimore physician, acting as agents of the United States government, purchased Cape Mesurado, near the mouth of the St. Paul's River some 225 miles south of Sierra Leone, from the local chieftains for less than $300. The third group of settlers arrived there in August, 1822, to augment those already brought back from Sierra Leone. By the middle of 1823 there were 150 colonists at the cape.[8] The population steadily grew, reaching the 1,000 mark in 1830. Under Jehudi Ashmun's energetic administration, Liberia, as the new colony was called, expanded from its original site on Cape Mesurado to an area encompassing miles of territory to the interior along the St. Paul's and other rivers and an Atlantic coastal strip southward. Ashmun pressured many a chieftain into granting the colony control over strategically held locations. Trading rights, on a most-favored-nation basis, were likewise acquired. Liberia gradually gained strength as it increased in population and size, but citizens displayed a marked aversion

8 *Ibid.*, pp. 50–66.

to agricultural enterprise, preferring to engage in petty barter activities.[9]

Under the American government's auspices, the Colonization Society had obtained the site for its settlement. From then on, however, it was obliged to carry on as a private agency dependent upon individual citizens for financial support. As its monetary needs increased, the body turned to fund-raising. The establishment of state and local auxiliaries to publicize the society's activities and the colony's progress as well as to raise money and to recruit emigrants became increasingly important. To carry out this objective, as well as to coordinate other society activities and to oversee the colony's administration from home base, Ralph Gurley, a young Yale graduate destined to spend most of his life in the service of the society, was chosen as resident agent in 1823. Thenceforth, the society's operations were widely extended.

Auxiliaries were founded both in New England and in the southern states. From time to time, traveling agents, some voluntary, others commissioned by society managers, toured the cities and countryside appealing for aid. A variety of arguments were employed to arouse interest: the missionary aspect of the effort was always stressed, and the evils of the slave trade were likewise harped upon. Colonization as an orderly method of emancipation was a favorite text in the North, while the approach in the South emphasized the potential of insurrection among the blacks and the need to provide a home for those whose owners wished to free them.[10]

The strikingly different appeals made to northerners and southerners pointed up a growing problem within the national movement. Early colonization advocates supported the society for different reasons. Northerners generally looked to it as a means of ending slavery, while southerners favored the scheme because it offered hope for removing freed blacks from their

---

9 *Ibid.*, pp. 152–56; see Charles Henry Huberich, *The Political and Legislative History of Liberia*, 2 vols. (New York: Central Book Co., 1947), vol. I.

10 Staudenraus, *African Colonization Movement*, pp. 80, 104–5.

midst. The extent of this sectional disagreement became apparent only when the cause became involved in politics. In 1824 the society renewed its efforts to secure federal aid. Encouraged by prominent colonizationists, the legislatures of such states as Ohio, Connecticut, and New Jersey endorsed federal assistance. Each, in its resolutions, also attacked the institution of slavery. The response from southern legislatures was a vehement denunciation of all colonization proposals as part of an abolition plot in interference with the right of each state to control and regulate its own affairs.[11] The subject, moreover, became a partisan issue in the 1828 presidential election. Henry Clay, as John Quincy Adams' Secretary of State, identified it with his own program; Andrew Jackson carefully preserved southern support by a cautious attitude.

Jackson's election, while dashing colonizationist hopes for immediate direct federal aid, did not affect the government's African agency or alter the naval protection accorded Liberia. These continued in spite of the disclosure that since 1819 the U.S. Treasury had paid out $264,710 for the repatriation and care of a mere 260 Africans rescued from illicit slave traders. Throughout this period of controversy the society in Washington and its secretary, Ralph Gurley, assumed a conciliatory and mediating role. Gurley declared that the body was not an abolitionist organization but, rather, one aiming at the removal of the free Negro population, which he characterized as ignorant, vicious, and unhappy.[12] Nevertheless, the battle between southerners and northerners continued to rage. Colonization remained an issue of partisan debate, with the consequence that direct federal aid was never received and that unanimity of feeling necessary for the complete success of any movement was absent.

Among colonization proponents, none was more sensitive to the factionalism within the organization than a small group of prominent Baltimoreans. After all, Francis Scott Key and Senator Robert H. Goldsborough were among the Marylanders present at the founding of the national movement. One of the first

11 *Ibid.*, pp. 169–73.
12 *Ibid.*, pp. 171, 178.

state auxiliaries was founded in Baltimore. In 1817 a group of citizens approved a constitution which stated that the body's object was "to promote and execute a plan to colonize (*with their own consent*), the free people of color in our country, either in Africa or such other place as Congress shall deem most expedient. . . ." [13]

Doctor Richard Randall, a native of Annapolis and a graduate of St. John's College, was colonial agent in Liberia before dying there in 1829 of fever.[14] Doctor Eli Ayres, so influential in the purchase of Cape Mesurado, was an active member of the Maryland auxiliary. Furthermore, Maryland interest in the cause is attested to by the reorganization of their branch in 1827. Meeting in Baltimore, these friends of colonization stressed the desirability of establishing as many chapters as possible in every town, village, and district of Maryland. They stated the object of their agency to be the improved efficiency of the parent society's operations, the procurement of members, the promotion and superintendence of emigration, the instruction of the public, and the collection of funds.[15] In the Maryland legislature that year, colonization interest was manifested by approval of an annual appropriation for the cause. Asserting its belief that the scheme was "the only one which can promise practical benefit to the country, or to that class of the community which it is intended to relieve," the legislature voted the sum of $1,000 a year to the state auxiliary for the establishment on the African coast of free people of color who had been actual residents of Maryland during the twelve months preceding their embarkation.[16] The attention in Maryland was thus upon the free Negro population; early colonizationists intended no interference with the institution of slavery.

In spite of the diligence of leading citizens and legislative

13 Maryland Historical Society, *Broadsides*, "Constitution for the Government of the Maryland Auxiliary Society, for Colonizing the Free People of Color of the United States," [1817].
14 Staudenraus, *African Colonization Movement*, p. 162.
15 Maryland Historical Society, "African Colonization. Proceedings of a Meeting of the Friends of African Colonization, Held in the City of Baltimore, on the 17 October, 1827."
16 *Maryland Colonization Journal*, n.s., IX, no. 12 (May, 1858), 183.

encouragement, the cause in Maryland languished. In 1829
emigration from the state was so small that the parent society
was unable to collect the state's subscription for that year. Moreover, the dearth of emigrants so discouraged supporters that all
interest seemed to die out.[17] However, the visit to Baltimore
early in 1831 of Robert Smith Finley, son of the Reverend
Robert Finley who had initiated the national movement, dras-
tically changed the situation. As a traveling agent for the parent
society, young Finley held meetings in numerous Baltimore
churches where he appealed to supporters for larger contributions. On February 14, 1831, he addressed "a large and respectable meeting" at the First Presbyterian Church. John
Latrobe, a Baltimore attorney about to become Maryland's
leading colonization advocate, described the gathering: "I introduced Finley, he carried the audience away, all present became Colonizationists. . . ."[18] On February 16 Finley spoke
at St. Paul's Church and on February 20 in the Methodist Protestant church on Pitt Street and at another on Liberty Street.[19]

The Finley visit coincided with a swell of feeling among
Marylanders that cooperation with the parent society was re-
tarding the movement in their state. Citizens began to ask what
good was being accomplished by the national organization.
They charged that contributions credited to them in the society's official journal, the *African Repository,* were not spent
for Maryland emigrants. Although large numbers were sent
from below the Potomac, the colonization movement north of
it was moribund.[20] The consequence of this more critical atti-

17 John Latrobe, *Maryland in Liberia. A History of the Colony Planted by
   the Maryland State Colonization Society under the Auspices of the State
   of Maryland, U.S., at Cape Palmas on the South-West Coast of Africa,
   1833–1853,* Maryland Historical Society Fund Publication 21 (Baltimore:
   John Murphy, 1885), pp. 11–12.
18 Quoted in John Edward Semmes, *John H. B. Latrobe and His Times,
   1803–1891* (Baltimore: Norman, Remington Co., 1917), p. 144.
19 *Baltimore Gazette and Daily Advertiser,* Feb. 15, 19, 1831.
20 Maryland State Colonization Society MSS (hereafter MSCS), *Corresponding Secretary Books,* vol. I, John Latrobe to Courtland Van Rensselaer,
   Baltimore, July 10, 1833.

tude was the founding of a new state society which, acting independently in fund collection and recruitment, was expected to produce a great exodus of free blacks to Liberia. The effort to bring this about forms a new chapter in colonization history.

I

The First Year

Maryland in 1831 was beginning to participate in a nationwide prosperity. Although since colonial times her one-crop dependence upon tobacco had resulted in soil impoverishment and economic depression from which her farmers had not yet recovered, the state was on the eve of a great agricultural thrust. Increasingly flour and grain were becoming major exports. Truck farming proved profitable as such population centers as Baltimore and Washington swelled in size. Diversified farming and attention to land improvement were the order of the day.[1] Significantly, slave labor fit into the new pattern as well as it had into the plantation system, although the fact was not generally recognized by nonslaveholders.[2]

In large measure the agricultural revival after 1830 was due to the new transportation network which enabled farmers to

1 Avery O. Craven, *Soil Exhaustion as a Factor in the Agricultural History of Virginia and Maryland, 1606–1860* (Urbana: University of Illinois, 1926), pp. 122–47.
2 *Ibid.*, p. 163.

get their products to market. Turnpikes, canals, and railroads were under construction in every part of the young republic and no less so in Maryland. The "great western road" from Cumberland to Ohio, with links to Baltimore and Washington, was the first to connect the back country with the entrepots along the eastern seaboard. In rapid succession the Chesapeake and Ohio Canal, the Chesapeake and Ohio Railroad, the Baltimore and Susquehanna Railroad, and lesser projects were undertaken.[3] Though completion was slow, these improvements encouraged agricultural as well as commercial development. Baltimore particularly benefited, as did Cumberland, Frederick, and Annapolis to a lesser extent. Baltimore harbor became the home of the great clipper ships which carried Maryland goods over the seven seas.

Yet, for all the outward appearances of boom, Maryland in the 1830's showed certain weak points. A most serious sign was the emigration of native sons and new arrivals to other parts, particularly the West. The fact that there was a mere 9 per cent increase, 27,000 persons, in the white population during the entire third decade is accentuated by evidence that more than 50,000 foreign immigrants entered through Baltimore in those ten years.[4] Avery Craven, in his pioneering study of soil exhaustion, attributed the emigration from Maryland to lost faith in the impoverished land.[5]

Another weakness was in Maryland's social system. The intermingling of whites, free blacks, and slaves constituted a basically unstable environment that allowed little change that was not seen as threatening to major groupings within it. In 1830 white inhabitants numbered 291,108; blacks totaled 155,932, of whom 102,994 were slave. Three southern counties, running from Baltimore to the Potomac River—Anne Arundel, Prince Georges, and Charles—held the greatest number of

---

3 J. Thomas Scharf, *History of Maryland,* 3 vols. (Hatboro, Pa.: Tradition Press, 1967), III, 153–70, 182–86.
4 U.S. Bureau of the Census, *History and Statistics of the State of Maryland According to the Returns of the Seventh Census of the United States, 1850* (Washington: Gideon and Co., 1852), pp. 20–21.
5 Craven, *Soil Exhaustion,* p. 122.

slaves. Free Negroes were fairly evenly scattered over the state, although 30 per cent lived in Baltimore City.[6]

In Maryland, as farther south, the Negro was presumed to be a slave. Many, especially in their local communities, moved about freely. As farm hands, laborers, and domestics, however, they were at the mercy of their masters. Frederick Douglass, in bondage at this time on the Eastern Shore, later testified that life was hard.[7] Perhaps the capriciousness of masters was the most oppressive aspect of servitude. A quarter of Maryland's white population must have been connected with slave ownership in 1830.[8] The average holding was about six, although one family owned more than 300.

The free Negro, however threatened with challenges about his background, enjoyed a wide liberty in getting a living. He could acquire and dispose of property and bring court action, although Negro rights were restricted in giving evidence against whites. There were limitations on assemblage, but these were local, often mild, and frequently overlooked. Concerning the legal status of the free black, one scholar concluded that "he was protected in his essential rights and was permitted to improve his condition."[9]

His essential rights, however, excluded the possession of firearms, enfranchisement, and participation in an educational program. The free Negro endured poor living conditions and, in fact, strived to eat and dress as well as slaves. Sanitation was bad, even by standards of that day, and in plague seasons as in normal times, the mortality rate for freemen ran higher than for the rest of the population, white or slave.[10] In many respects

6 U.S. Bureau of the Census, *Fifth Census, 1830* (Washington: Duff Green, 1832), pp. 82–83.

7 Frederick Douglass, *My Bondage and My Freedom* (New York: Miller, Orton and Co., 1857).

8 U.S. Bureau of the Census, *A Century of Population Growth from the First Census of the United States to the Twelfth, 1790–1900* (Washington: U.S. Government Printing Office, 1909), p. 138. In 1790 slave ownership involved 38.7 per cent of the population; in 1850, including the District of Columbia, it involved 21.9 per cent.

9 James M. Wright, *The Free Negro in Maryland, 1634–1860* (New York: Columbia University, 1921), p. 129.

10 *Ibid., passim.*

free blacks suffered a lower status in society than slaves, for whereas slaves were often the object of sympathy and solicitation, freemen were almost universally treated with suspicion and contempt. Slaveholders considered free blacks the greatest threat to that institution which they held so dear while even abolitionists harbored biases.

This was the scene in Maryland when interest in colonization revived. By invitation to the general public published in the *Baltimore Gazette and Daily Advertiser* on February 21, 1831, colonization advocates met in the parlor of the Athenaeum that evening. Nicholas Brice of the Baltimore City Court presided and both Robert S. Finley, concluding his speaking tour in the city, and John Latrobe, heretofore active in the American Colonization Society, addressed the group. Stirred by their eloquent pleas, the audience voted that the idea of a colony of free Negroes from the United States on the African coast was "perfectly practicable." Moreover, it recognized that a greater concentration of effort and multiplication of resources than previously attained were urgently needed if success were to be achieved. The group immediately formed a state society and adopted a constitution, drawn up in advance by Latrobe. Although dissatisfied with delays encountered in sending Maryland emigrants to Liberia and conscious of the growing rift between northern and southern supporters of the Washington society, Maryland colonizationists still considered themselves a part of that national movement. Article 2 of their constitution declared, "The object to which it [the society] shall be exclusively directed shall be to aid the Parent Institution at Washington, in the colonization of free people of color of Maryland with their own consent to the coast of Africa."

With this specific objective proclaimed, the new society set about to erect a framework for the organization. At this historic February meeting terms for membership and for administration were laid down. An annual contribution of at least one dollar was necessary for membership; a lump payment of $20 or more made the donor a life member. There were to be three presidents, delineated as first, second, and third. Three vice-presidents, twelve managers, a secretary, and a treasurer rounded out the leadership. The Board of Managers, including all the other officers as *ex officio* members, was to transact society business, fill vacancies, and draw up bylaws. Annual open meetings were to be held each second Monday of December in Baltimore.[11]

Several days later the officers met at Judge Brice's chambers and adopted the bylaws. Except for special occasions, the Board of Managers was to meet quarterly. The highest-ranking officer would preside. An Executive Committee of three was established to carry on day-by-day operations. It was, however, prohibited from taking any major step. It could not decide upon emigration, charter a vessel, or spend more than $100 without board approval. Recognizing that women would undoubtedly constitute an important element of the society, the board stipulated in one bylaw that female subscribers could vote by proxy at all elections for society officers.

The question of an agent to traverse the state was one of the first to occupy the new officers. They resolved to appoint an agent who would organize auxiliary societies, keep an accurate list of members and donations, recruit emigrants, and prepare and supervise their embarkations to Liberia. On March 7 Doctor Eli Ayres was named to fill this important post. While not traveling for the society, he was to serve as resident agent in Baltimore. His salary was set at $1,000 per annum, plus daily expenses while in the field. The latter monies were to come exclusively from collections he made but, when stationed in Baltimore, the salary was to be paid from society funds. The Executive Committee was to issue his instructions.[12]

The list of officers elected at the Athenaeum in Baltimore that February night is an impressive one. George Hoffman, selected first president, was one of the organizers of the Baltimore and Ohio Railroad and for many years served as one of its directors. The second president, Thomas Ellicott, was president of the Union Bank of Maryland. Nicholas Brice, the third president, was the chief judge of the Baltimore City Court. Doctor

11 MSCS MSS, *Records of 1831*, Feb. 21, 1831.
12 *Ibid.*, meetings of the Board of Managers, Feb. 24, Mar. 7, 1831.

Thomas E. Bond, a vice-president, was a prominent city physician. A founder of the University of Maryland Medical School, he was a devout Christian layman who retired from his medical practice in 1844 to become editor of the *Christian Advocate*, the official organ of the Methodist Episcopal Church. The body's first treasurer was John Hoffman, a highly successful businessman. The secretary, James Howard, came from an old-line Maryland family. He held a number of important posts in the community during a long and busy life, including the presidency of the Baltimore and Susquehanna Railroad and of the Franklin Bank.

More men of eminence were found among the society's managers. Moses Sheppard, successful both in the grocery business and as a manufacturer of cotton twine, is today remembered as the donor of the bulk of his estate, some $600,000, for the founding of the Asylum for Curable Insane in Baltimore County. Peter Hoffman was also a successful businessman, continuing the dry goods firm founded by his father. Solomon Etting participated in a number of ventures. Early in his life he ran a hardware store and later organized the city's Union Bank. He was a founder of the Baltimore and Ohio Railroad and served it as a director. At another time he operated a general shipping and commercial enterprise.[13] Doctor Samuel Baker was a professor at the University of Maryland and at the Maryland College of Medicine. Just prior to his participation in the Maryland colonization movement, he completed a six-year term as the Baltimore Medical Society's president.[14] Latrobe, himself selected a manager at the first meeting, later remarked that "in place of filling the Board with clergymen, the directors chosen

13 See *Baltimore: Past and Present* (Baltimore: Richardson and Bennett, 1871); Richard Henry Spencer, ed., *Genealogical and Memorial Encyclopedia of the State of Maryland*, 2 vols. (New York: American Historical Society, 1919), vol. I; *Biographical Cyclopedia of Representative Men of Maryland and District of Columbia* (Baltimore: National Biographical Publishing Co., 1879); and Abraham D. Glushakov, *A Pictorial History of Maryland Jewry* (Baltimore: Jewish Voice Publishing Co., 1955).

14 Eugene F. Cordell, *The Medical Annals of Maryland, 1799–1899* (Baltimore: Medical and Chirurgical Faculty of the State of Maryland, 1903), p. 310.

were businessmen of intelligence and character—a good business arrangement, but one that prejudiced the Society then and ever afterwards with the clergy." [15]

Of all the new state society officers, none was to play a more significant role in its history than John H. B. Latrobe. In addition to his election as a manager, he shortly thereafter became a member of the Executive Committee. Latrobe was born in Philadelphia in 1803. His father, the architect Benjamin H. Latrobe, was called to Washington in 1807 to complete the Capitol. John entered West Point Military Academy in December, 1817, but withdrew during his senior year, following his father's death. He then began the study of law in Baltimore in the office of his father's friend, General Robert Goodloe Harper. It was here that he first became aware of colonization, the movement to transport free blacks across the Atlantic, for Harper's two leading interests were internal improvement and African settlement. Through Harper's efforts Latrobe met the leading men of Baltimore. He also became acquainted with Doctor Ayres after Ayres's trip with Lieutenant Stockton to purchase Cape Mesurado. With Ayres's help he drew the first map of Liberia.[16] Although Latrobe grew in prominence as a lawyer and enjoyed a notable legal career, a significant portion of his energies from early manhood to old age went into the colonization movement.

The enthusiasm of the new Colonization Society's officers was reflected immediately by their decision to send an emigrant vessel to Liberia in June, 1831. This was considered wise strategy for gaining public confidence, promoting the formation of auxiliary societies throughout the state, and acquiring funds.[17] At the same time the board directed the secretary to correspond with the parent society about arrangements for receiving the Maryland emigrants at Liberia.

It was now that the Maryland society learned how it was

---

15 Quoted in John Edward Semmes, *John H. B. Latrobe and His Times, 1803–1891* (Baltimore: Norman, Remington Co., 1917), p. 144.

16 *Ibid.*, pp. 139, 141–42.

17 MSCS MSS, *Records of 1831*, meeting of the Board of Managers, Mar. 7, 1831.

viewed in Washington. The American Colonization Society's Board of Managers looked upon the new venture as a mere adjunct to the parent organization, promoting the objects of that group and raising funds within Maryland. It expected all money to be handed over to the central treasury and all arrangements for expeditions to be made through its offices. The Maryland society was not to be an independent movement, although the Washington board was willing to concede some direction of funds.[18]

The Maryland society's attitude was a willingness to cooperate in sending expeditions but an insistence upon the exclusive management and appropriation of its own funds. Citing the inefficiency of the earlier system of auxiliary societies, the Baltimoreans stoutly declared that if the new movement were crushed, Maryland must hopelessly continue to endure her free colored population. They predicted that injurious consequences would reach beyond their state and affect the whole colonization cause.[19]

Negotiations, proposals, and counter-proposals dragged on through spring and summer. The June expedition was naturally cancelled. Apart from minor side issues, the central dispute between the two groups came down to whether the American Colonization Society, as the parent organization and founder of Liberia, would handle whatever monies were collected by state auxiliaries and pay expenses for all emigrants traveling to the colony or whether state auxiliaries could collect and manage their own funds, paying the parent body a per capita sum for each colonist it sent out.[20] Proponents of independent state action argued that the discordant views of northerners and southerners which had heretofore diluted the society's effectiveness

18 American Colonization Society MSS (hereafter ACS), *Board of Managers Minutes: 1828–33,* Mar. 14, 17, 1831.
19 MSCS MSS, *Records of 1831,* meeting of the Board of Managers, Mar. 26, 1831.
20 ACS MSS, *Board of Managers Minutes: 1828–33,* Apr. 4, 1831; MSCS MSS, *Records of 1831,* meetings of the Board of Managers, Apr. 12, May 4, 1831.

could be satisfied if each state directed the application of its funds according to its own ideas on colonization. The Washington board, they claimed, was still necessary to procure unity of action and to provide for the government of the colony.[21]

Although failing to reach a settlement, the Maryland society went ahead blindly in the fall with plans to send an expedition. It apparently thought that once it had gathered emigrants, chartered a vessel, and completed arrangements to sail, the parent board would be obliged to comply with a request that the colonists be accepted in Monrovia. This was refused. With the schooner *Orion,* chartered at the rate of $550 a month, lying at anchor in Baltimore harbor and loaded with emigrants, the Marylanders had no alternative but to throw themselves on their opponents' mercy. Pledging that never again would they get up an expedition without the parent board's authority and approval and agreeing to reimburse whatever expenses were incurred for the maintenance of the new settlers in Africa, the Maryland society dispatched its first company.[22] The basic question concerning the relationship between the two colonization groups was unresolved.

That an emigrant expedition sailed in the fall of 1831 was largely due to the perseverance of the agent, Doctor Eli Ayres. Appointed in March, he was instructed by the Executive Committee to set out from Baltimore on March 15 for a six-week canvass of the state. He was to go first to Bel Air in Harford County, north of Baltimore, and then to Port Deposit, Havre de Grace, and Elkton. Proceeding around the head of Chesapeake Bay and on to the Eastern Shore, Ayres was directed to visit Chestertown, Church Hill, Centreville, and Denton. The last leg of the trip included Cambridge, Vienna, Salisbury, Snow Hill, Princess Anne, and back to Cambridge in order to catch the steamship for Baltimore. He was to hold a public meeting

21 MSCS MSS, *Records of 1831,* meeting of the Board of Managers, May 4, 1831.

22 *Ibid.,* Ralph Gurley to James Howard, Washington, Oct. 10, 1831; meeting of the Board of Managers, Oct. 12, 1831; ACS MSS, *Board of Managers Minutes: 1828–33,* Oct. 17, 1831.

at each place and to attempt the organization of an auxiliary to the State Colonization Society.[23]

This circular route, designed to cover many of the Maryland counties systematically, was never completed. Doctor Ayres left Baltimore on March 15, as instructed, and opened his agency with a public meeting at Bel Air. He found Harford County citizens favorably disposed to the idea of colonization and readily established an auxiliary. Operating on the theory that the most auspicious places and times to found auxiliaries were during court sessions at the county seats when citizens were already gathered for other business, Doctor Ayres concluded that to continue on to Cecil County where the court would not convene until later in the month would be of no value.

He therefore returned to Baltimore and was sent to Chestertown in Kent County, where court was then sitting. He formed a second auxiliary there. In May he shifted operations to central and western Maryland, visiting Frederick and Hagerstown and establishing a county auxiliary in each place.

Late in June Ayres returned to the Eastern Shore. His efforts in Easton, Cambridge, Denton, and Centreville produced auxiliaries in these towns too. From this period of travel, he collected a total of $214.03. Traveling expenses came to $83.68, leaving a balance of $130.35. Since his salary of $1,000 per annum was to come from his collections except when stationed in Baltimore, it is evident that his exertions were unprofitable not only to the society but to himself as well.

In spite of this unhappy pecuniary aspect, Doctor Ayres was generally encouraged by the attitudes toward colonization encountered about the state. On his first trip, to Harford County, he noted how admirably the area was situated for comparing the effects of free and slave labor. Across the line in Pennsylvania, soil improvement, population increase, and wealth accumulation stood in marked contrast to the soil deterioration, slow increase of the white population, and low land prices of Harford County. He also pointed to the immensely higher yield

23 MSCS MSS, *Proceedings of Executive Committee of Managers . . . ,* Mar. 9, 1831.

per acre on land cultivated solely by whites even in Harford County as proof that free men, who felt an interest in their labors, were superior to slaves. Ayres was confident that realization of this fact would result in support for the Colonization Society. His visit to Frederick County convinced him even more that white farmers had accepted the idea of free labor over a servile regime. He reported that, in consequence of frequent manumissions, the free blacks had become a public burden. Whites loudly called for modification of the laws regulating manumission. In Washington County Doctor Ayres speculated that both free blacks and slaves were decreasing in number (in fact, only bondsmen were becoming more scarce). He attributed this to both the simultaneous increase in whites and the recent heavy demand for land. He observed that, although from eighty to a hundred miles from market and of markedly inferior quality, land was selling readily for $30 an acre. It appears not to have occurred to him that the steady westward movement across the Baltimore Turnpike and the National Road plus hopes held for the new canal and railway systems might explain western Maryland's prosperity.

While remaining optimistic, Ayres reported a different situation on the Eastern Shore. Time and again he was accused of being a Georgia slave dealer. The Negroes frequently professed belief that those of their number who had previously emigrated under American Colonization Society auspices were sold back into Georgia slavery. In Cambridge Ayres found black opposition rooted in an actual case of misfortune. Some of Liberia's earliest colonists had come from this town and when they were killed or wounded in African attacks upon the settlement, their friends abandoned the idea of joining them there. The Negro attitude carried over to their white masters, who also lost interest in colonization.

Another hindrance to the rekindling of the colonization spirit on the Eastern Shore was the deception practiced by some blacks. There were some cases in which a Negro family, pretending to be going to the colony, toured the neighborhood. With money and goods collected from white sympathizers, the family moved on to Baltimore and settled. Ayres was convinced that the proper antidote to all these rumors and occurrences lay in the dissemination of correct information. He concluded that when the blacks knew Africa as he did, there would not be one in all America who would not want to go there as soon as possible.

From his months of travel throughout the state, except southern Maryland, Doctor Ayres surmised that the taxable inhabitants of Maryland were willing to share the cost of transporting free colored people to Liberia. Moreover, every thinking man desired that slavery be abolished if the slaves could be conveyed from this country to a place where their condition would improve. Finally, Ayres believed, all that was necessary to end slavery was to demonstrate to slaveholders how much cheaper white laborers were than the maintenance of the all too numerous idlers among the slaves. He noted, however, that as interesting as his findings regarding slavery were, only the free blacks' situation required attention. Ayres's statements show a contradiction in purported colonization goals and personal objectives. While the society's program supposedly aimed at the freemen, he was less interested in their condition than in ridding slaveholders of 100,000 slaves whose labor was considered less productive than that of white men. What Ayres was essentially striving for was a white society.

Apart from his views on the readiness of the people to support the colonization scheme in Maryland, Doctor Ayres speculated on its cost. He estimated the total expense per emigrant at $20. With 50,000 free blacks and 300,000 whites, he calculated that each white would be responsible for only $3.33. This would be the cost if all free colored were to return to Africa in one year. But if migration were spread over thirty years, the supposed society goal, and if freight were carried on the return passage, the figure could be reduced to a mere 7½ cents per white person. Recognizing that only about one-fifth of the white inhabitants were taxable, Ayres concluded that the sum would amount to about 31 cents per annum. In thirty years' time, of course, each white person would have been assessed more than $9.

The prospects of a commercial arrangement with Africa were even more appealing to Doctor Ayres. In his opinion, the establishment of Liberia was the most important cause for the drastic decline of the slave trade off the West African coast. The consequence for the Africans, however, was deprivation of supplies they were accustomed to receiving for the exchange of slaves. Were the colonists to call for rice, dyewood, or other indigenous products, Africans from miles around would supply them. Abolition of the slave trade would turn their attention to soil cultivation. Rice, ivory, indigo, gold, and other items could be exchanged for the implements Africans needed in their agricultural pursuits. Estimating the African population at 150 million, Ayres speculated that they would demand 300 million pairs of shoes a year. To clothe them would require the entire cotton production of America and England. But, Ayres stressed, Americans had the advantage over all other countries which might try to compete because the colonists were, in fact, agents stationed there. They would gather the raw materials to be supplied the United States in exchange for manufactured products.[24] Such visionary calculations from an ordinarily practical man who had visited the coast and had participated in the purchase of the first American colony were sure to wield a powerful influence upon his hopeful colleagues.

The unrealistic nature of Doctor Ayres's project for the emigration of Maryland's free colored population became apparent much sooner than the fanciful qualities of his mercantile expectations. Gathering emigrants for departure on the *Orion* readily demonstrated that only hard work and constant attention would bring success. The schooner was capable of transporting more than sixty passengers and their personal goods. Sixty became the goal of the first voyage but, although about that number applied to go, the *Orion* carried only thirty-one when it sailed from Baltimore on October 25. A variety of reasons was responsible for this sharp reduction in the number of emigrants.

24 *Ibid.*, Mar. 23, Aug. 9, 1831; *Records of 1831,* meeting of the Board of Managers, Aug. 5, 1831.

Some could not procure conclusive evidence respecting their emancipation in time for the sailing; others were unable to settle small matters and complete arrangements.[25]

The chief obstacle came from leading free blacks in Baltimore and special envoys from neighboring districts. As preparations for the voyage became known, opposition increased and organized. Prospective emigrants were repeatedly visited by agitators who made bold assertions and misrepresentations. Even public meetings were held ostensibly to warn potential colonists of their fate. At last, when sailing day came, but half the original number of applicants was willing to go. The final effort of voyage opponents was to follow intending emigrants on board, begging them to return to shore rather than sail to certain death in Africa.[26]

With the first expedition at length en route, the Maryland society managers settled down to paying bills and re-evaluating their methods. One of their first considerations was money. Provisions and stores to supply the original sixty applicants for six months in Africa had been sent aboard the *Orion*. They had now to be paid for. Doctor Ayres's salary was another responsibility. His collections were not even enough to provide for this. The $1,000 state appropriation was the best immediate hope for avoiding bankruptcy. Maryland colonizationists requested the American Colonization Society, originally designated as the recipient of the annual sum, to pass it along to them.[27] The parent society actually paid over $930, allowing $30 for each of the thirty-one emigrants transported aboard the *Orion*.[28]

The board decided to canvass the city of Baltimore personally to cover the balance. Dividing the city into twelve wards and assigning three members to each, it launched an active campaign for contributions. This plan was not successful, since numerous ward chairmen and collectors failed to secure results.

25 MSCS MSS, *Records of 1831,* meeting of the Board of Managers, Nov. 16, 1831.
26 ACS MSS, *Letters Received,* vol. XXXV (1831), Charles Howard to Gurley, Baltimore, Nov. 15, 1831.
27 *Ibid.*
28 ACS MSS, *Board of Managers Minutes: 1828–33,* Nov. 28, 1831.

A third effort to obtain funds involved the newly formed auxiliaries in the state. They were asked to send any cash they had raised. Moreover, persons who had earlier pledged sums to the society were now requested to pay up. As a last resort, the managers decided to release Doctor Ayres. Asserting that the existing state of society finances did not justify the continued employment of an agent, the board resolved to discontinue the office.[29] Ayres was, however, not notified of this action and remained on as agent until the following spring, and the board was obliged to pay him nevertheless.[30]

At the end of the year the Maryland State Colonization Society was heavily in debt. The expenses of the *Orion* expedition alone had been more than $3,200.[31] Contributions were highly disappointing. It was apparent to colonizationists that the future of their movement rested upon a steady source of income. To obtain this became their goal for 1832.

29 MSCS mss, *Records of 1831,* meetings of the Board of Managers, Nov. 16, 18, Dec. 6, 1831.
30 MSCS mss, *Miscellaneous Letters & Minutes, Package of Reports of the Board of Managers, etc., for 1832,* Eli Ayres to the Board of Managers, Baltimore, Apr. 24, 1832.
31 *Thirteenth Annual Report of the Board of Managers of the Maryland State Colonization Society* (Baltimore: John D. Toy, 1845), p. 13.

II

Legislative Action
and Early Expeditions

The Maryland State Colonization Society was backed against the wall. Its funds were depleted, creditors sent notice after notice of unpaid bills, contributions were negligible, and applicants for passage to the colony were few. Yet this picture does not accurately reflect the interest of white Maryland citizens in colonization or existing support for society goals. Doctor Eli Ayres, in his canvass of the state in 1831, found prevalent a general apprehension respecting the free blacks and the future of slavery. His emphasis on the problem of slave versus free labor in counties such as Harford and Frederick harmonized with attitudes being expressed elsewhere in the state. *Niles' Register* editorialized in October, 1831, that the continuation of slavery below the Susquehanna River would drive out the white laboring classes. It declared, "Free labor and slave labor *cannot* abide together. In preferring the latter . . . the former seeks a new location in which it is *protected* or

HONORED; and hence the one becomes stronger and stronger as the other becomes weaker and weaker. . . ." [1]

White citizens were also united in the view that free colored people were a nuisance. Henry Brawner, representing Charles County in the Maryland House of Delegates, deplored the evils growing out of the unrestrained association of free blacks with slaves. Although regretting the existence of slavery, he considered the unrestricted power of manumission as potentially more dangerous. Noting that the proportion of free Negroes to the white population in Maryland was steadily growing, he complained that employment was increasingly being taken from the white laboring class. He called for a consideration of colonization as a means of diminishing the proportion between the two groups. [2] Again, *Niles' Register,* professing hatred of Negro slavery per se, reminded its readers that "we *have* the blacks, and must make the best of the unhappy condition in which we are placed that we can. . . ." It declared certainty that a large majority of the slaves were better fed and clothed, more comfortable and virtuous, than were the free Negroes, the pests of society in Baltimore, Philadelphia, New York, and other northern cities. Emancipation without removal merely increased problems. [3] Thus *Niles' Register* publicized what most thinking Marylanders had already come to accept: manumission must be accompanied by removal. Yet all these expressions assumed that slavery was better than abolition and that Maryland should handle her problem without interference.

While these ideas were gaining wide support of their own accord, they were given immense new import by events in Virginia. Late in the summer of 1831 the fears of watchful citizens were realized by servile outbreaks in southern districts and in North Carolina. Known as the Southampton Rebellion, the murder of some fifty-five whites, largely in Southampton County, Virginia, created panic among Caucasians of neighboring states. Led by Nat Turner, a self-styled Baptist preacher, a

1 *Niles' Register,* Oct. 15, 1831, p. 130.
2 Maryland, *Journal of Proceedings of the House of Delegates* (December Session, 1830), p. 136.
3 *Niles' Register,* Sept. 17, 1831, p. 35.

band of sixty-odd slaves roamed the countryside plundering and killing. In the crisis army and navy troops hastened in to restore order.

Eventually the insurrectionists were captured and tried. Many, including Turner, were executed. For weeks thereafter reports of murder and treachery elsewhere in Virginia and in other southern states swept the country. In some towns, such as Wilmington, North Carolina, martial law was declared as citizens prepared to ward off armies of slaves. Volunteer militias were organized in numerous areas. The movements of all Negroes, both free and slave, were studied for suspicious signs. Even in Delaware and on Maryland's Eastern Shore authorities arrested many Negroes while citizens sent urgent pleas for arms and men and general excitement prevailed.

In the midst of the speculation, accusations, and demands for action, one moderating influence was the editorial voice of *Niles' Register,* which from the outset sought to sift rumor from fact in its accounts of the widespread disorders. While it sympathized with citizens who suffered from current agitations, it counseled against further oppressive measures upon the black population. The weekly applauded colonization as the best solution to the growing tension between the races. "Let the way be prepared," it suggested, "that humane owners of slaves shall not feel themselves checked in manumitting them, that they may have a country and a home,—and become *men."* Several weeks later the paper called for a nationwide effort to develop some practicable project which would afford the hope of security to whites and offer prospects of an improved condition to the slaves.[4]

In Maryland the Nat Turner rebellion fostered a rapidly growing movement to regulate slavery more closely, including limitation upon the introduction of new slaves into the state, and to curtail liberties of the free blacks who were held responsible for inciting the outrages below the Potomac. White citizens held

---

4 *Ibid.,* Sept. 3, 1831, pp. 4–5; Sept. 24, 1831, p. 67; Oct. 15, 1831, pp. 130–31; Nov. 19, 1831, p. 221.

public meetings in numerous towns to prepare memorials for the approaching session of the state legislature. The gathering at the Upper Marlboro Courthouse in Prince Georges County was typical. A committee appointed to investigate the recent outbreak and to recommend measures countering tendencies for similar occurrences in their area laid chief blame upon certain Boston and New York publications which spread malicious doctrines among the blacks. Prince Georges citizens accused itinerant colored clergymen of promoting these views and criticized local colored preachers for the secrecy of their movements. The committee further cited the mounting free black population and its association with slaves as a sore and growing evil.

The resolutions offered by the group were far-reaching. The governor of Maryland was requested to take all constitutional steps available to punish the editor or publisher of any paper circulated in Maryland designed to produce insurrection among the slaves. They called for the prohibition of local and itinerant colored preachers traveling about Prince Georges County. Another resolution called upon the next session of the Maryland General Assembly to pass a law forbidding future emancipation of slaves within the state unless their old owners provided for transmission to Africa. Moreover, colored persons were to be permitted to travel into or through Prince Georges County only if they possessed certificates, signed by some well-known and respectable white, stating their business and attesting to their good character. If possible, free blacks were to be required to give security of good behavior.

Concluding the report, the committee sought to avert any misconception of its motives by announcing that the objects of the several recommendations were the safety and welfare of white *and* colored people. "To see . . . [the colored population] on all proper occasions availing themselves of the opportunities of public worship and necessary instruction from those who are able and willing to teach them their duties both to God and man, will at all times, afford us the truest gratification." Another committee of eight was then appointed to visit

Annapolis during the approaching legislative session to seek the passage of laws suggested in these resolutions.[5]

The Prince Georges County memorial was among the many presented to the December session of the Maryland legislature by various counties. Collectively, they proposed legislative action in four areas: (1) prohibition of future emancipation of slaves unless provision were also made for their removal from the state, (2) appropriation of funds for the removal of those already free, (3) establishment of a police system to keep closer check upon free blacks, and, from several parts of the state, (4) the complete abolition of slavery.[6] The memorials were referred to the Committee on Grievances and Courts of Justice, chaired by Henry Brawner, which was expanded to a joint House and Senate board.

A basic assumption by the congressmen was that the black population's presence was injurious to Maryland's prosperity. They pointed out the great disparity in land values in servile and free states and concluded that slavery's existence alone accounted for the difference. The continuance of slavery, the committee predicted, would sink Maryland to lowest rank in the Union, but the removal of this evil would raise the state's land values so that, proportional to her territory, she would rank among the highest in total worth. The object of any legislation should be to remove all or almost all of the colored population, both free and slave, from Maryland.

Estimating the cost of removal and the support of emigrants in Africa until they could maintain themselves at $30 per head and calculating, by an intricate scheme, that the annual increase of the colored population was then 868, the delegates "proved" that a mere $26,040 yearly would eliminate the entire group from the state's population. At that rate, only one generation would be necessary to eradicate the problem. The increased value of property, if only $1 for each of Maryland's nine million acres, would be more than sufficient to finance the project.

5 *Maryland Gazette,* Jan. 12, 1832.
6 Maryland, *Journal of Proceedings of the House of Delegates* (December Session, 1831).

Another argument which the Brawner committee raised concerned white workers. It blamed slavery as the leading cause of the laboring whites' emigration from the state. The resultant sparse population presented an obstacle to the increase and improvement of free schools. While every means possible was to be employed in removing free black folk and to prevent an increase of slaves in the state, the committee refused to propose abolition. It pointed out that the people of Maryland had voluntarily emancipated a third of their slaves without any inducement. It predicted that the removal of emancipated slaves from the state would encourage slave owners to release even more bondsmen.[7]

Simultaneously with the Brawner committee's deliberations, the officers of the nearly defunct Maryland State Colonization Society were arranging the formal chartering of their organization under Maryland laws. The reciprocal effect of the existence of a state colonization society and the legislature's consideration of that body's charter upon the study of the colored problem in Maryland can only be estimated. Society supporters included leading citizens throughout the state. The proposed legislation depended for its success upon the operation of the society, while the latter could not survive without the funds accompanying such legislation. The charter was swiftly granted.

Two legislative proposals came from the Brawner committee. The first, "An Act Relating to the People of Color in This State," was approved by the General Assembly in March, 1832.[8] Its wording indicated its dependency upon the Colonization Society and its object was clearly the free black population. It stipulated, first, that the governor and council appoint a Board of Managers, consisting of three members of the Maryland State Colonization Society, whose duty would be to remove from the state persons of color already free, and those thereafter freed, to Liberia or some other place outside the bounds of Maryland.

7 Henry Brawner, "Report of the Committee on Grievances and Courts of Justice, of the House of Delegates, Relative to the Colored Population of Maryland," *Baltimore Gazette and Daily Advertiser,* Mar. 17, 1832.
8 Maryland, *Journal of Proceedings of the House of Delegates* (December Session, 1831), pp. 94, 114, 304, 543, 557.

The state treasurer was instructed to pay the Board of Managers whatever sums it needed, not exceeding $20,000 the first year nor more than $200,000 over a period of twenty years. The clerks and registers of wills of the Maryland counties were to report to the Board of Managers within five days any deed of manumission or will admitted to probate which freed slaves and the managers were then to inform the Colonization Society.

Should that body decline to accept and remove the person or persons manumitted or should such individuals refuse to be removed to some designated place, it then became the duty of the three managers to banish them beyond the limits of the state. Should a freed ex-slave refuse to depart, the state managers must inform the local sheriff, who would then arrest the recalcitrant and transport him outside the state. Experience was to prove this feature unenforceable because of its lack of details.

An exception to this general rule for the removal of free colored persons was contained in a provision allowing the state Orphans' Court or the Baltimore City Court to grant annually a permit to any ex-slave to remain in his county if he could produce respected testimony of his exceptional good conduct and character.

To raise monies for the accomplishment of these several goals, the law specified the amount which each county was to supply from its assessment of taxable property within its limits. To determine the number of potential emigrants, the sheriffs were directed to take a census of the free colored in their counties and to report details of names, sexes, and ages to the county clerks and the state Board of Managers. Penalties and compensations were established to give sheriffs a proper incentive. In addition to the census which the sheriffs were to take, they were, starting in June, to report from time to time the names and circumstances of any free persons willing to leave the state.[9]

The second proposal submitted by the Brawner committee and passed into law was "An Act Relating to Free Negroes and Slaves," which severely restricted the colored population's liberty within Maryland and sought to prevent the settlement of any

9 Maryland, *Laws of Maryland* (1831), Chapter 281.

additional free blacks or slaves within the state. No free Negro or mulatto could move into the state or even stay there for more than ten successive days without incurring a fine of $50 for each week he continued there. Employers were forbidden, also under penalty of fine, to hire free Negroes or mulattoes who settled in Maryland after June, 1832. Moreover, it became unlawful thereafter to bring into the state by land or water any Negro, mulatto, or other slave for sale or for residence.

Free Negroes and mulattoes were forbidden to possess any kind of firelock, military weapon, or gunpowder and lead unless they had obtained from the local authorities a license, renewable annually and subject to withdrawal at any moment. It became generally unlawful for free Negroes or slaves to assemble or attend any meetings for religious purposes unless a white clergyman or some other respectable white person of the neighborhood conducted them. There were two exceptions: an owner of slaves could permit his servants to hold religious services upon his own land and, in the cities of Baltimore and Annapolis, worship not lasting beyond 10 P.M. was permitted with the written consent of an ordained white preacher.

For any free Negro, mulatto, or slave to sell such goods as bacon, pork, corn, or tobacco, he had to present a certificate from a justice of the peace or from three respectable persons of his neighborhood that he had come honestly into possession of the articles placed on sale. Another section of this far-reaching act made it illegal for any retailer or storekeeper to sell liquor, gunpowder, shot, or lead to any free Negro, mulatto, or slave unless he brought either a license or a permit from his master. The final section carried an ominous warning: any free Negro or mulatto thereafter convicted of a crime not punishable by hanging might be sentenced to the penalties and punishments provided by law, "or be banished from this state by transportation into some foreign country." [10]

These several acts resulted from a combination of circumstances in Maryland bringing to a head public concern for the Negro population. Evidence suggests that there was not a slave-

10 *Ibid.*, Chapter 323.

holders' conspiracy to inflate the value of their bondsmen. Already many slaves were being sold south as farmers began to seek fresh capital and new agricultural methods. These laws seem clearly a response to an aroused citizenry, three-quarters of whom owned no slaves. An energetic colonization society was made the instrument of state policy. Assured of a steady income for two decades, the society, to hold a position of esteem in Maryland, needed only to prove itself capable of alleviating the tension growing between the two races and of altering the racial balance in favor of the whites.

With a charter and an annual appropriation, Colonization Society officials met in Judge Brice's chambers in the Baltimore Courthouse on March 24, 1832, to formalize the body's organization in line with recent developments. Among its first actions was the recommendation to the governor and council of Moses Sheppard, Charles Howard, and Charles C. Harper as managers. Several days later the group adopted new bylaws and reorganized the administration of the society. There was now to be only one president but six vice-presidents. Moreover, there was no stipulation that the Board of Managers should meet quarterly. Under the new laws it was invested with full authority to act for the society whenever seven officers were present. The Executive Committee of three continued. George Hoffman, first chief executive in the earlier organization, was elected president, and most of the former officers again held positions of authority. John H. B. Latrobe became corresponding secretary, a position of more significance than the title implies.

Hoping to capitalize upon recent attention given colonization by the passage of legislation affecting the whole black population, the society considered the formation of auxiliaries throughout Maryland as the best means of enlarging its operations and its funds. The three state managers hired Robert S. Finley as agent for a term of six months at a salary of $500 and traveling expenses. His remuneration was to come from the state appropriation; traveling expenses were to be paid by the Colonization Society from its voluntary contributions. Agent Finley was instructed to form as many auxiliary branches and to obtain as many new members as possible throughout the state. He was to be mindful of his role in persuading Negroes to emigrate. No specific date for the departure of another expedition was set at this time, but all agreed that it would be necessary to dispatch one within the year in order to hold public attention.[11]

Agent Finley left Baltimore early in May, 1832, for a canvass of the Eastern Shore, taking with him a large quantity of colonization literature. His first report, from Chestertown on May 7, spoke of widespread interest and of the good reception accorded the literature. One Negro, he wrote, carefully read a pamphlet, proclaimed it the best work that he had ever seen and a very satisfactory one too since it "came straight from Headquarters." Finley happily related that a large meeting of whites and blacks had been held in the Methodist Episcopal Church where an Episcopalian rector had offered prayer, a Reformed Methodist clergyman had officiated as clerk, and the local pastor had presided.

For five weeks he visited the principal Eastern Shore towns, forming auxiliary societies in many of them. His mode of operation was to call public meetings which the colored people were urged to attend, to address the audience, and then to distribute colonization pamphlets. Whether the meetings were biracial in character or only for the blacks, Finley invariably arranged for the local clergy to participate and for other respected citizens of the community to attend and to make beneficial remarks. Finley found colonization popular among Eastern Shore whites. The best that he could say for the colored population was that the recent legislation affecting them was causing them to begin thinking seriously of leaving the state.

A tour of the Western Shore counties in June and July uncovered the fact that the white population there, too, was generally favorable to the idea of colonization and cooperative in arranging meetings. But Finley found the Negro population

---

11 MSCS MSS, *Records,* vol. I, meetings of the Board of Managers, Mar. 24, 28, Apr. 11, 24, 1832; *Manumission Books,* vol. I, meeting of the Board of State Managers, Apr. 18, 1832; *State Managers Book,* Charles Howard, Moses Sheppard, and C. C. Harper to Board of Managers, Baltimore, Apr. 23, 1832; Harper to Ralph Gurley, Baltimore, Apr. 17, 1832; ACS MSS, *Letters Received,* vol. XLIII (1832), Howard to Gurley, Baltimore, Sept. 3, 1832.

downright hostile to the movement. He attributed such opposition to the circulation of falsehoods and rumors by Baltimore free blacks.

From his hundreds of miles of travel throughout Maryland in
the few months following the legislature's action, Finley concluded that the great obstacle to colonization success among
the Negro population was their lack of confidence in the plan.
He found almost universal among them the belief that the
legislation originated in sordid white motives of fear and interest. He encountered everywhere the conviction that the laws
were designed to perpetuate and to strengthen slavery. Moreover, many respectable and intelligent Caucasians shared these
views. Finley urged the Board of Managers to make a public
declaration of its views on slavery in such clear and simple
language that the most obtuse intellect could not misunderstand
them and so explicit that the most malicious could not pervert
their meaning. He advised the society to push for legislation
which would bring the gradual abolition of slavery in Maryland.
Even if the effort were unsuccessful, it would favorably impress
the black people and skeptical whites.[12]

The most encouraging reports could not disguise the dearth
of applicants for the colony. Even the state managers' efforts
in notifying each sheriff, each clerk of the courts, and each
register of wills of his additional duties produced few results.
Soon after the enactment of the legislation, the state managers
addressed a circular to the clerks and registers which requested
cooperation in reporting all new manumissions and in ascertain-
ing the attitude of the Negro population toward removal to
Africa. The traveling agent was frequently supplied with a list
of manumitted slaves in the area he was visiting and asked to
notify such people of recent legislation and of the alternatives
before them. Early in June, 1832, sheriffs were reminded of
their new responsibilities. Each was furnished with a list of
persons manumitted in his county since the passage of the law.

12 MSCS MSS, *Letters,* vol. I, Robert S. Finley to Sheppard, Chester River,
   May 7, 1832; Finley to John Latrobe, Baltimore, Aug. 8, 1832; Finley to
   managers of the State Colonization Fund, Easton, May 15, 1832.

He was instructed to inquire of these people when he took the census of his county's free black population about their willingness to depart to Liberia. Many a sheriff reported opposition. The Calvert County officer notified the state managers that, among the free blacks within his jurisdiction, there was unanimous voice against leaving the state without the privilege of returning. The sheriff of Queen Annes County reported the same situation. In actuality the Colonization Society had already dismissed the goal of removing all free blacks and was concentrating on prospective manumissions.[13]

Beginning in July, as sheriffs' reports were checked against lists of newly manumitted slaves from the clerks and registers of wills, the state managers notified each sheriff of the persons in his county who were violating the law by remaining in the state. The implication was that the sheriffs should remove them forcibly. Difficulties in the interpretation of the law actually resulted in few of the penalties written into it being enforced. One notable example occurred in Frederick County. There the sheriff, with the names of several Negroes manumitted since passage of the law, confessed confusion as to what compensation he was to receive for the transportation of each Negro, where and when he was to be granted such payment, and, more important, where he was to take the Negroes. He reported that both Virginia and Pennsylvania forbade the importation of free Negroes. In exasperation he exclaimed, "Indeed I cannot conceive how the legislature, should require them to be transported beyond the limits of the state and not specifically provide some place for their reception." [14]

The state managers conceded that they had expected these

13 MSCS MSS, *State Managers Book,* "Circular to Clerks of Courts and Registers of Wills," Baltimore, n.d. [1832]; Howard to Finley, Baltimore, May 9, 1832; "Circular to the Sheriffs," Baltimore, June 7, 1832; *Miscellaneous Letters & Minutes, 60 Letters to the Board of Managers,* Henry L. Harrison to Howard, Lower Marlboro, Aug. 1, 1832; Thomas Ashcom to Howard, Centreville, Aug. 28, 1832.

14 MSCS MSS, *State Managers Book,* Sheppard, Howard, and Harper to Henry Green, Baltimore, July 3, 1832; "Circular to the Sheriffs," Baltimore, Oct. 1, 1832; *Miscellaneous Letters & Minutes, 60 Letters,* Peter Brengle to Howard, Frederick, Oct. 11, 1832.

difficulties. But they argued that their duty was merely to inform the different sheriffs of the violators within their respective districts. Pledging to direct the legislature's attention to the ambiguities of the law at its next session, the state managers understated the situation when they replied to the baffled sheriff that, in their opinion, the legislature had not explained with sufficient detail its intentions on compensation and the places to which the newly freed were to be removed. That other officials were equally uncertain about sections of the law for which they were responsible is attested by a letter from the register of wills of St. Marys County. He reported that Moses, a recently manumitted slave, had come in for his "pardon papers." Asked if he were willing to remove to the colony of Liberia, the black had replied in the negative. He had, however, been willing to move to the District of Columbia. The register had attempted to persuade Moses to emigrate to Liberia and when that worthy had persisted in his refusal, he had been denied a certificate of manumission.[15]

Fall was fast approaching and Finley, capable and enthusiastic, wished to return to his former field of labor in Ohio. He was consequently appointed to the American Colonization Society's Western Agency. From Columbus in August he wrote, "I have again safely arrived within my own diocese." To replace him, the state managers now appointed William McKenney, a Norfolk, Virginia, native, hired specifically to spend two months on the Eastern Shore enrolling emigrants for a fall expedition. The situation on the Western Shore was such that the society despaired of gaining any there, blaming northern abolitionists and fanatical emancipationists for creating violent opposition to emigration among the blacks.[16]

Rather than taking up work immediately, McKenney was de-

15 MSCS MSS, *State Managers Book,* Howard to Brengle, Baltimore, Oct. 16, 1832; *Miscellaneous Letters & Minutes, 60 Letters,* E. J. Millard to Howard, Leonardtown, Saint Marys Co., Oct. 11, 1832.
16 ACS MSS, *Letters Received,* vol. XLIII (1832), Finley to Gurley, Baltimore, Aug. 11, 1832; Finley to Gurley, Columbus, Ohio, Aug. 22, 1832; MSCS MSS, *State Managers Book,* Howard to William McKenney, Baltimore, July 25, 1832; Howard to E. K. Wilson, Baltimore, Aug. 15, 1832.

tained until October by family illness. Meanwhile, the Colonization Society distributed among the auxiliaries literature especially prepared to advertise the colony and the plan. One publication, *The Statement of Facts,* put a full account of the Liberia colony before both races. It also demonstrated that while the black population would never be violently driven out, the force of circumstances would eventually compel it to leave Maryland. The purpose, furthermore, was to publicize the fact that an asylum where they could enjoy real liberty and happiness, which they could never obtain in the United States, awaited them in Africa. Another pamphlet, *News from Africa,* through its simplicity, was intended for circulation only among the blacks. It was principally addressed to residents of rural areas and villages. The state managers, who paid for the printing of these publications, encouraged friends of colonization to lend them to good prospects rather than give them away.[17]

McKenney began his actual work on the Eastern Shore early in October, 1832. The prospects for getting an expedition off before the end of the year immediately improved. A Methodist minister by profession, McKenney possessed inordinate persuasive ability. Like agent Finley before him, he operated through the local churches. He reported from numerous towns that after he had spent several days in the area, a general excitement overtook the free blacks. He proceeded at a rapid pace and from almost every town reported a number of emigrants willing to embark that autumn. McKenney was also an individual inclined to speak for his employers before first consulting them. He soon took the liberty of declaring that a vessel would sail from the Cambridge area or from Baltimore between the middle and the end of November if there were sufficient prospective emigrants. Before the end of October McKenney was confident that there would be at least eighty applicants and he urged the Colonization Society to advertise for a suitable vessel. Early in November McKenney advised Charles Howard that there would be not one less than 100, if

17 MSCS MSS, *State Managers Book,* Howard to Wilson, Baltimore, Aug. 15, 1832; Harper to Gurley, Baltimore, Aug. 1, 1832.

not 125, departees. Several days later he revised his estimate upward to 140-150 persons.[18]

On December 9, 1832, 146 emigrants left Baltimore on the *Lafayette* bound for Monrovia. Clergymen representing various city churches, the state managers, and other Colonization Society members went aboard the vessel to conduct services. Prayers, hymns, Scripture reading, and a short address lent a solemn and sacred air to the farewell.[19] The cholera epidemic persisting in Baltimore through the summer and early fall and the continued opposition from the city's free blacks had not prevented the sailing of a large complement of passengers to Africa.

Negro opposition in Baltimore continued unabated. Wanting to avoid a repetition of events such as those which had occurred before the sailing of the *Orion* the previous year, Charles Howard, writing for the state managers, requested the Captain of the Watch in the eastern district of Baltimore City to instruct his officers to protect persons then arriving for embarkation to Africa. Howard reminded the official that they were going out at state expense and that they were entitled to all the security they might need. He asked specifically that the city blacks be prevented from molesting the emigrants and from attempting to spread lies among them.[20]

Procurement of a large group of colonists within two months' time was due chiefly to the work of two men. One of those, agent McKenney, was instrumental in spreading a favorable view of colonization in every hamlet and town of the Eastern Shore. Besides his personal qualities, the fact that he was an ordained Methodist minister undoubtedly contributed to his success. The second individual playing a leading role in forming the expedition was Jacob W. Prout, an early settler in Liberia and register of wills there, who was back in the United States for a visit. The knowledge that Prout would be

18 MSCS MSS, *Letters,* vol. I, McKenney to Howard, Cambridge, Oct. 15, 1832; McKenney to Howard, Salisbury, Oct. 26, Nov. 5, 1832.
19 *Baltimore Gazette and Daily Advertiser,* Dec. 14, 1832.
20 MSCS MSS, *State Managers Book,* Howard to the Captain of the Watch, eastern district, Baltimore, Nov. 25, 1832.

the expedition leader induced many emigrants to go that autumn.[21] His trips in the state testified to the actual existence of a colony, to the keen satisfaction of a resident with his new home, and to his willingness to return to Africa.

The liberal terms offered emigrants were also a factor in getting together such a large number for the *Lafayette.* Not only were they promised passage and provisions for the voyage and for six months after their arrival in the colony but free land as well. Each emigrant was to receive immediately a certificate for a town lot of five acres. In addition, each married man was to receive two acres for his wife and one acre for each child accompanying the parents. However, no family could receive more than ten acres in town. If, within two years after its arrival, the family had cleared and enclosed the lot, had built a substantial house, and had brought two acres of land under cultivation, it could exchange the certificate for a deed in fee simple. Should the emigrant, upon arrival, wish to settle in the country at least three miles from town, he would receive forty acres with the option of purchasing as many as another fifty at 25 cents each within the next five years.[22]

The contrast between the *Orion*'s thirty-one emigrants and the *Lafayette*'s 146 produced a feeling of satisfaction among Maryland colonizationists. It demonstrated to them that sufficient effort by a capable man could change their opponents' hearts. Mindful of McKenney's role in all this, the state managers conveyed to him an expression of their whole-hearted approbation along with an offer of continued employment as their agent.[23] The factor which they expected thereafter to have the greatest sway among the colored population of Maryland, however, was favorable word from departees in the *Lafayette.* This they eagerly awaited. Unfortunately, they were to be bitterly disappointed and to be thrust into a new period in their history.

---

21 ACS MSS, *Letters Received,* vol. XLV (1832), Howard to Gurley, Baltimore, Nov. 3, 1832.
22 MSCS MSS, *State Managers Book,* Howard to Frisby Henderson, Baltimore, Oct. 31, 1832.
23 *Ibid.,* Howard to McKenney, Baltimore, Dec. 14, 1832.

In February a handful of letters arrived with the returning ship. Jacob Prout, the expedition leader, assured his employers that the *Lafayette* passengers had arrived safely after a forty-one-day sail from Cape Henry to Monrovia. Liberia at this time controlled about sixty miles of coastline and contained some 1,900 ex-Americans. Prout described the new settlers as being as satisfied as many immigrants who had been in the colony for such a short duration and perhaps even more so. He reported that most of his late charges were then living in a comfortable building at Caldwell, a settlement several miles inland, being acclimatized. Only a few had suffered from the fever which had struck down so many earlier immigrants who had settled in the coastal lowlands. The one hint that all was not harmonious came in Prout's proposal that steps be taken to prevent murmuring and complaining letters being sent to America. These he dismissed as generally coming from widows apprehensive of their fate after the initial six months.[24]

Quite another picture was presented by six of the *Lafayette* group. In a joint communication to Moses Sheppard, they reported deplorable conditions. First, they complained that their weekly rations had been reduced by the Monrovian citizens to a pound of spoiling beef, a pound of putrid fish, and a quarter pint of molasses per person, all left over from previous voyages while good supplies sent aboard the *Lafayette* were being held by the Monrovians. The new immigrants claimed that they had received no tea, coffee, or sugar since their arrival. They described Caldwell as overrun with mangrove which gave off such an offensive odor when they began turning the soil that it gave them fever. They charged further that no land had been cleared and that there was no way of doing so. Moreover, at the cape, settlers with a little capital traded with the Africans and sent back glowing but false reports concerning the colony in order to entice more emigrants, whose provisions they then took over.[25]

24 MSCS MSS, *Letters,* vol. I, Jacob W. Prout to Howard, Monrovia, Feb. 7, 1833.
25 *Ibid.,* abstract of letter from James Price and five others to Sheppard, Caldwell, Feb. 3, 1833.

Another Maryland immigrant, a shoemaker by trade, requested the Board of Managers to send him leather, declaring it to be either unavailable or too expensive in the colony. He conceded that Caldwell was in reality a good place for a new settlement but complained that prior settlers were hostile to newcomers.[26]

Governor Joseph Mechlin's account of the new arrivals told still another story. He attributed the "little dissatisfaction" among the Marylanders to the rations reduction and to the quality of one barrel of beef which had been accidentally damaged. He considered this insignificant in comparison to the indiscretion of the *Lafayette*'s second officer who reputedly advised the disappointed immigrants to relay their grievances to friends back home. Concluding his report on the new arrivals, Mechlin stated that in his opinion most problems had been worked out; he then went on to one of his favorite topics: the recruitment of emigrants. He complained of the extravagant promises made to prospective colonists by well-meaning but overzealous friends. Many emigrants, he said, came expecting every comfort and many of the luxuries of civilized life. They apparently believed that they had only to tell the agent of their wants to realize them. As for the *Lafayette* emigrants, Mechlin laid their unhappiness upon friends who "excited hopes which can never be realized: of course their dissatisfaction will be equally great with their disappointment. . . ." [27]

Dismayed by these messages, Baltimore colonization leaders sought first-hand accounts from ship officers and crew members. Captain Robert Hardie and his top-ranking men met with society representatives. Hardie had been ashore regularly during the sixteen days the ship lay off Monrovia. He found the houses far apart, no sign of industriousness among the settlers, and an atmosphere of suspicious watchfulness. Local Africans went about in a state of near nakedness and were called upon by the settlers to perform all their menial tasks. He inferred from what

26 *Ibid.*, abstract of letter from A. James Reese to Board of Managers, Caldwell, Feb. 2, 1833.
27 *Ibid.*, Joseph Mechlin to Harper, Liberia, Feb. 10, 1833.

he heard and saw that the land allowance was used to influence the election of civil officials in the colony. Moreover, he had never heard that any settlers were compelled to work and thought the colony rife with jealousy, envy, and selfishness. The captain had also received a very unfavorable impression of Caldwell. Expecting to see cleared lands and fields, he found the country-side a wilderness. When he had rebuked Mechlin for issuing the new immigrants beef which was literally green and fish so rotten that it scarcely hung together, Mechlin had argued that the bad must be used first.

The *Lafayette*'s crew verified the captain's statements. The first officer, David C. Landis, who was served brandy when he dined at Prout's house, remarked that were he to judge the colonists' morals by their church attendance, he would think favorably indeed of them. But were he to judge their morals from other factors, he must need assume that there were rogues among them. Landis also reported unfavorably upon Prout's conduct during the passage to Liberia. That man, it appeared, was prone to assume airs. With the authority vested in him by the state managers, he had access to the provisions and pampered his appetite. Although a major duty was to care for ill passengers, Prout ignored them and the comfort of everyone else when he could. Landis further charged that Prout was familiar with the women on board, committing the only indecency of the voyage. The second officer, James F. Cooksey, completed the description of this sordid affair by recounting his departure from Caldwell. The women called after him, saying that they were willing to be slaves in America for the rest of their lives to anyone who would feed and clothe them. The *Lafayette*'s crew thus concluded that under the present government colonization must go backward rather than forward.[28]

The Maryland colonizationists' chagrin was deep and they called upon the parent society to launch an immediate investigation. Ralph Gurley was incredulous. Doubting the accuracy of the emigrants' statements, he expressed skepticism that the

28 MSCS MSS, *Miscellaneous Letters & Minutes,* "Capt. Hardie and crew's statement in regard to Emigrants per Ship Lafayette," Apr. 11, 1833.

colonial agent Mechlin, with such ample instructions to leave nothing undone for their comfort and general satisfaction, should allow the abuses reported. The accounts of Captain Hardie and his officers could not, however, be refuted. Hardie was widely respected in Baltimore. The information from Cooksey, the second officer, likewise received credence because of his special interest in the trip. He had gone out to ascertain the condition and prospects of the colony in order better to advise friends and relatives in Virginia who were considering emancipating their slaves for the purpose of sending them to Liberia.[29]

Before the parent board had time to make a move, Maryland colonizationists received another packet of letters from the colony via a passing vessel. The situation appeared to have improved somewhat since departure of the *Lafayette* but was still far from satisfactory. Moses Sheppard, addressing Gurley as a private individual, noted that the two chief sources of dissatisfaction were lack of shelter and subsistence. Reminding Gurley that frames for two houses went out aboard the *Lafayette*, Sheppard expressed amazement that they had not been erected. In addition, he asked why it was that when the construction of cabins was so simple anywhere, the carpenters in the colony had not been put to work building houses for settlers and the expected new arrivals. "To send lumber across the Atlantic to be carried into the *woods* of Africa presents a case on which I will not venture a single remark. I know building stone were brought from England to Alexandria and Brick were imported from Holland and dragged over the sand to Schenectady, but these things were not done in the 19th century." Sheppard also took Gurley to task respecting the provisions. He queried why the colonists, with highly productive soil right under their feet, depended upon supplies from the Africans around them, from passing ships, and from the United States.[30]

Pressed to meet an apparently critical situation, the American

29 MSCS MSS, *Letters,* vol. I, Gurley to Harper, Washington, Apr. 12, 1833; ACS MSS, *Letters Received,* vol. XLVIII (1833), Howard to Francis Scott Key, Baltimore, Apr. 13, 1833.
30 ACS MSS, *Letters Received,* vol. XLVIII (1833), Sheppard to Gurley, Baltimore, Apr. 16, 1833.

Colonization Society immediately dispatched a shipload of provisions to the colony and summoned Mechlin home to explain the various matters of conflict. It consented to the resolution of the Maryland society that all provisions, agricultural implements, and other goods sent out for or with the Maryland emigrants be stored apart from the general colonial depository. It agreed to allow the Maryland society to appoint an agent residing in Africa to disburse and superintend those supplies. Finally, it assured that body that the surveying of the colony would be accelerated so that suitable lots and lands could be assigned the immigrants as soon as they were able to begin work.[31]

The parent board, however, was not without supporters. One colonist informed it that there would always be false reports from casual visitors who sought sensational news from the lazy and improvident rather than an impartial picture. He replied in some degree to every accusation made against the colony. He declared that everyone stood on a basis of equality before the law and that the Africans, rather than suffering ill treatment, were thought to receive preferential handling from magistrates. Conceding that some complaints concerning agriculture might have a semblance of truth, he predicted rapid correction of the situation. Finally, he defended the liquor traffic on the basis that to disrupt it would destroy commerce with the Africans and result in revival of the slave trade.[32]

A well-known defender of the colony was John Brown Russwurm, an 1826 graduate of Bowdoin College and now editor of the *Liberia Herald* in Monrovia. He was by no means blind to faults existing in the settlement. He admitted that agricultural pursuits were far from the minds of the colonists and that they preferred trading with the Africans to planting crops. This commerce all too often involved rum, of which the Africans and many settlers were excessively fond. Russwurm advocated that the importation of liquor into the colony be prohibited.

---

31 MSCS MSS, *Letters,* vol. I, Gurley to Harper, Washington, Apr. 25, 1833; *Records,* vol. I, meetings of the Board of Managers, May 18, June 28, 1833.

32 ACS MSS, *Letters Received,* vol. LI (1833), C. M. Waring to Gurley, Monrovia, Aug. 1, 1833.

Respecting the complaint of old settlers' unfriendliness, he denied any obligation to take "Tom, Dick, and Harry because they were colored men to my table and honor as equals. . . ." He asserted, indeed, that in many cases the fault lay with the newcomers who expected special consideration and felt themselves above any work assigned them. In a remark which portended a modern-day problem in Liberia, the editor summarized the prevailing spirit: "It is human nature that the old settlers should be a little lifted up with the success which has crowned their efforts, and new emigrants ought not to expect to be placed on par with them unless they bring undoubted letters of introduction and recommendation from home. . . ." A similarly haughty attitude, while not with the approval of Russwurm, was held toward the Africans: ". . . they [the colonists] are unwilling to divest themselves of the idea of inferiority whenever circumstances have thrown educated native Africans in their society. 'He is native' is enough." [33]

Disheartened and disillusioned by this lamentable turn of events, the Maryland society's Board of Managers agreed that the establishment of a new colony on the coast of Africa was its only hope. In reality, a new settlement had been considered and debated by leaders of both the Washington society and the Maryland branch during the past several years. The idea originated with Latrobe. At an annual meeting of the American Colonization Society in 1829 Latrobe had first advocated a settlement at Cape Palmas, some distance south of Cape Mesurado where the first colony was situated. He appears to have been influenced by scraps of information picked up from Doctor Ayres and from other travelers and traders he met in Baltimore. With the knowledge he had gleaned in this informal way, Latrobe had concocted a plan whereby northern Negroes would settle above Sierra Leone on Bulama Island, while those from the middle states would live at Mesurado and those from the South at Cape Palmas.[34] That the British occupied Sierra Leone

---

33 *Ibid.*, John B. Russwurm to Gurley, Liberia, Aug. 6, 1833.
34 John Edward Semmes, *John H. B. Latrobe and His Times, 1803–1891* (Baltimore: Norman, Remington Co., 1917), pp. 142–43.

apparently did not bother Latrobe, but nothing came of his proposal.

In 1831 and 1832 Latrobe had sought information on the desirability of a second colony, likely locations, and means for carrying out its establishment from George R. McGill, a Baltimorean who had emigrated to Liberia in 1827. McGill believed that any place on the African coast was preferable to the Monrovian site where the soil was infertile and mangrove swamps dominated the landscape, but he advocated a spot below Monrovia between the Sestos River and Cape Palmas, although Cape Palmas itself was very suitable. He estimated that, should the Maryland society obtain such a place of its own, it could reduce expenses by three-fourths within two years. The most effective mode of founding a new settlement, McGill reported, would be to send a small vessel with emigrants, supplies, and ammunition, pick up some Marylanders from Liberia, and proceed down the coast and purchase the desired area. McGill also favored the formation of a colony consisting only of Maryland emigrants because Liberian citizens were disputing the superiority of the several states from which they had come. This was apparently the factor behind Latrobe's original proposal in 1829.

Russwurm, also approached by Latrobe for information, corroborated McGill's estimate of the Cape Palmas country. He reported that one of Monrovia's most respectable citizens had been offered land within sight of the cape for $200 worth of trade goods. Russwurm quoted a Massachusetts ship captain as calling Cape Palmas' advantages too great to be ignored, especially with the English anxious to extend their settlements along the western coast.[35]

With these letters from McGill and Russwurm, the Maryland Board of Managers had appointed a committee of three—Latrobe, Brice, and Harper—to suggest what steps the state society should take in relation to a new settlement. The coming fall expedition had required hasty consultation with the parent

35 MSCS MSS, Letters, vol. I, George R. McGill to Latrobe, Monrovia, Sept. 2, 1831, July 12, 1832; Russwurm to Latrobe, Liberia, July 18, 1832.

body. Harper had warned Gurley that Cape Palmas was such an important site that it must be secured as soon as possible. He had inquired what assistance the national organization could give the Marylanders in effecting this. Insisting that they had no intention of founding an independent colony but only of settling another portion of the Liberian area, Harper had talked of lining the whole coast with American settlements which would spread laterally until they met and then penetrate far into the interior. All colonies in Africa, he had emphasized, would be parts of one great confederacy.[36]

The American Colonization Society's response had been farsighted and judicious but had shown a lethargic tendency. Agreeing that Cape Palmas was an important point which should be quickly secured, Secretary Gurley had cautioned that the Africans' savage disposition there would make settlement difficult. He had warned that, should the Maryland society attempt to plant an establishment at Cape Palmas, it must count upon substantially the same expense, hazard, and calamity which had accompanied the early years at Cape Mesurado. Gurley had suggested that Maryland colonizationists join in an exploring voyage along the coast as far south as Accra or the Niger delta. The purchase of as many sites as possible would substantiate Liberia's claim while she gradually extended her coastal settlements. Rather than founding such additional colonies with new emigrants, as the Maryland society was now proposing, Gurley had advocated that Monrovian colonists be the pioneers.[37]

However, nothing was done. The *Lafayette* with its large complement of colonists had gone on to Mesurado in December, 1832, and it was news of their difficulties which gave final impetus to the establishment of a new colony for Maryland emigrants. On April 30, 1833, the Board of Managers unanimously voted to found a new settlement at Cape Palmas. The extirpation of slavery in Maryland, by proper and gradual efforts, was the primary object. Colonization was not only to benefit her black

36 MSCS MSS, *Records*, vol. I, meeting of the Board of Managers, Oct. 4, 1832; ACS MSS, *Letters Received*, vol. XLV (1832), Harper to Gurley, Baltimore, Oct. 7, 1832.
37 MSCS MSS, *Letters*, vol. I, Gurley to Harper, Washington, Oct. 10, 1832.

people but to spread the lights of civilization and the Gospel in Africa. The principle of abstention, except for medicinal purposes, was to be incorporated into local government and no emigrant was to be permitted to go to the settlement or to hold public office unless he swore to abstain from the use of or traffic in alcohol. In linking colonization and temperance, the society believed that the best interests of both would be promoted. Moreover, agricultural pursuits were to be the chief economic effort in the proposed colony.[38]

The first tasks before Maryland colonizationists were to choose a suitable person to proceed to Africa to carry out their plans and to secure funds for the project. The man who immediately came to mind as best qualified to purchase territory and establish a new colony was Doctor James Hall. An 1822 Medical School of Maine graduate, Doctor Hall had sailed to Liberia aboard the *Orion* late in 1831 to serve as the American Colonization Society's colonial physician. During his tenure there both Ayres and Latrobe corresponded with him about the colony's affairs. Early in 1833 ill health forced Hall to return to the United States and the news he brought confirmed earlier reports of maladministration at Monrovia. His appointment to lead the Maryland expedition that fall bolstered hopes that the venture would succeed.[39]

Underwriting the extra costs accompanying such an audacious effort proved more difficult. The society sought funds from northern colonization supporters, but to no avail. It was forced to rely upon whatever voluntary sums or public monies it could secure in Maryland. Contributions were so negligible, in spite of professed colonization interest among the citizenry, that the society was dependent upon the goodwill of those allotting the legislative appropriation. To convince officials that the General Assembly's act warranted the use of public funds for

38 MSCS MSS, *Records,* vol. I, meetings of the Board of Managers, Apr. 30, June 28, 1833.
39 *Ibid.,* special meeting of the Board of Managers, July 19, 1833; *Corresponding Secretary Books,* vol. I, Latrobe, Howard, and Frank Anderson to James Hall, MSCS Office, Sept. 10, 1833; Latrobe to Finley, Baltimore, July 22, 1833.

the purchase of a remote colonial site overseas and the outfitting of an expedition was indeed a major task. These officials were quite amenable to advancing the money for land purchase and arming and provisioning the colony, but they would not give outright any funds except those to be spent directly for the emigrants. A compromise was finally reached in which the society was paid $30 per emigrant transported to Africa that year and lent an additional sum to cover the extra outlay.[40]

An issue which created quite a stir among society officers was the means of paying for the territory at Cape Palmas. The question was whether the society would hold to its professed temperance principle or adhere to the universal practice along the African coast of bartering with rum. Relying upon Doctor Hall's experience, the Board of Managers authorized its expedition to carry whatever amount of liquor thought necessary to accomplish the purchase. Affirming its belief that no territory could be bought in Africa without rum, the board claimed, nevertheless, that it was not violating the abstinence principle. Opposition among board members resulted in a further resolve to avoid this mode of business if possible, even if the cost involved an increased expenditure of other articles.[41]

A final item to be examined is the relation between the Maryland society and the parent organization and between their respective colonies in Africa. The Marylanders expected to continue settling at Monrovia or Grand Bassa, a newly opened area near Monrovia, those emigrants who preferred those locations. Moreover, if the Maryland attempts to settle Cape Palmas failed, they expected the parent society to allow them to make special arrangements for the temporary settlement of emigrants under exclusive Maryland control in Liberia. While the Washington board blessed their efforts and expressed willingness for Maryland emigrants to remain in Monrovia or Grand Bassa upon the same conditions regulating earlier voy-

---

40 MSCS MSS, *Letters,* vol. I, George Hoffman, Anderson, and Latrobe to Sheppard, Howard, and Harper, Baltimore, Sept. 7, 1833; *Manumission Books,* vol. I, meeting of the Board of State Managers, Sept. 9, 1833.
41 MSCS MSS, *Letters,* vol. I, Will G. Read to Board of Managers, Oct., 1833; *Records,* vol. I, meeting of the Board of Managers, Oct. 9, 1833.

ages until the new settlement was prepared, nothing was said about what the relations between the two colonies in Africa should be if the Maryland venture at Cape Palmas succeeded.[42]

And so the bold decision to form a new colony for Maryland blacks was made. An old Africa hand, Doctor Hall, was ready to lead the expedition, and state monies were to underwrite expenses. All that was needed were emigrants. William Mc-Kenney, the agent so successful in building up the *Lafayette* party, had been reappointed back in January, 1833. He renewed his efforts in March, once more concentrating on the Eastern Shore. From Snow Hill he wrote that it was essential that the first authentic news from the *Lafayette* passengers immediately be spread, for nothing effective could be done until then. A few days later he reported meetings in Berlin, Saint Martin's Parish, and Newark. At each one listeners seemed more interested than previously in colonization. In fact, McKenney was so swayed by the prospects that he took the liberty of stating that the Colonization Society would probably dispatch a vessel to Africa early in June. Two weeks later McKenney again begged for all the good news that might have been received from the *Lafayette* and predicted that there would not be the least difficulty in getting off an expedition of 200 by June 1 if reports were favorable.

The subsequent bad news from Africa nearly crushed the colonization movement in Maryland. The society lay blame upon inefficient management and improper official conduct in the colony itself, stressing that there was nothing in the soil or climate of Liberia to prevent the realization of a successful colony. McKenney was instructed to explain the difficulties to the white and black population in this light, assuring them that the Maryland society would not advise any person to emigrate until it was convinced that the evils were remedied. To backtrack over the hundred-mile circuit, explaining the situation and promising that an expedition would certainly sail that fall,

42 MSCS MSS, *Corresponding Secretary Books,* vol. I, Harper to the president and managers of the ACS, Baltimore, Sept. 20, 1833; *Records,* vol. I, meeting of the Board of Managers, Oct. 9, 1833.

took McKenney several weeks. The *Lafayette*'s deleterious influence is seen in the fact that not one Eastern Shore recruit went to Cape Palmas that November.[43]

With prospects on the Eastern Shore diminished, McKenney covered central and western Maryland in October with orders to obtain not less than twenty nor more than thirty emigrants. They were to be able to choose Monrovia, Grand Bassa, or Cape Palmas as their home. Only persons with exceptional moral character, preferably adult men who would subscribe to the society's abstinence policy, were desired. In Frederick McKenney found two highly recommended Negro families considering colonization. The members of both groups were slaves. In one case, the Jacob Gross family was offered its freedom if it consented to go to the Maryland colony. In the other, the family, offered emigration or resale, had delayed its decision two years. The owner now demanded an immediate answer. Traveling westward to Williamsport in Washington County, McKenney could report no prospective colonists but he did form an auxiliary and received a contribution of four $500 banknotes from the president of the Bank of Washington County.[44]

The dearth of emigrants did not delay preparations for the voyage. Society officers set about to charter a suitable vessel and purchase supplies and armaments. On November 28 at 9 A.M. the brig *Ann* sailed from Baltimore under a favorable wind. The usual prayers and blessings solemnized the departure. Atop the mast flew the newly adopted colony flag. Similar to the United States one, it substituted a cross of equal arms for the stars of the American ensign. Nineteen colonists from Frederick and Washington counties and from Baltimore were aboard. Of these, only ten were at least eighteen years old and only seven were men. They included two barbers and four

43 MSCS MSS, *Letters*, vol. I, McKenney to Howard, Snow Hill, Mar. 27, Apr. 2, 1833; McKenney to Howard, Church Hill, Apr. 14, 1833; *State Managers Book*, Howard to McKenney, Baltimore, Apr. 13, 1833; *Letters*, vol. I, McKenney to Howard, Salisbury, Apr. 23, May 4, 1833.
44 MSCS MSS, *Records*, vol. I, meetings of the Board of Managers, Sept. 9, Oct. 16, 1833; *Letters*, vol. I, McKenney to Howard, Frederick City, Oct. 23, 1833; McKenney to Latrobe, Williamsport, Oct. 30, 1833.

farmers. Accompanying them were Doctor Hall, the agent in charge, John Hersey, assistant agent, and two missionaries of the American Board of Commissioners for Foreign Missions (ABCFM). Latrobe's private prayer that their efforts might benefit the cause of freedom and religion and that he might not have to reproach himself with the loss of lives or any unhappy matter attending them was now to be tested.[45]

45 MSCS MSS, *Records,* vol. I, meeting of the Board of Managers, Dec. 7, 1833; Maryland Historical Society, *Diary of John Latrobe, August 2, 1833–May 1, 1839,* Sept. 29, 1833.

III

Establishment of Maryland in Liberia

The Maryland State Colonization Society, as an active organization, was less than three years old when it embarked upon the project of establishing its own colony in Africa. Until this time it had worked with the parent society in Washington and had sent its emigrants to one of the several settlements in Liberia. Now the Marylanders were intent upon founding an independent establishment south of Liberia. Ostensibly the impetus came from the fiasco and disappointment attending the *Lafayette* venture. But other reasons of a more serious nature were numerous. For one, society officers underwent a change of attitude during the first two years of their effort. In founding the group in 1831, they announced their aim to be the removal of the state's willing free people of color to Africa.[1] When the legislature incorporated the society in 1832, its objective was given as the "colonizing, with their own consent,

---

1 MSCS MSS, *Records of 1831*, Feb. 21, 1831.

in Africa, the free people of color of Maryland, and such slaves as may be manumitted for the purpose. . . ." [2] Obviously, Maryland colonizationists expected a great voluntary exodus by the free and by ex-slaves to their ancestral land. This failed to materialize. Only extraordinary effort got off less than 200 emigrants aboard the *Orion* and *Lafayette*. Even severely restricting legislative measures and the threat of banishment to some foreign country would not budge Maryland blacks. Now, in mid-June, 1833, the society came out for the complete eradication of slavery in Maryland. The new objective was to convert Maryland into a free state and to make the Potomac River, rather than the Mason-Dixon line, the slaveholding states' boundary.

The assertion of its hopes for the extinction of slavery in Maryland did not mean that the colonizationists had become abolitionists. The society emphasized that it viewed the end of slavery as a natural event, the result of voluntary action by slaveholders. It stressed that it intended in no way to enter upon a crusade against a time-honored and legally entrenched institution. Society heads reiterated that colonization differed from abolition in that it refrained from any interference with slavery other than encouraging owners to manumit their Negroes for the purpose of colonizing them in Africa.[3]

Fifty years later Latrobe, in an address before the Maryland Historical Society, remarked that his listeners might think it strange that there was any question as to the propriety of adopting such a resolution. But he reminded them that half a century before, slavery in the states where it existed was regarded as permanent. Even men who deplored its presence considered it a necessary evil upon which their prosperity depended. The constitution of the American Colonization Society had declared its object to be "the removal of the *free* people of color, with their own consent, to Africa," and Maryland legislation in 1832

2 Maryland, *Laws of Maryland* (1831), Chapter 314.
3 MSCS MSS, *Records*, vol. I, meetings of the Board of Managers, June 28, 1833, Jan. 8, 1834; *Corresponding Secretary Books*, vol. I, John H. B. Latrobe to Courtland Van Rensselaer, Baltimore, July 10, 1833.

had received support from citizens who believed that it would reinforce slavery. The action of the Maryland State Colonization Society in declaring that its ultimate object was the extirpation of slavery in Maryland was more advanced than anything that had been done in the slaveholding states. Latrobe acknowledged that society deliberations took into account both the principle involved and the effect of the resolutions upon the public and especially their impact on the legislature, upon which the society depended for funds.[4]

Latrobe's admission that the society considered the slavery extirpation principle because of its possible public effect points out the key issue. In reality, the society's decision to support gradual decline of slavery in Maryland aimed at gaining financial backing from the northern states. The determination to sponsor this new program was rooted in the annual American Colonization Society meeting held in Washington early in 1833. The storm which had been brewing between the southerners, who supported the parent society largely because it promised aid in dealing with the free blacks and protecting slavery, and the northerners, who considered colonization a means of ending slavery, now broke out in full fury. This feud within the national movement had been a prime reason for the establishment of a new state organization in Maryland in 1831. It now became a major reason for Maryland colonizationists to form their own African establishment. The heated arguments, the discord, and the general confusion attending the annual meeting convinced Maryland observers that a compromise between the two factions could never be effected. Southern participants complained that northern society members dominated its policies; they insisted that abolition, rather than colonization, was becoming the organization's objective and that they were about to be deprived of their right, guaranteed by law, to possess slaves. Representatives from the North alleged that the parent

---

4 John H. B. Latrobe, *Maryland in Liberia. A History of the Colony Planted by the Maryland State Colonization Society under the Auspices of the State of Maryland, U.S., at Cape Palmas on the South-West Coast of Africa, 1833–1853,* Maryland Historical Society Fund Publication 21 (Baltimore: John Murphy, 1885), pp. 19–20.

society's trend was to perpetuate slavery because it would not undertake a crusade against the institution in the South but, rather, contented itself with colonizing free blacks and slaves freed for settlement in Liberia. Maryland participants concluded that such arguments expressed more political feeling than was desirable for a purely philanthropic institution. They became convinced that the two groups could not operate under the same roof and that the whole movement would ultimately be destroyed unless drastic steps were taken.[5]

As a slaveholding state herself, Maryland was just as zealous as any in that camp in seeking to prevent interference with her domestic Negro policy. Maryland colonizationists therefore would not support meddling in their southern neighbors' affairs. However, if dissension within the national movement destroyed the Liberian project, what would become of Maryland interests and efforts in its behalf? The formation of an independent colony operated exclusively by the Maryland state society was the obvious answer. Maryland representatives, to a great degree, took the side of their northern colleagues at the Washington meeting in 1833. While they refused to cooperate in a general antislavery crusade, they now emphasized their hope for slavery's gradual extinction in Maryland and underscored the probable beneficial example their success would have upon other slaveholding states.[6]

Maryland colonizationists also expected, by the creation of their own colony, to be the heirs of Liberian interest in the United States following the probable disintegration of the American Colonization Society. Southern states, following the Maryland precedent, would undertake the management of colonization within their own borders for whatever reasons suited them. Northern champions of West African settlement would channel their contributions through the Maryland society.

5 MSCS MSS, *Corresponding Secretary Books,* vol. I, Latrobe to Van Rensselaer, Baltimore, July 10, 1833; *Records,* vol. I, meeting of the Board of Managers, Jan. 8, 1834; Maryland Historical Society, *Diary of John Latrobe, August 2, 1833–May 1, 1839,* Nov. 27, 1833, Jan. 15, 1834.
6 MSCS MSS, *Records,* vol. I, meeting of the Board of Managers, Oct. 2, 1833.

With a new establishment resting upon Christian and temperance principles, with the advantageous location of Baltimore, with a program advocating the extirpation of slavery but committed to noninterference, the Maryland society looked forward to taking the lead and soon heading the colonization movement in the United States. As the parent society in Washington progressively weakened, the Maryland society would, if necessary, take over the existing Liberian establishment. Baltimore, a natural port of preparation and embarkation, would keep Maryland at the front of the movement. These rather visionary expectations were among the primary motives attending the establishment of a new African colony.

Another factor in the Maryland society's determination to launch such an undertaking was its view that Liberia could not expand its facilities rapidly enough to accommodate the anticipated flow of Maryland emigrants. The original colony's capacity was limited and was likely to enlarge so slowly that the parent society would have to apportion the number of settlers going out in any given year among the various states with persons awaiting departure. But were the emigration movement to expand, as the state society officers believed it would, the quota allowed Maryland might materially impede her colonization efforts. This bleak prospect made a multiplication of settlements imperative for Maryland society success.[7]

The Marylanders' lack of confidence in the parent society's ability to accommodate increasing numbers of colonists in Liberia was symptomatic of their general disapproval of the way that enterprise was being run. A severe charge leveled against the Liberian settlements was their commercial character. Some settlers had actually acquired considerable wealth by trading with Africans and with passing vessels. Many others had turned to traffic with back-country residents as the only means of supporting their families. Destitute after reckless consumption of the conventional six-month supply of provisions given upon arrival,

7 MSCS MSS, *Corresponding Secretary Books,* vol. I, Latrobe to R. S. Finley, Baltimore, Sept. 5, 1833; Latrobe to William McKenney, Baltimore, July 24, 1833.

newcomers commonly went into the swamps to saw timber for the colonial government. For this they received, at inflated prices, trade articles at the agency store. Such wares were then taken into the interior to exchange for food. The consequence was that the immigrants were cheated by the Africans, known as keen traders, and returned to their families, remaining behind on the coast, worse off than before. The Maryland society wanted its colonists to avoid such practices. It believed that not only were most settlers likely to be more successful farmers than businessmen, but that close relations with the Africans would engender vicious habits and make the colonists less receptive to and protective of religious and moral demands. An agricultural community, spreading gradually into the interior, would present a better example to the heathen and provide greater facilities for a rapidly increasing emigration from the United States than would commercial centers.[8]

Another charge against the west coast settlements was mismanagement of affairs. Reports from the *Lafayette* emigrants and crew were sufficient to convince the Maryland society's Board of Managers that conditions were highly unsatisfactory. Letters from established colonists corroborated such accounts. One asserted that duties on tobacco, gunpowder, and spiritous liquors, designed to pay the salaries of colony teachers, amounted to more than $5,000 annually. There were three teachers, each employed at $400 a year, but they could not collect their pay and one even had to resign for lack of resources.[9]

Shortly after the Maryland society had dispatched the *Ann,* committing itself to the new course of action, even more damning evidence of the state of Liberian affairs reached the parent board in Washington. George McGill, acting as the American Colonization Society's agent while Governor Joseph Mechlin returned home to explain the tangled situation in the colony, reported that there was not one dollar in the treasury and that

8 MSCS MSS, *Records,* vol. I, meeting of the Board of Managers, Oct. 2, 1833; *Letters,* vol. I, Remus Harvey to C. C. Harper and Moses Sheppard, Liberia, July 29, 1833.

9 MSCS MSS, *Letters,* vol. I, Hilary Teage to Harper, Liberia, July 29, 1833.

insurmountable debts had accumulated. The schools had all closed because the teachers had gone unpaid and had abandoned them to seek other means of livelihood. Shelves in the public store were almost bare because no new supplies had arrived and all public property was in a state of dilapidation. He described the colony as in ruins and attributed this to the improper handling of the provisions and agricultural equipment which had been provided. The Maryland society had suspected this all along and had already come to the conclusion that the only alternative to the abandonment of colonization was the establishment of a new colony.[10]

A fundamental problem of the original settlement, thought the Marylanders, lay in the character of the emigrants and their preparation for a new life in Africa. Long before they determined upon a colony of their own, Maryland society officials were cautious in screening their applicants. They stressed to all inquirers that they must carry with them legal proof of freedom. Slave owners were admonished to manumit their hands according to law, with a deed to become effective at the time of their emigration.

Another precaution which the society took was the insistence that all married persons carry marriage certificates with them. If outgoing couples possessed none and could not obtain proof of wedlock, they were to be remarried before embarkation. Agent McKenney was advised that the high tone of moral feeling in the colony was such that new arrivals would be looked upon askance were there any doubt about their having been legally married.[11] Although this regulation was initially adopted to make Maryland emigrants acceptable to the Liberian colonists, it was enforced just as rigorously after the new Cape Palmas colony was established.

Adherence to this rule was at most a nuisance to couples

10 ACS MSS, *Letters Received,* vol. LIV (1833), George R. McGill to board of the ACS, Monrovia, Nov. 16, 1833; MSCS MSS, *Corresponding Secretary Books,* vol. I, Latrobe to Van Rensselaer, Baltimore, July 10, 1833; Latrobe to Finley, Baltimore, July 22, 1833.
11 MSCS MSS, *State Managers Book,* Charles Howard to McKenney, Baltimore, Oct. 30, Nov. 8, 1832.

without the necessary evidence, but a real problem faced many slave families contemplating emigration when the husband or wife was owned by an individual who refused to allow the partner to join the departing group. Families were frequently deterred by their inability to go to Africa together. Even in cases where wives were willing to leave and to take their families with them, the Colonization Society sought to prevent their emigration because such women had so little to offer in building up a settlement.

Single females were, however, another matter. With adult unmarried women eligible for the same allotments of land given men, their prospects for early marriage after arrival in Liberia and at Cape Palmas were excellent. Young females were encouraged to go to Africa under the protection of respectable families with which they could live until they married.[12]

The Maryland society also sought to provide better guidance for their emigrants than those already in Africa appeared to have received. Persons preparing to move could take two barrels of baggage apiece. The society urged them to include their beds, bedding, and cooking utensils. Bulky items such as tables and chairs were excluded because they were worth less than the freight charges. Where departees were too poor to provide such basic needs, auxiliary branches of the state society and private individuals were encouraged to donate suitable goods. The Maryland Board of Managers was particularly anxious to have emigrants decently clothed and equipped when they were destined for settlement in one of the Liberian communities. Nothing, thought the Maryland officers, would be so prejudicial to the future welfare of the colonists as a squalid and comfortless appearance which would create a bad initial impression. The officers, however, soon found by experience that some items sent from the United States were inferior to those available on the African coast. Agricultural implements with edges, such as axes, were useless because of the humidity of the coast and their

12 MSCS MSS, *Letters,* vol. I, Frisby Henderson to Howard, Elkton, Nov. 14, 1832; Ralph Gurley to Howard, Washington, Oct. 10, 1832; *Miscellaneous Letters & Minutes, Collection of 75 Letters from William McKenney,* McKenney to E. Bosworth, Baltimore, Oct. 14, 1833.

poor quality. Other equipment was found unsuited to colonist needs. Emigrants were consequently supplied with money to buy axes and other tools from visiting traders carrying superior English goods after they actually got to Africa.

While the Maryland society encouraged citizens and auxiliaries to furnish indigent emigrants with their needs, it would not condone attempts to secure prospective colonists whose only hindrance was unpaid debts. It received numerous requests for monies to release applicants from financial encumbrances, but the organization deemed it bad policy to apply funds in this manner, since donors might object to the practice. To individuals seeking such assistance, the standard reply was that in the few cases where persons actually received aid in paying off bills, the cash came from personally solicited donations of the philanthropic.[13]

A regulation which was not immediately established, but which became part of the Maryland society's bylaws late in 1834, was the stipulation that all emigrants be vaccinated before they embarked for Africa. Doctor Benjamin Waterhouse had introduced this safeguard against smallpox into the United States in 1800; Waterhouse was a Boston physician and Harvard professor whose European training had opened the way for correspondence with Edward Jenner, developer of the procedure. The country rapidly accepted it, partially because such prominent men as Thomas Jefferson advocated the practice. The first vaccine institution in the United States was established in Baltimore in 1802. Considering these facts, it seems unusual that this preventive practice had not been adopted with departees long before. Now both vaccination and general health certificates issued by a qualified physician were required.[14]

Another lesson Marylanders learned from observance of the

---

13 MSCS MSS, *State Managers Book,* Howard to Henderson, Baltimore, Oct. 31, 1832; Howard to L. H. Patrick, Baltimore, Sept. 19, 1832; *Records,* vol. I, meeting of the Board of Managers, Nov. 24, 1832; *Minutes and Proceedings of the Executive Committee . . . ,* Oct. 15, 1832.

14 MSCS MSS, *Records,* vol. I, meeting of the Board of Managers, Dec. 30, 1834; John B. Blake, *Benjamin Waterhouse and the Introduction of Vaccination: A Reappraisal* (Philadelphia: University of Pennsylvania Press, 1957), pp. 11, 42, 62–63.

Liberians was the necessity of investigating the character of their applicants. Aware of the numerous lazy citizens already in the west coast American settlements of Africa, the Maryland society warned its auxiliary chapters not to accept worthless vagabonds. This admonition became particularly important after the society decided to plant its own colony at Cape Palmas. McKenney, seeking candidates through the state, was instructed to accept no one unless he was of exceptional moral character and to give preference to those distinguished for piety and learning. In keeping with its determination to prohibit the use of liquor in the new colony, the Colonization Society drew up a pledge before the *Ann*'s departure which each emigrant was obliged to sign: "We the persons whose names are hereunto signed do hereby solemnly promise and declare that we will severally support and obey the foregoing Constitution, and we do hereby also solemnly promise and declare that we will abstain from the use of ardent spirit except in case of sickness." [15]

Once an applicant was approved, had fulfilled all the requirements, and had taken the oath, he was still bound by regulations. Emigrants were divided into groups or messes during their voyage to Africa. The ship captain or some individual named as overseer by the Maryland society selected group leaders to supervise the distribution of provisions and the cooking of meals. Each of them was responsible for the order, good conduct, and cleanliness of his charges. All emigrants, save for the sick, were to be up and to wash on deck by sunrise. Experience showed that they tended to remain in their berths and between decks much of the day. Overseers were consequently urged to prevent this when the weather permitted passengers to remain outside. Regulations for scrubbing the decks and living quarters aimed at maintaining sanitary conditions. Religious observance, too, was an important feature of the voyage. Family prayers were to be held before breakfast and after supper. On Sunday two public services were to be held and an addi-

15 MSCS MSS, *Letters*, vol. I, McKenney to Dr. Martin, Salisbury, Nov. 3, 1832; *Records*, vol. I, meetings of the Board of Managers, Sept. 9, Nov. 22, 1833.

tional one was scheduled for each Wednesday. Officers of the Maryland society were worried lest idleness during the long voyage lead to improper conduct. They urged such passengers as could do so to spend much time reading to others and devoting as much effort as practical to teaching those wishing to learn.[16]

Once in Africa, the new arrivals were entitled to provisions for six months. Although the variety, quantity, and quality of goods varied with circumstances, the standard weekly allowance per person was about three pounds of meat, some fish, six quarts of bread, tea, and a half pint of molasses. Rice and palm oil were also distributed in small quantities when they could be purchased from the Africans.[17]

The brig *Ann* was en route to Africa. The state society board had studied every aspect of founding a new colony. The nineteen emigrants were deemed suitable material for the nucleus of the proposed settlement at Cape Palmas. Doctor Hall possessed detailed instructions covering every conceivable problem. These stipulated that the *Ann* should sail first to Monrovia. Hall was to show the person in charge there the American Colonization Society resolutions which gave blessings to the attempt at settling Cape Palmas. Monrovian citizens were to be procured to accompany the *Ann*'s passengers to Cape Palmas, but they, too, were to sign the pledge respecting support of the colony and abstinence from ardent spirits. Should no volunteers for the venture appear in Monrovia, Hall was to proceed down the coast to Grand Bassa and repeat his effort there. He was at all times to speak in friendly terms of the parent society and to repudiate the idea that the Maryland body was either an opponent or a rival. Cape Palmas, because of both its desirability and the public attention already given it, was to be the site of the new settlement, if at all possible. The Reverend John Hersey was employed to assist Doctor Hall. His specific duties were to

16 MSCS MSS, *State Managers Book,* directions to J. W. Prout, Dec. 7, 1832; *Corresponding Secretary Books,* vol. I, Latrobe and others to James Hall, Baltimore, Nov. 25, 1833.
17 MSCS MSS, *Letters,* vol. II, Hall to Latrobe, Cape Palmas, June 10, 1834; Hall to [Latrobe], Cape Palmas, Oct. 1, 1834.

supervise the survey and allotment of the land and to superintend the settlement's agricultural pursuits.[18]

Although the brig left Baltimore on November 28 in good weather, she encountered storms and contrary winds down Chesapeake Bay. Hall discovered that the vessel was a poor sailor; the log revealed that on the previous voyage she had averaged only three knots an hour. He also found that the cargo was so badly arranged that he had to repack in order to get at necessities. Moreover, a fire broke out which, Doctor Hall estimated, would have completely destroyed the ship had it blazed another fifteen minutes. All this occurred while the *Ann* was still in the bay. The rest of the voyage was at least as difficult. During the first month at sea, a continued gale kept the decks wet. The emigrants' berths were filled with sea water. Hall found that the captain, lacking a chronometer or nautical almanac, had little knowledge of longitude. Worried that they might reach the African coast south of Monrovia and then be unable to sail against the prevailing northeast winds, Hall made soundings off Gambia and decided to pick the way south. However, they were now plagued with the calms and, fearful that they might not reach their destination before the annual rainy season set in during April, Hall, Hersey, one of the two missionaries from the American Board of Commissioners for Foreign Missions, and four emigrants left the brig in an open boat some 350 miles at sea. After great fatigue and exposure to the sun and the night dews, they reached Monrovia five days later on January 27. The *Ann* arrived the next day, having experienced good winds from the time the seven had left the vessel.

Another difficulty confronting Hall on this initial voyage as agent for the Maryland society was the conflict between his assistant, John Hersey, and nearly everyone else aboard. Hersey almost immediately became embroiled with the ship's captain, a heavy drinker possessed of a violent temper and profane speech. As an ordained minister, Hersey protested such conduct. Matters worsened. On Christmas morning the captain suggested

18 MSCS MSS, *Corresponding Secretary Books,* vol. I, Latrobe and others to Hall, Baltimore, Nov. 25, 1833.

that the emigrants celebrate with a dance. Hersey objected. He also complained to the captain that one of his crew had ridiculed religion before the passengers. The more his protests were ignored, the more Hersey became obsessed with the idea that he was being abused by all aboard the *Ann* and that his was the lone righteous soul in the multitude.

While still at sea, Hersey considered resigning his post upon reaching Monrovia. He decided upon further reflection to sacrifice his own feelings and to continue on with the party to Cape Palmas. This he did. But by that time he was complaining that he had no specific duties, and hence no actual authority, and that he was forced to submit to the commands of Doctor Hall who did not regard the Bible as the Word of God. His resignation and return home were honestly regretted by Hall, who still considered his potential services valuable, but his departure reduced the ranks of chronic complainers.[19]

The arrival of the *Ann* in Monrovia was hailed by some citizens as evidence that deliverance from the badly managed existing colony was at last possible. Hall made the necessary contact with colonial authorities and received permission for a number of the old settlers to remove to Cape Palmas. Meeting with potential cape colonists both publicly and privately, he soon found great opposition to the project among almost all persons not originally from Maryland. He attributed the hostility principally to a jealousy of the new colony and to the desire of the wealthy to maintain their existing labor force. Persons anxious to move to Cape Palmas were often deterred by unpaid debts in Monrovia, by promises of assistance in case they remained, and by threats if they left. Both ordinary citizens and at least one colonial employee, Doctor George P. Todsen, the physician, resorted to these measures. Additional opposition came from English traders who endeavored to discourage colonists from moving and to dissuade the Africans from forming contracts with the Marylanders. British denunciation of temperance regu-

19 MSCS MSS, *Letters*, vol. I, Hall to Latrobe, brig *Ann*, near Cape Henry, Dec. 2, 1833; vol. II, Hall to [Latrobe], Monrovia, Jan. 29, 1834; John Hersey to McKenney, at sea, Jan. 14, 1834; Hersey to Latrobe, Monrovia, Feb. 3, 1834.

lations which would bind persons going to Palmas also wielded great influence.

Fearing that English merchants might arrive at the cape before the Maryland expedition and worried that the quest for additional settlers in Monrovia would heighten opposition, Hall departed on February 4. With thirty Monrovians, including nineteen adult males, added to his original company, Hall anchored off Bassa the following morning, recruited five more men there, and set sail for Palmas soon after. The *Ann* arrived at Garroway, about fifteen miles from the cape, on the 10th. Doctor Hall immediately sent an African friend from Palmas, who had been in Monrovia awaiting his arrival and had joined him there, ahead in a canoe to inform the inhabitants that the Americans would arrive the following day. News that the emigrants were en route had actually reached the area some days before. Even at Garroway fifty to a hundred Africans had greeted the ship, begging for rum and tobacco. Late in the afternoon of February 11, 1834, the *Ann* anchored at its destination.[20]

Selection of Cape Palmas as the new colony's site was one of the Maryland society's easiest decisions. As Americans and Europeans gained accurate information respecting the African west coast, the promontory was habitually referred to in highly laudatory terms. Observation soon taught visitors and merchants that the steady northwest trade winds made return voyages to Europe or America easy, whereas farther south, toward the Biafra Bight, calms and currents made sailing difficult. Furthermore, only a few years before, in 1830, the mouths of the Niger River had finally been identified. Latrobe believed that Cape Palmas, with its Cavally River and a good harbor for small ships, would become a maritime victualing station akin to that at the Cape of Good Hope. Although Governor Mechlin reported the area's inhabitants to be savages, a considerable number of Liberian settlers claimed that the cape people were mild-

---

20 *Ibid.*, Hall to [Latrobe], Monrovia, Jan. 29, 1834; John B. Russwurm to Latrobe, Liberia, Feb. 23, 1834; Hall to [Latrobe], brig *Ann* off Drov, Feb. 9, 1834.

mannered and industrious and that they were anxious to have Americans locate there. The surrounding country was reputedly fertile, producing rice, palm oil, ivory, and camwood, a valuable hard timber. For a colony whose basis was to be agriculture, unanimously favorable soil reports were one reason for the cape's selection.[21]

Another major reason for its choice was the accepted opinion in Africa and America that it was healthier than the Monrovia area. When the Board of Managers announced its plans for a new settlement, it pointed out that the country from the Senegal to the St. Paul's River was intersected with streams rising far in the interior. All brought vast quantities of alluvial deposits to the ocean, thus giving rank luxuriance to the mangrove swamp. Assuming this to be the cause of the dreaded fever, the board noted that no rivers of any length existed between the St. Paul's near Monrovia and the Assinie, close to Cape Three Points on the Gold Coast. It concluded that the absence of streams bringing rich deposits from the interior was further evidence that Cape Palmas must be one of the healthiest spots on the coast.[22]

Doctor Hall's first reports gave heart to the anxious colonizationists in Maryland. He wrote that the appearance of the country, the bay, and the river was exceedingly fine and that no place could be more desirable for a settlement. The Africans were anxious for a settlement in the area. George McGill, the Baltimorean who had corresponded frequently with Latrobe since 1827 following his settling in Liberia, was among those accompanying the *Ann* to Cape Palmas and reported that the inhabitants welcomed the party with open arms. They told the colonists that they had long wanted the Americans to settle there in order to have someone to teach them English, to buy their produce, and to supply them with merchandise. According

---

21 MSCS MSS, *Records,* vol. I, meeting of the Board of Managers, Oct. 2, 1833; *Corresponding Secretary Books,* vol. I, Latrobe to Van Rensselaer, Baltimore, July 10, 1833; *Letters,* vol. I, McGill to Latrobe, Monrovia, July 12, 1832.
22 MSCS MSS, *Records,* vol. I, meeting of the Board of Managers, Oct. 2, 1833.

to this exceptionally able informant, Palmas was held in as high esteem among the Africans themselves as Cape Mesurado and Sierra Leone. Even John Hersey, the disaffected assistant agent, stated that vegetation grew as luxuriously at the cape as on the best lands back home in America. He confirmed the popular view that Palmas was much healthier than Monrovia and declared that there was little danger of sickness among the Maryland emigrants.[23]

The task of negotiating with native residents called for expert maneuvering. Hall had been chosen specifically for the job because of his knowledge of African ways. His instructions from the Board of Managers were to purchase as much land as possible. Boundaries, so far as possible, were to be streams of water. While the Marylanders hoped to purchase the land in fee simple, they were willing to agree to any of a variety of other arrangements to gain a foothold. Hall was ordered to use rum only if the territory could not be purchased without it.[24]

Hall found that the Cape Palmas area was under the control of three African groups, each taking the name of the region in which it dwelled and all Grebos, related to the Kru people. He had, consequently, to deal with the king of Cape Palmas, immediately dubbed King Freeman, the Grahway headman, thereafter known as King Will, and the king of Grand Cavally, nicknamed King Joe Holland. The party, including Hall, McGill, and the two ABCFM missionaries, J. Leighton Wilson and Stephen R. Wynkoop, went ashore on February 12 to arrange a palaver. An immense multitude of Africans lined the beach to watch. Jangling bells and chains suspended from their necks and ankles created an almost deafening noise. The conical-shaped houses with high thatched roofs were so close that only one person could pass between them at a time. The visitors found King Freeman, a stout but dignified man, seated upon a low stool with a small striped umbrella over his head. His

23 MSCS MSS, *Letters,* vol. II, Hall to [Latrobe], brig *Ann* off Drov, Feb. 9, 1834; McGill to Latrobe, Monrovia, Mar. 8, 1834; Hersey to Latrobe and the Board of Managers, Baltimore, July 21, 1834.
24 MSCS MSS, *Corresponding Secretary Books,* vol. I, Latrobe and others to Hall, Baltimore, Nov. 25, 1833.

dress consisted of a black hat with a red cap underneath and a knee-length striped loin cloth. A string of beads around his neck, several iron rings around his waist, and at least a half-dozen coarse iron rings about each ankle completed his attire. Behind him stood his wives. Hall gave a "dash," as gifts were called in Africa, and in return received a bleating black goat. The grand palaver with the other two kings was amicably set for the following day.

Negotiations with all three kings took place in equally colorful surroundings. King Joe Holland's apparel matched that of King Freeman, but King Will was dressed in American fashion. Appearing in a blue broadcloth coat with metal buttons, white trousers which came only halfway down his legs, and dirty ruffled shirt, he strained to personify dignity. At a short distance sat a group of old men who participated in deliberations via messenger. In one day's time Hall secured a deed for as much land as the society could possibly desire at a price far less than anticipated. Although twenty puncheons of rum were among the items sought, that demand was easily dismissed when Hall insisted that his master had sent him to purchase land without rum. In reality, Hall's success must be attributed to the work done by the African friend who met him in Monrovia. Though under protest, this person lobbied among the petty rulers before negotiations opened and had largely pushed aside the insistence upon liquor.[25]

Hall signed a deed of cession with Kings Freeman, Will, and Joe Holland for land extending some twenty miles along the seashore and twenty into the interior. Ownership gave possession of all the rivers, bays, creeks, anchorages, timber, and mines on it, except for one tract of land deeded to King Yellow Will of Little Cavally sometime back by the Grahway headman and lands already under cultivation or occupied by the Africans as towns and villages. The Africans reserved the right to travel by

25 MSCS MSS, *Letters*, vol. II, Hall to [Latrobe], brig *Ann* off Drov, Feb. 9, 1834; Houghton Library, ABCFM Papers, *Correspondence, Letters from Missionaries to Africa*, vol. I (West Africa, South Africa, previous to 1838), journal of J. Leighton Wilson on a missionary tour to western Africa in 1834.

stream and to traverse all sections of the country not inhabited by Maryland colonists. The society was deeded the land for its own special benefit in perpetuity, but the Africans retained the right of governing any groups of their own people who might wish to occupy any part of the territory. They acknowledged themselves "members of the colony of Maryland in Liberia, so far as to unite in common defence, in case of war or foreign aggression." Hall, in the society's name, guaranteed the reserved rights, agreed that neither person nor property of the kings and their dependents would be trespassed upon or molested, and accepted the stipulation that no lands under cultivation, towns, or villages would be taken over save by special contract and the payment of compensation agreed upon. Finally, the Maryland society was to establish within one year a free school for the children at Palmas, Grahway, and Grand Cavally.[26]

Besides the twenty puncheons of rum, residents sought an extensive list of items, among them twenty cases of guns, twenty and a half barrels of gunpowder, twenty bales of cloth, twenty cases of looking glasses, a hundred dozen red caps, a hundred iron pots, twenty hogsheads of tobacco, a box of umbrellas, and a wide assortment of ornamental and practical articles. A comparison of the items requested with those finally given for Cape Palmas reveals that Hall had justifiably earned his reputation for skill in handling the Africans. First, they got no rum whatsoever. Save for a small quantity reserved for the infirmary, all was poured overboard. Instead of twenty cases of guns, they received only four. Likewise, the Africans received twenty kegs of powder rather than twenty and a half barrels, a considerable difference in quantity. Then, too, they got only twenty hats and three hogsheads of tobacco. All else was likewise reduced in quantity.

Hall was a cunning agent in other respects as well. For example, the deed specified no exact bounds to the society's territory. The terms delineating property under the colony's

26 "Deed for Maryland in Liberia" in the Appendix to the *Third Annual Report of the Maryland State Colonization Society* (Baltimore: John D. Toy, 1835), pp. 29–30.

jurisdiction were such terms as "a cocoanut tree, known as the large cocoanut," "one day's journey," "six-hours' walk," and "running along the beach." Other portions of the deed bearing upon African claims were likewise indefinite. A principal reason for such vagueness was Hall's ignorance of the country's potential and the most arable tracts. Furthermore, knowing that English traders whose self-interest would prompt them to block the society's purchase were due any day from Cape Mesurado, Hall wanted to lay claim to as much coastline as possible. A deed in which the Africans' possessions could not be clearly distinguished from the society's property, and which in fact made Cape Palmas appear almost under joint ownership, afforded outsiders scant opportunity to interfere with society aims.

Another adroit move on Hall's part was arranging to send a son of each of the three rulers to the United States for schooling. In this initial phase of good feelings the kings were enthusiastic and acquiesced. Hall considered it a judicious measure, for the boys could be held as hostages should relations between colonists and Africans grow unfriendly. In addition, the presence of three African princes in their midst was certain to inspire the Christian public at home to work harder for the colonization cause.[27]

Doctor Hall's orders from the Board of Managers for the creation of the colony were specific. His first task was to build a large stockade. Detailed instructions for every aspect were given. As soon as the site had been chosen, a wide street was to be laid out perpendicular to one side of it. Lots with 300 feet in frontage and 726 feet in length were to be marked off. Each family or single adult immigrant was to be assigned a town and a farm lot. Lots nearest the stockade were to be held for public purposes and could be divided into smaller lots for distribution to immigrant traders. Other streets were to be laid out parallel to the first and occasional narrow cross streets were to afford access between the main streets. Each grantee was to be responsible for keeping the road in front of his lot in good repair and

27 MSCS MSS, *Letters,* vol. II, Hall to [Latrobe], brig *Ann* off Drov, Feb. 9, 1834; Hall to Latrobe, Cape Palmas, Apr. 16, 1834; "Deed for Maryland in Liberia," pp. 29–30.

clear of brush to the center. In making town and farm allotments, compactness of the settlement was to be kept in mind.
The assigning of farm lands was to be undertaken as soon as
the stockade had been built and the colonists were comfortably
housed. Later, townships approximately four miles square were
to be delineated.[28]

Although orderly development was desirable, Doctor Hall
found that local circumstances prevented such step-by-step procedures. Aware that English traders opposed Maryland efforts
at Palmas, Doctor Hall deemed that secure possession of the harbor was the most important goal. Consequently, the site he chose
for the stockade and town, while possessing many inconve-
niences, was on the northwest point of the cape overlooking the
harbor. It was some distance from the landing spots along the
beach and necessitated spreading the farm lots a considerable
distance from the town. Moreover, the timber for the stockade
was found to be of improper size, leaving the settlement without means of building a defense. The government house was
built in two weeks' time but only with great difficulty. Although
the frame had been sent out aboard the *Ann,* the colonists found
that mistakes had been made in framing and marking the different pieces. The frame was entirely too slender for the height
of the house, which then had to be reduced by some four feet.
Hersey, still at the colony, admitted that part of their problem
stemmed from lack of acquaintance with this type of work.
Though unaccustomed to house construction, he thought the
government building had the most slender frame he had ever
seen in a structure of its size and cost.[29]

By mid-April Hall could write that most were in their own
houses and that most town lots were fenced. Not a single colonist had died of fever. But other parts of his report were far less
favorable. Hall had known from the beginning that the settlers
were not the most desirable ones for establishing a colony. As

28 MSCS MSS, *Corresponding Secretary Books,* vol. I, Latrobe and others
to Hall, Baltimore, Nov. 25, 1833.
29 MSCS MSS, *Letters,* vol. II, Hall to [Latrobe], brig *Ann* off Drov, Feb. 9,
1834; Hersey to Latrobe and the Board of Managers, Baltimore, July 21,
1834.

they sailed from Monrovia to Cape Palmas, Hall had written that "our emigrants are not exactly what I could wish, although some few are sterling men. . . ." His low estimate of this human stock was borne out when actual development got under way in the colony. His first letter from Cape Palmas noted that "much public work is to be done; and I do assure you with such emigrants as I now have but little can be effected. There is not the least particle of public spirit or patriotism in them, and it is with utmost effort that I can produce unanimity of feeling sufficient to enable them to mess together. . . ." Hersey also testified that upon their arrival at Cape Palmas the emigrants not only revealed a marked disinclination to work but also became hostile toward the Africans and argumentative among themselves.

Another difficulty plaguing the colony was the need for food and supplies. Many provisions sent aboard the *Ann* had been left at Monrovia and Bassa for the families of the men volunteering to settle Palmas. Most of these pioneers would never have left the older settlements had arrangements not been made for their dependents in the interval before the cape was ready to receive them. By April most families had arrived. The lateness of the season unfortunately prevented them from planting crops. Matters were made worse by a scarcity of rice along the coast. The Africans, knowing of the colonists' need, were determined to charge them at least twice the amount paid by passing trading vessels. They even prevented Doctor Hall from making purchases from neighboring tribes. He concluded that the only way to avoid war with the Africans was to go along with them until a small schooner could be sent for the colony's use. With it, the Marylanders could obtain rice at reasonable rates. While acknowledging that such a vessel would be expensive, Hall warned the Board of Managers that it was absolutely necessary for the safety and welfare of the colony. It was several years, however, before a ship actually arrived.[30]

---

30 *Ibid.*, Hall to [Latrobe], brig *Ann* off Drov, Feb. 9, 1834; Hall to Latrobe, Cape Palmas, Apr. 16, 1834; Hersey to Latrobe and others, Baltimore, July 21, 1834.

With Cape Palmas purchased, the government house erected, and most colonists settled on their own allotments, the next task was the establishment of government. The Maryland society's managers, seeking to meet every eventuality, had sent with Hall a constitution and an ordinance for the colony's temporary administration. The name chosen for it was "Maryland in Liberia," suggested by Robert S. Finley, who happened to pass through Baltimore as preparations for the *Ann*'s voyage were under way. While a committee of three was entrusted with drawing up the documents, Latrobe had done the actual work. He studied the charters and constitutions of the different states of the United States and selected from them the best features. He then took Nathan Danes's ordinance of 1787 for the government of the Northwest Territory and modified it for use in the Maryland colony. He introduced a clause into the bill of rights making it a penal offense to drink and would have done away with trial by jury in civil cases but "was deterred by a decent respect for the opinions of mankind." He considered it a rare opportunity for a young lawyer to lay the foundations of what might become a great nation.[31]

By this constitution, the Maryland State Colonization Society retained full power and the right to make the rules, regulations, and ordinances for the territory in Africa until that body withdrew its agents and placed control wholly into the colonists' hands. Every adult immigrant was required to sign a pledge to uphold the constitution and to refrain from the use of liquor save in case of illness. Local Africans were to be treated justly and their property, rights, and liberty were never to be invaded or disturbed, "unless it may become necessary to do so, to repel aggressions on their part." No taxes were to be levied except for purposes of defense, internal improvement, education, and the support of local government. The society, however, reserved the right to impose duties and port charges.

All elections were to be by ballot, with the state society setting voter qualifications. The seventh article of the constitution

---

31 John Edward Semmes, *John H. B. Latrobe and His Times, 1803–1891* (Baltimore: Norman, Remington Co., 1917), pp. 146–47.

embraced a bill of rights. This guaranteed the citizens of Maryland in Liberia the rights to worship as they pleased; to speak, write, and publish freely their personal views in all matters; to assemble freely and to apply for redress of grievances; as well as the enjoyment of a wide range of additional activities. Finally, the constitution, save for the bill of rights which might never be touched, could be altered only by the unanimous consent of a meeting of the Board of Managers or by a two-thirds vote of the members present at two successive meetings of that body.[32]

The evangelical goals propounded in the decision to establish a new colony in Africa were entrusted to the American Board of Commissioners for Foreign Missions in Boston. Experience had proven to the ABCFM that it was preferable for missionaries of different societies, and especially of different denominations, to labor apart, if possible, and thus it eagerly accepted the offer to send two representatives to Cape Palmas to inspect the country and to investigate mission possibilities. The Reverend J. Leighton Wilson of South Carolina and Stephen R. Wynkoop of Pennsylvania were chosen to sail on the *Ann* and to arrange for a station in the colony. Their reports on Africa as a field for operations were enthusiastic. Wilson commended the Marylanders on "the *rumless* purchase" of Cape Palmas and judged Doctor Hall as uncommonly expert in managing settlement affairs. ABCFM officers, anxious to get a foothold in West Africa and aware of the provision in the Cape Palmas deed that three schools were to be established within a year, voted to found and conduct them. Their object was to train and employ a competent African agency. Assuming that the climate was uncongenial to white men, they determined to bring forth a legion of Africans as school teachers, readers, distributors of Bibles and tracts, and preachers. The ABCFM accepted a society offer to grant them a mission house site in the colony and Wilson, with his wife and two Negro male assistants, sailed from New York aboard the schooner *Edgar* on November 7, 1834. The

---

32 "Constitution of Maryland in Liberia," in the Appendix to the *Fourth Annual Report of the Maryland State Colonization Society* (Baltimore: John D. Toy, 1836), pp. 62–66.

response of the ABCFM prompted the board to offer to the members of all religious denominations every facility in their power to establish schools and to carry on missionary work in the colony. It was two years, however, before other denominations, the Methodist Episcopal and the Protestant Episcopal, launched plans to establish stations at Cape Palmas.[33]

The Maryland society board's reaction to news of Doctor Hall's accomplishments was one of approbation and gratitude. The only matter which the board requested Hall to alter concerned the lands reserved by the Africans as their own. He was instructed to secure to the society a pre-emption, thus preventing the chieftains from selling their areas to outsiders. Hall's plea for immediate supplies was heeded by dispatch of the *Sarah and Priscilla* in June, 1834. The cargo embraced such provisions and conventional items for the colonists as flour, pork, molasses, and soap, together with such agricultural implements as handsaws, axes, and files, and plank, bricks, and nails for building operations. Numerous trade goods—tobacco, beads, and wash basins—were also sent, but instead of the dining chairs and cocked hats and feathers requested by the three African kings, the board sent multicolored silk umbrellas. Latrobe, writing for his colleagues, confessed that they were somewhat at a loss as to what would be suitable presents but, he concluded, "I don't know why they [the umbrellas] may not answer as well as a cocked hat to designate Royalty." [34]

The colony in June, 1834, stood in a precarious position.

---

33 MSCS MSS, *Corresponding Secretary Books,* vol. I, Latrobe to Board of Foreign Missions, [Baltimore], Sept. 10, 1833; *Letters,* vol. I, B. B. Wisner to Latrobe, Boston, Sept. 14, 1833; Wisner to Latrobe, Philadelphia, Oct. 5, 1833; vol. II, J. Leighton Wilson to Latrobe, New York, Apr. 15, 1834; R. Anderson to McKenney, Boston, Nov. 11, 1834; vol. IV, Anderson to Ira A. Easter, Boston, Feb. 17, 1836; vol. V, John Clark and James R. Williams to the managers of the MSCS, Baltimore, Oct. 26, 1836; Hall to Easter, Hot Springs, [Va.], Aug. 28, 1836; *Records,* vol. I, letter from Anderson (read at a meeting of the Board of Managers, Apr. 29, 1834); vol. II, meeting of the Board of Managers, June 23, 1836; Houghton Library, ABCFM Papers, *Miscellaneous, Instructions to Missions,* vol. I (1828–1836), Prudential Committee to Wilson, Oct., 1834.
34 MSCS MSS, *Records,* vol. I, meetings of the Board of Managers, Apr. 22, May 22, 1834; *Corresponding Secretary Books,* vol. I, Latrobe to Hall, Office of the MSCS, June 2, 1834.

Government buildings completed were a large kitchen and storehouse for rice, a stockade fort and jail, and one large and two small houses for arriving immigrants which could accommodate 150 persons. The original colonists had built twelve frame houses and were finishing two stone dwellings. Though most town lots were cleared, fenced, and planted, what food could be expected from them would be insufficient to keep the colonists alive. Public funds were nearly exhausted and Doctor Hall, periodically ill, was without any assistant to survey the lands, inspect public affairs, or advise settlers on the best course of their work. Fortunately, the Africans were peaceable.

The arrival of the *Sarah and Priscilla* in Cape Palmas harbor on August 9 found the colony rather well supplied. Not knowing when to expect relief from home, Hall had traded with several passing vessels. He paid specie to a captain from Salem, Massachusetts, for cloth and gunpowder. A few days later a Spanish schooner anchored in the harbor and Hall bartered a half hogshead of tobacco for iron and cloth. A week before the *Sarah and Priscilla* arrived, Hall exchanged palm oil for crockery with a Philadelphia captain. Nevertheless, Hall was glad to have the new shipment, although it proved a mixed blessing. Sight of the goods bred great dissatisfaction among the Africans over the amount agreed upon and received when they had sold Cape Palmas a few months before. They now laid claim to half the cargo. Hall was perturbed. If he gave in, the price would be high, for only a considerable amount of goods would mollify them. Moreover, there would be no end to their extortions. But to refuse their claims would cause constant clamor among them, much ill will, and the continual possibility of war. Hall chose the latter course, swearing never to grant their unreasonable demands. Aware that the society would have to support newcomers then in the colony beyond the customary six months, and repeatedly warned of financial difficulties at home, Hall opted to retain a full larder.

The disappointing feature of the *Sarah and Priscilla*'s arrival was the complete lack of immigrants. Hall had kept the Africans at a distance by regularly reminding them that he daily expected at least a hundred new colonists. Two houses, or receptacles, as they were called, stood ready for occupancy. He was mortified that only cargo came and pleaded with the state society to send him settlers. He realized that the Africans would never attach much importance to the colony until it had more people and ample stores of guns, powder, tobacco, and cloth. By the end of the next year the board had sent out three additional loads of immigrants. The *Bourne* with fifty-eight aboard arrived at the cape on January 24, 1835, twenty-seven passengers went out on the *Harmony* in June, 1835, and at the end of 1835 thirty-nine sailed on the *Fortune*.

The Africans' attitude at the docking of the *Sarah and Priscilla* and their obstinacy in refusing to sell rice or allowing Hall to purchase from neighboring tribes epitomized strains developing between colonists and Africans. An equally serious problem was theft. One ship captain who frequented the West African coast called the native inhabitants at the Maryland settlement the greatest thieves between Cape Mesurado and Palmas. Many of them considered theft commendatory, especially if carried out adroitly. Seldom were they punished, save when colonists took matters into their own hands. This usually worsened relations without any beneficial consequence. The headmen shared articles stolen from the colonists or from vessels, with the pilfering individual retaining half the loot. Even a constant guard of two men could not prevent nightly theft. There were cases in which thieves slipped their hands through the wattling of houses and stripped bedclothes from the sick. Since the colony was too weak to risk a major conflict with the indigenes, only palavers with the kings were employed and they, too, proved ineffective.[35]

The colonists also practiced theft, against both the Africans and the colonial store. The constant loss was reflected semiannually when the agent made his financial report to the Maryland State Colonization Society. One early accounting noted that

35 MSCS MSS, *Letters,* vol. II, Hall to Latrobe, Cape Palmas, Apr. 24, June 27, Aug. 17, Oct. 15, 1834; Richard E. Lawlin to Latrobe, New York, July 21, 1834; vol. III, Hall to Latrobe, Cape Palmas, Jan. 27, Aug. 26, 1835; Oliver Holmes, Jr., to Latrobe, Cape Henry, Dec. 27, 1835; *Records,* vol. II, meeting of the Board of Managers, Dec. 5, 1835.

nearly two barrels of beef, probably stolen by the colonists, were missing from the government warehouse. Hall concluded that "this thief palaver is one grand attendant expense on all establishments in this country. Night watch, locks, mare traps, and watch dogs are of no avail." He sought to balance financial records by charging at least 100 per cent profit on goods sold in the agency store.[36]

The six-month subsistence for colonists was to end in August, 1834. Aware that the people had no resources of their own, Hall continued to provide them with meat and bread for another four weeks. Having missed the traditional planting time, they would have to wait another year before their first harvest came. Under the circumstances Hall inaugurated a public works program. Making it a point to have every able-bodied man work for his fare, even when the work was of little consequence, he undertook the construction of a stone warehouse, a wharf, and a tower. The society had to bear the additional expense.[37]

Public employment rescued the settlers from certain starvation and insured gradual improvement in the colony, but it did not improve their quarrelsome nature. As the spring of 1835 came and the citizens finished the clearing and planting of their farm allotments, they began to complain about the manner in which land was being distributed. While each adult immigrant came with the expectation of receiving the minimum five acres promised colonists at the other American settlements, he found that Hall limited the size of outlying plots to two acres. Consequently, after receiving his town lot, the new colonist was given the choice of a two-acre lot beyond the village, with the right to three acres more even farther out after he had met deed requirements for the first two, or he might take five acres immediately at some more remote location. Most newcomers had chosen the two-acre plan, but once they got to attending their farm lots they became dissatisfied and charged Hall with deceiving them as well as failing to follow his instructions from the Board of

36 MSCS MSS, *Letters*, vol. III, Hall to Latrobe, Cape Palmas, Apr. 1, 1835.
37 *Ibid.*, vol. II, Hall to Latrobe, Cape Palmas, Oct. 15, 1834.

Managers. Hall, believing that two acres was the maximum amount any one man could cultivate, placed the chances at a hundred to one that a colonist might be so ambitious that he required more than the five acres as he had set it up.[38]

A project which the Board of Managers took personal delight in was the establishment of a public farm. Doctor Hall was urged to try different agricultural methods and crops to determine the most successful for the Cape Palmas area. He was to pay immediate attention to cotton and tobacco cultivation, but not to neglect plans for producing coffee and palm oil. Coffee, because it was not raised in the United States, was a potentially important export crop. The board expected that the public farm's success would encourage the colonists and provide work opportunities for those unable to make a living at their own occupations or temporarily destitute.[39]

Doctor Hall complained of ill health in letter after letter following his arrival in Africa. His condition worsened as he struggled to keep the colony going. Early in June, 1835, he informed society officers that he could not continue to act as their agent either with advantage to the colony's development or in safety to himself. By his own experience on the African coast and through observation of the sacrifices to health and life by Europeans visiting Africa, Hall had become convinced that if a colony were to flourish, it must be under the direction of "some spirited, intelligent, patriotic coloured man" acting in behalf of the Board of Managers. The frequent interregnums at Monrovia were enough, in Hall's mind, to corroborate his opinion that Africa meant death for most white men. The contrast between his own chronic illness and the general healthiness of the black colonists further confirmed the belief. The board took the attitude, nonetheless, that only a white man could replace Hall. Charles Howard wrote, "However confident [you] might be in the abilities of a Coloured person as your representative in your absence[,] yet some years must elapse before such an one will be

38 *Ibid.*, vol. III, "Petition of Colonists to the Agent [Hall]," n.d. [June 24, 1835]; Hall to Latrobe, Harper, June 1, 1835.
39 MSCS MSS, *Corresponding Secretary Books,* vol. II, Latrobe to Hall, Baltimore, Feb. 21, 1835.

viewed with respect that is accorded to a white man. . . ." [40]

Fearful that Doctor Hall, whose letters evinced progressive physical deterioration, might soon die, the board chose Oliver Holmes, Jr., a twenty-eight-year-old Maryland dentist, to lead a group of emigrants leaving aboard the *Fortune* in December, 1835. Volunteering to go to Africa for six months, Holmes was to assist Hall, but should Hall leave during that time, Holmes was to assume powers as governor pro tempore. Latrobe advised Holmes to emulate Hall in handling the Africans and colonists. Restating the society's philosophy, Latrobe wrote:

> It would seem that his [Hall's] success with the natives has been the result of his firmness of purpose, not less than the Justice of his course. A vacillating conduct is the worst possible, with ignorant men in any country, and essentially [especially] bad in Africa. It has been the policy of many colonists heretofore to drive out the aboriginies—as in the case of the colonies in this country of our own. . . . Such is not our policy, however. We would amalgamate the native with the colonist, raise the Farmer [former] to the standard of the latter, and then carry both on together to the highest eminences of civilization and the Gospel. In doing this, great care is necessary to prevent the colonist sinking to the native standard. This work of amalgamation should be managed discreetly, and the native should be made to feel, that it is a privilege to be considered the equal of the colonist. In a word, let the natives be taught to look on your colonists as benefactors and brothers, not as conquerors and enemies. [41]

Upon Holmes's arrival in West Africa early in February, 1836, Hall immediately surrendered to him the colony's property and interest, although he remained for some weeks until passage could be secured. Hall's accomplishments during his two-year tenure were remarkable. He succeeded in enlarging Maryland State Colonization Society territory from approximately twenty square miles to control of an area largely in the

---

40 MSCS MSS, *Letters,* Hall to Latrobe, Harper, June 1, 1835; Hall to [Latrobe], Cape Palmas, Mar. 1, 1835; *Corresponding Secretary Books,* vol. II, Howard to Hall, Office of the MSCS, May 30, 1835.

41 MSCS MSS, *Corresponding Secretary Books,* vol. II, Latrobe to Hall, Office of the MSCS, n.d. [late 1835]; Latrobe to Holmes, Office of the MSCS, Dec. 18, 1835; Latrobe to Holmes, Baltimore, Feb. 11, 1836.

interior from 600 to 800 square miles. He had accomplished this mostly in the last six months as he sought to carry out the board's instruction to gain pre-emptions on the African reserves specified within the original deed. Hall had also been able to establish contacts with tribes neighboring the cape, Grahway, and Grand Cavally peoples. All such groups had a vague hope of benefiting from their connection with the colony and deeded their land believing that the Marylanders would never be able to find a use for it. The sole good which many tribes counted on was the advantage of free trade. Hall reasoned that the colony could now expect unrestrained intercourse with all adjacent tribes and that it had obtained a legal right to territory of almost unlimited extent, to take over when, in due course, it might be needed.

Visible evidence of Hall's achievements was to be seen in a large agency house, which served both as his home and as the public courtroom; a two-story stone warehouse; a long wharf; a public farm of which some ten acres were cleared, enclosed, and partly cultivated; a country house for the farm superintendent; a jail; and three large structures to accommodate newly arriving emigrants. Four miles of road, named Maryland Avenue, had been built and were open. The town itself, called Harper for the late Robert Goodloe Harper, contained twenty-five frame houses belonging to private individuals arranged along Baltimore Street. On the farm lots beyond town limits, there were eight frame dwellings and twelve temporary structures. The ABCFM mission, named Fair Hope, embraced a number of buildings for worship, study, and housing. The colony's population was about 220, of whom sixty were adult males. The colonists had planted more than sixty acres of land with sweet potatoes, cassava, corn, beans, and other foodstuffs. Tobacco and cotton were also under cultivation. In Hall's view the colony could, in 1836, be considered as beyond the threat of famine.[42]

Hall's accomplishments were highly commendable. In comparison to the early history of Monrovia, Maryland in Liberia

42 MSCS mss, *Letters,* vol. IV, Hall to Latrobe, brig *Luna,* at sea, May 1, 1836.

had far surpassed what might reasonably have been expected in so short a time. Most of the success was directly attributable to Doctor Hall's perseverance, astuteness, and effort. There were, however, flaws in his operations and transactions. Hall permitted settlers to incur heavy debts by extending unreasonable credit at the public store, where he marked up most items to balance petty theft and loss through other circumstances. After he left the colonists complained that their debts were largely due to the mark-up. There was, likewise, no uniformity of pay for the public employment provided hard-pressed colonists. It was difficult to equate the worth of different services and settlers grumbled about supposed inequities. Without exception they believed that wages paid for working on public projects were too low. Much to the consternation of the society and of his successor, Hall had a propensity for keeping tallies of commercial transactions in his head rather than in the agency books.

Unpleasant and contrary reports of Holmes's stewardship soon superseded evaluation of Hall's administration. Possessed of a critical and fretful nature, Holmes proved to be mentally unstable and unsuited for his duties. Although he undertook some projects in the colony, most notably the digging of a well, he rapidly became a controversial figure. Throughout his brief tenure the new administrator engaged in a dispute with Charles Snetter, the newly appointed colonial secretary and bookkeeper. While useful in managing governmental affairs, Snetter had only a limited knowledge of accounting, a deficiency enabling Holmes to lay blame for colonial problems and financial disputes upon him. Before long the citizenry was divided into those supporting Holmes or defending Snetter. Another charge against Holmes was his offering to African workmen and others a drink he called wine but which was in reality a mixture of water, molasses, and rum personally prepared by him, obviously a breach of the basic no-liquor regulation. A final unfavorable aspect of the acting governor's stay in the colony was the serious mental derangement he suffered periodically as a result of the fever.[43]

43 *Ibid.,* Hall to Holmes, Harper, Mar. 18, 1836; Holmes to Latrobe, Harper, July 13, 1836; Wilson to Latrobe, Fair Hope, Feb. 8, 1836;

A problem for which the Board of Managers attempted remedial action during Holmes's administration concerned the establishment of a monetary system to replace barter. One difficulty of barter, even if the relative prices of goods were established, was bringing together parties each of whom had what the other wanted. It often happened that a person wanting to buy cotton cloth, for example, had only rice to exchange for it. But if the person possessing cloth had no use for the rice, one of them would have to make a sacrifice of his property in order to induce the other to effect a transaction. In order to create an exchange medium, the board in February, 1836, made cotton grown in the colony legal tender at the rate of 10 cents a pound. The colonial agent was responsible for purchasing and handling it. The board expected the set value of cotton to regulate trade and produce prices in the colony. If there was demand abroad for cotton and the set price rose, the cost of things in the colony would fall, and vice versa. Since some cotton was already being successfully grown, this ordinance was seen as the best means of stimulating the colonists to become agriculturalists.[44]

While Holmes was seeking to keep the colony running as he deemed best, the Board of Managers in Baltimore was considering a successor. The slowness of communication between the United States and Africa necessitated early action in order to have his replacement on the scene when his six months were up or as soon thereafter as possible. Hall, who advocated the appointment of a Negro governor, arrived in Baltimore early in June, 1836. During that month the board seriously deliberated the proposal and ultimately unanimously voted to appoint John Brown Russwurm, a resident of Monrovia for almost ten years. Believing that Russwurm possessed all the qualifications necessary for the position, the board expected that illness, which had

the Committee of Report to the Board of Managers, n.p. [Cape Palmas], June 15, 1836; vol. V, Wilson to Latrobe, Fair Hope, Sept. 6, 1836; James M. Thomson to Latrobe, Harper, Sept. 6, 1836; *Corresponding Secretary Books,* vol. III, Latrobe to committee of the citizens of Harper, Baltimore, n.d. [fall, 1836]; *Records,* vol. II, meeting of the Board of Managers, Sept. 13, 1836.
44 MSCS MSS, *Records,* vol. II, meeting of the Board of Managers, Feb. 19, 1836.

reduced Hall's and Holmes's effectiveness, would not interfere with his work. In its *Annual Report* to Maryland supporters, the board explained that ultimately the government of the colonies on the coast of Africa had to pass into the hands of the colonists and the tutelage of the societies in the United States had to cease. Were the colonists ever to assume self-government, they had to be inspired with the belief that they were competent for it. This could never be accomplished with perpetuation in Africa of the system of white overseers to which most colonists were accustomed in the United States. A final argument was the colony's small size and the opportunity to install a new administration which later immigrants would accept as the established order.

The board fully realized that its decision was a gamble. It could only hope that Russwurm would command respect from both colonists and Africans. It risked the colony's future on its belief that the new governor would prove competent. Society officers acted upon the conviction that the black race was capable of the same mental improvement expected of whites. In their letter of appointment they reminded Russwurm that they bore a heavy responsibility for their act and besought him to aim at a high reputation and honorable fame.[45]

When news of his appointment as Maryland State Colonization Society agent and governor of Maryland in Liberia reached Russwurm at Monrovia late in September, Holmes had already released the Cape Palmas community to a three-man committee rule. Also in Monrovia, Holmes agreed to return to Harper to settle accounts and to continue in control until Russwurm could take over some weeks later. Apparently mortified that a Negro was appointed as his successor, Holmes remained at Cape Palmas less than twenty-four hours. Charles Snetter, the beleaguered colonial secretary, now came to a defense of his own work, charging that during Holmes's administration he had never seen the society's books. The Board of Managers, investigating the colony's financial accounts, found that a great portion of them

45 MSCS MSS, *Corresponding Secretary Books,* vol. II, Latrobe to Holmes, Baltimore, n.d. [June, 1836]; Latrobe to Russwurm, Baltimore, June 30, 1836; *Fifth Annual Report of the Maryland State Colonization Society* (Baltimore: John D. Toy, 1837), p. 8.

were absolutely unintelligible. Part of the difficulty arose from the lack of system in bookkeeping in the colony at the outset. The society now resolved to establish improved accounting procedures.

Of Holmes's unhappy and unsuccessful stay in Africa, one charitable colonist reported that the type of men Holmes had to deal with had been enough to dampen the zeal and perseverance of any person of his years and experience. He concluded that Holmes had managed the colony's affairs as judiciously and discreetly as had been possible. Whether a Negro governor could inspire the confidence and cooperation denied two white predecessors now became the test of Russwurm's administration.[46]

46 MSCS MSS, *Letters,* vol. V, Holmes to Latrobe, [Cape Palmas], Sept. 7, 1836; Thomson to Latrobe, Harper, Sept. 6, 1836; vol. VII, Russwurm to Latrobe, Monrovia, Sept. 28, 1836; Charles Snetter to Latrobe, Cape Palmas, July 7, 1837; *Records,* vol. II, meeting of the Board of Managers, Sept. 29, 1837.

I V

Home Operations
1833-1840

The generous state appropriation to Maryland colonizationists dating from 1832 largely covered the expense of sending emigrants to Monrovia and the other American Colonization Society Liberian settlements. When, however, Marylanders decided to found their own colony, the question was raised as to whether the legislation allowed fund managers to apply state monies to such a venture. The law read that the managers were given authority to "make such preparations at the said colony of Liberia, or elsewhere, as they may think best, which shall seem to them expedient for the reception and accommodation of the said persons so to be removed, until they can be enabled to support themselves. . . ." Society officers asserted that the act's phraseology fully warranted the application of monies to any cost connected with establishment of a settlement. Demurring, state managers advanced $30 per emigrant who went to the new colony in 1833 and lent an additional amount, making the total outlay $8,000.[1]

This sum was only a small portion of the amount the Colonization Society deemed necessary for its project. John Latrobe, as corresponding secretary, contacted state society headquarters in Boston, New York, and Philadelphia, informing them of the need for another $10,000. While hoping to raise several thousand dollars in Baltimore, the Marylanders counted upon the northern states for the balance, expecting $2,500 to be raised in each of these cities. Unhappily for the Maryland colonizationists, their requests to the North produced little cash. Robert S. Finley, hopscotching from agency to agency and now employed by the New York Colonization Society, informed Latrobe that his auxiliary's constitution prevented any contribution to the Maryland enterprise. The New York society naturally continued committed to parent society support. Yet, before the year ended, it had decided to spend its money to send out and settle emigrants independently within the bounds of the original Liberian colony. Boston colonizationists, already finding other movements of more interest and promise, gave scarcely more support than the New Yorkers. John Tappan, deeply involved in the temperance cause, could promise nothing from his city but personally contributed $100. The Pennsylvania Colonization Society, holding itself obligated to assist the national body, declined to aid the Marylanders. Although it did not entirely approve of the parent board's course, it considered itself bound to aid that debt-ridden organization.[2]

When written requests to the northern societies failed to bring in funds, the Maryland group decided to send up envoys in the

---

1 Maryland, *Laws of Maryland* (1831), Chapter 281; MSCS MSS, *Records,* vol. I, meeting of the Board of Managers, Sept. 9, 1833; *Corresponding Secretary Books,* vol. I, John Latrobe to Courtland Van Rensselaer, Baltimore, July 10, 1833; *Manumission Books,* vol. I, meeting of the Board of State Managers, Sept. 9, 1833.

2 MSCS MSS, *Corresponding Secretary Books,* vol. I, Latrobe to Robert S. Finley, Baltimore, Oct. 11, 1833; *Letters,* vol. I, Finley to Latrobe, New York, [Oct.], Dec. 31, 1833; John Tappan to Latrobe, Boston, Oct. 16, 1833; James Bayard to Latrobe, Philadelphia, Oct. 22, 1833.

summer of 1834 to solicit contributions. The society's agent, William McKenney, was accompanied by the Breckenridge brothers, John and Robert. Natives of Kentucky, both were deeply committed to colonization. The star attraction on this trip was the African princes who, according to the Cape Palmas purchase agreement, had been sent to the United States for education. Each of the three kings sent a son, but one boy became so ill by the time they reached Monrovia that he was sent back home. The other two, John Cavally and Charles Grahway, landed in New York in April, 1834. Their arrival in Baltimore created great interest in Africa. The Board of Managers arranged meetings in numerous city churches to display the princes and to take up collections for the society's benefit. Their appearance with McKenney and the Breckenridges in the Northeast was likewise calculated to enhance society coffers.[3]

The entourage arrived in Boston early in August and held meetings in a number of churches. Lack of success and opposition from many quarters induced the group to cut short its tour and return home. Numerous factors account for the debacle. A more unfavorable time for the tour could hardly have been selected. General economic conditions in the country, reflecting the Jackson-Biddle bank fight, were so bad as almost to prohibit philanthropists from contributing to a new cause. Moreover, Orthodox Congregationalists in Boston were under pledge to allow the Reverend Lyman Beecher to solicit funds for the Lane Theological Seminary in Cincinnati, of which he was the first president, and he was expected daily. Another timing difficulty was that New York had lately experienced a violent clash between colonizationists and members of the recently formed American Anti-Slavery Society. Bostonians suspected that they might suffer the same clamor, a realistic fear since William Lloyd Garrison, a rabid abolitionist, publisher of the *Liberator,* and a founder of the new national antislavery organization, was

3 MSCS mss, *Records*, vol. I, meetings of the Board of Managers, Apr. 22, June 23, 1834; *Letters*, vol. II, J. Leighton Wilson to Latrobe, New York, Apr. 15, 1834; D. M. Reese to William McKenney, New York, May 17, 1834.

a local citizen. The mayor sought to forbid colonization meetings, declaring that such gatherings would draw unruly mobs, but several were held despite his protests. The greatest deterrent to financial success in Boston was the failure of the Maryland party to make clear the urgent need for further money to keep the colony going. Apparently no one gave a satisfactory explanation of why the state appropriation was proving insufficient. The trip showed that, at least in Boston, where abolition and colonization advocates within congregations made pastors reluctant to allow any meetings which might further divide their flocks, little could be gained by working with religious bodies. Colonization was done permanent damage in Boston by presentation of the Maryland plan which left the impression that Negroes in the state must either emigrate to Africa or suffer extermination. Garrison thereafter had great success in impressing upon the community the belief that Maryland laws were designed to drive blacks into the arms of the colonizationists.[4]

As for the African princes, their presence seems to have had little influence upon the more sophisticated Bostonians. Unfortunately, Charles died of an undisclosed illness in November, 1834, and it was decided to return John to Cape Palmas immediately to tell of their good treatment. The Board of Managers, fearful that Charles's death might bring bad consequences, sent a special envoy, the Reverend R. B. F. Gould, to the colony with the dead boy's belongings and a generous peace offering for his parents and family. The gifts included a black and gilt looking glass, a dozen tumblers, a pair of glass pitchers, a half-dozen china cups and saucers, a set of castors, nine dozen beads, and one pair of lusterware pitchers.[5]

Later efforts to gain financial aid in the North likewise failed. The New York Colonization Society again declined on the ground that only when it sent emigrants from the port of New York could it raise funds. Members claimed that any evidence

---

4 MSCS MSS, *Letters*, vol. II, B. B. Wisner to Latrobe, Boston, Aug. 5, 1834; Reese to McKenney, New York, May 17, 1834; vol. III, S. R. Wynkoop to Latrobe, Princeton, June 25, 1835.

5 MSCS MSS, *Corresponding Secretary Books*, vol. II, Nathaniel Williams to James Hall, Baltimore, Dec. 11, 1834; Williams to Weak Bolio, king of Grahway, Baltimore, Dec. 9, 1834.

of cooperation with a slaveholding state would doom its chances of success in that city.

The American Union for the Relief and Improvement of the Colored Race, a short-lived Boston organization, refused agent McKenney's plea for funds because its members no longer considered colonization an adequate remedy for slavery's evils. Many were former colonizationists who now considered that effort primarily a means of introducing civilization and Christianity into Africa. Whatever benefit it might have on the Negro population in the United States would be indirect.

Even Doctor James Hall, just returned from his service at Cape Palmas, could do nothing for the Maryland society in his native New England. He felt that the leading citizens were now doubting the Marylanders' benevolence because of abolitionist arguments that they were motivated by self-interest. Moreover, even those community elements disposed to aiding colonization could not now switch commitments from the parent society to the Maryland group without adding fuel to the abolitionists' fire. Hall concluded that only a gradual grass-roots adoption of the colonization cause could turn the elite of New England back to its support.[6]

The American Colonization Society was naturally hostile to and jealous of Maryland activities in the North, particularly the Breckenridge tour. Elliott Cresson of Philadelphia complained to the parent society that poachers had invaded their field. But Ralph Gurley, recalling that John Breckenridge now headed the Young Men's Colonization Society of Philadelphia, speculated that Cresson and the Breckenridges were collaborating with the Maryland society to gain northern support. Friends of the national movement followed Finley's actions with particular interest since he had originally been in their employ, in turn taking up the Maryland cause and then that of New York. They were thoroughly disillusioned to see him espouse separate state action and encourage both Louisiana and Mississippi to follow the Maryland example in founding their own African colonies. They

6 MSCS MSS, *Letters*, vol. IV, Reese to Latrobe, New York, Apr. 7, 1836; E. A. Andrews to McKenney, Boston, May 3, 1836; Hall to Latrobe, New Haven, July 5, 1836.

were also disturbed by the Marylanders' increasing indifference toward the parent group. Many held Maryland's aggressiveness in pursuing a state program and in wooing outside support to be a menace to the founding body.[7]

Maryland colonizationists were exceedingly disappointed at the results of their efforts. When the *Ann* left Baltimore in November, 1833, the society had but $500 left. Upon the vessel's return, $3,500 was due for the voyage. The *Sarah and Priscilla* expedition with supplies ran to more than $1,700. Adding Doctor Hall's $2,000-a-year salary, payable quarterly, society obligations in 1834 mounted to $6,000. In the summer, when creditor pressure and the realization that voluntary contributions would not be forthcoming weighed heavily on the Maryland board, it took matters into its own hands. Nineteen officers were assigned amounts ranging from $50 to $3,000 which they were to raise during the following week. But personal solicitations were scarcely more successful than previous efforts had been. Only $975, of which $500 was raised by one person, was obtained in this manner.[8]

The debt remained nearly $6,000. The Maryland colonizationists were in a dilemma. They could not raise funds to meet outstanding bills, yet they felt it imperative to dispatch another expedition that fall in order to demonstrate to skeptics that they were actually engaged in carrying out the society's ambitious program. Signs of activity and accomplishment would stimulate contributions. Insolvency was temporarily averted when society officers reached into their own pockets to maintain organizational credit. Meanwhile, a number of measures to correct the financial situation were launched. The allowance per emigrant from the legislative appropriation was raised from $30 to $50. The society published an open letter to the public, assuring it that the smallest contribution would be welcome. Then, too, a

7 ACS MSS, *Letters Received*, vol. LVIII, pt. 2 (1834), Elliott Cresson to Joseph Gales, Philadelphia, Aug. 3, 1834; pt. 3 (1834), Ralph Gurley to Gales, Annfich near Millwood P.O., Aug. 18, 1834; vol. LXI, pt. 1 (1835), Gurley to P. R. Fendall, Baltimore, Nov. 27, 1835.

8 MSCS MSS, *Corresponding Secretary Books*, vol. I, Latrobe to Finley, Baltimore, Nov. 25, 1833; *Records*, vol. I, meetings of the Board of Managers, July 3, 11, 1834.

special committee called upon all the pastors of the city's churches, asking that special collections be taken for colonization.

But little was achieved and the sailing of the *Bourne* in December, with fifty-eight emigrants aboard, left the Maryland society's finances in the same embarrassing state—its indebtedness continued to stand at $6,000. Officers again applied to the group in charge of the state appropriation to refund them a sum for the purchase of territory and the establishment of a colony at Cape Palmas. The state managers, always cautious, declined.[9]

An idea to advertise colonization as well as to raise funds resulted in the publication of a journal containing extracts from the correspondence of the governor and citizens of Cape Palmas, lists of donors, and general information of interest about Africa. The society appointed a committee of officers to prepare materials for a quarterly entitled the *Maryland Colonization Journal*. The first number, appearing in May, 1835, went to editors of all political, literary, and religious newspapers in Maryland with requests that they comment editorially upon the publication and reprint extracts. The committee continued its control of the paper for more than a year and issues appeared intermittently, depending upon receipt of news from Africa and accumulation of suitable material. Late in 1836 the local agent in Baltimore assumed reponsibility for publication and issues began to appear bimonthly.[10]

While this worthy paper no doubt increased public awareness of the Cape Palmas colony and the society's pecuniary needs, profits accruing from the venture were still insufficient to relieve the Marylanders of their debts. They now resorted to begging the state fund managers for an advance payment on future emigrants. In October, 1835, more than $4,000 was borrowed to pay off the most pressing notes. The practice of running up debts

9 MSCS MSS, *Records*, vol. I, meetings of the Board of Managers, Sept. 18, 25, Dec. 23, 1834; vol. II, meeting of the Board of Managers, Oct. 13, 1835; *Letters*, vol. III, Charles Howard to Latrobe, Baltimore, Jan. 2, 1835.

10 MSCS MSS, *Records*, vol. II, meetings of the Board of Managers, Feb. 24, Apr. 3, May 7, 1835; *Corresponding Secretary Books*, vol. III, Latrobe to Elisha Whittlesey, Baltimore, Sept. 14, 1836.

and then asking for state monies became the society's lifetime pattern.[11]

As the society's successive efforts to obtain voluntary support came to naught and as attempts to recruit emigrants turned up painfully few, the Board of Managers began to study its organization and operational methods. The subject of closest scrutiny was the agent employed to canvass the state. William McKenney, initially hailed as a hero in getting up the large complement of passengers for the *Lafayette* in December, 1832, had become a controversial figure. He was never very successful in raising cash, and the auxiliary societies he formed in some areas of the state were often temporary creations which withered after his enthusiastic and emotional messages were viewed in the light of practical experience. His voluminous correspondence reveals a propensity for the dramatic, the exaggerated. He was known as a hypochondriac and a procrastinator. The board feared that his tactlessness made more enemies than friends for the cause.

The most serious charge against McKenney was in the area of his greatest ability: recruitment. Joseph Mechlin, governor of Liberia when the *Lafayette* arrived with 149 immigrants from Maryland, complained that immediate dissension had arisen among them due to the extravagant promises made by overzealous friends in the United States. Remus Harvey, a public school teacher at Caldwell where most *Lafayette* emigrants settled, noted that the newcomers' minds had been filled with unreasonable prospects back home. A colonist who sailed to Cape Palmas aboard the *Bourne* in December, 1834, informed McKenney that he found things pretty much as the agent had described them, except that there was no team of horses essential to cultivation.

McKenney was indignant over this grumbling. He insisted that the inducements he had held out to prospective colonists were: (1) free passage and subsistence in the colony for six months, or more if absolutely necessary; (2) a town lot and a

11 MSCS MSS, *Manumission Books,* vol. I, meeting of the Board of State Managers, Oct. 14, 1835.

five-acre farm in the surrounding country with a native house and a half acre of cleared land (in return for this service, the colonist was to build a house and clear the same quantity of land on another farm being staked out for a future immigrant); (3) distribution by the Colonization Society of agricultural hand tools to persons unable to furnish them. Given McKenney's persuasive nature, it is easy to see that even these fairly accurate statements could be misunderstood in the heat of his oratory.[12]

In a general administrative reorganization the Board of Managers decided to replace McKenney. His demand to know the circumstances resulted in an about-face, but his supervision was turned over to the state managers who had paid his salary all along. Under their command, he was directed to work at the recruitment and transportation of emigrants. The board meanwhile decided to hire a new agent to establish auxiliaries and collect funds. In October, 1835, Ira A. Easter, a Methodist minister then collecting funds for the Maryland State Bible Society, was selected for the post. In time, his duties embraced some responsibilities formerly borne by McKenney.[13]

The effort to ease McKenney out of the scene by returning his supervision to the state managers and to break Easter into the recruitment job left a gap in society administration—the full-time collection of funds and the establishment of local chapters. This vacuum was filled when the Young Men's Colonization Society, a newly created Baltimore organization adjunct to the parent group, appointed John H. Kennard. When McKenney finally resigned, effective as of November, 1836, the administrative shuffling was complete. Easter became the home agent, re-

12 Maryland Historical Society, *Diary of John Latrobe, August 2, 1833– May 1, 1839*, Mar. 23, Oct. 22, 1835; MSCS MSS, *Letters*, vol. I, Joseph Mechlin to C. C. Harper, Liberia, Feb. 10, 1833; Remus Harvey to Harper and Moses Sheppard, Liberia, July 29, 1833; vol. III, Alexander Hance to McKenney, Cape Palmas, Mar. 14, 1835; vol. II, McKenney to Latrobe, Anne Arundel Co. near Owingsville, Sept. 24, 1834.
13 MSCS MSS, *Records*, vol. II, meetings of the Board of Managers, May 21, June 16, Oct. 16, 19, Dec. 28, 1835; *Agent's Books*, vol. I, McKenney to committee of the Board of Managers, Baltimore, June 9, 1835; *Letters*, vol. III, Ira Easter to Hugh D. Evans, Baltimore, Oct. 29, 1835.

sponsible for bookkeeping, office work, and, when possible, the solicitation of funds in Baltimore. Kennard took over emigrant recruitment.[14]

During this internal upheaval in the Maryland society's home operations, efforts still went on in the state to gather emigrants and funds. James Reid, a resident of Hagerstown, served temporarily as agent in western Maryland. He had a hard time of it. The areas covered were generally mountainous and the population sparse. Many people were entirely unaware of the numerous benevolent organizations of the day, including the Colonization Society. On his first tour in September, 1834, Reid covered 450 miles but collected only $148.88 which, less his 25 per cent commission, did little to enlarge the society's treasury. Other tours, in the dead of winter, were even more difficult and less remunerative. Unable to earn much and affected by severe weather, he became discouraged and resigned.[15]

McKenney, touring southern Maryland early in 1835, found that his best efforts were of little avail in persuading Negroes to depart. Only direct messages from friends who had already taken the step tempted them. A common practice among departees was to take a small token which they enclosed in their first letters from Africa. Only when the promised letters arrived with these inside were they considered authentic. Nevertheless, correspondence between those who settled in Africa and their friends at home was difficult because most blacks, on both sides of the ocean, were so unaccustomed to sending or receiving letters that they misdirected them or did not think to inquire at the post office. McKenney explained their reluctance to believe whites as a consequence of their training from infancy that white men were "uncartin." Three years afterwards he found that the dis-

---

14 MSCS MSS, *Letters*, vol. IV, William F. Giles to John H. Kennard, Baltimore, Mar. 25, 1836; *Agent's Books*, vol. I, McKenney to Messrs. Howard, Harper, and Peter Hoffman, [State] Managers of the State Colonization Society, Emigration and Colonization Office, [Baltimore], n.d. [May, 1836]; *Records*, vol. II, meeting of the Board of Managers, Sept. 13, 1836.

15 MSCS MSS, *Records*, vol. I, meeting of the Board of Managers, June 23, 1834; *Letters*, vol. II, James Reid to McKenney, Hagerstown, Sept. 25, 1834.

astrous results of the *Lafayette* expedition had done more than all other causes combined to discourage departure.[16]

Despite success in persuading numerous slave owners to manumit their bondsmen for settlement in the Maryland colony, many Negroes preferred slavery in America to freedom in Africa. This was a baffling problem to slave owners and colonizationists alike. On many occasions, it was not the longtime owner himself who faced the dilemma but heirs or executors who sought to carry out the benevolence of the deceased. For example, in Easton, Doctor Nicholas Hammond by his will freed several male servants upon condition that they emigrate. Much to the distress of his widow and his executor, the men refused the offer, fearing, they said, that they might stop in New Orleans. Doctor Albert Ritchie of Frederick, an executor of his brother's estate in Tallahassee, was burdened for five years with the support of two young men who had the option of going to Liberia or being sold upon reaching their majority. Petitioning the Maryland legislature, Ritchie was able to bring them into the state during the interval. Both men refused to choose either alternative at the end of that time and were hired out temporarily. Their unsatisfactory work and unruly ways exasperated Ritchie until he sought immediate relief from his responsibility by placing them in jail and requesting the Colonization Society to transport them to Africa.

Although Ritchie's men were at length persuaded to depart, the use of force suggested in his letters raised an issue which the society had heretofore avoided. Latrobe, confronted with the request to take the Ritchie slaves, asserted that to his knowledge the society had never kept emigrants in confinement until departure or even sent Negroes out against their will and declared that such was not the intention of the legislature. His interpretation was in direct contradiction to specific terms of the law.

16 MSCS MSS, *Letters,* vol. III, McKenney to Howard, Herring Bay, Mar. 30, 1835; McKenney to Latrobe, Friendship, Apr. 10, 1835; McKenney to Latrobe, Baltimore, Sept. 10. 1835; vol. VIII, Henry Hollingsworth to Easter, Elkton, May 5, 11, 1838.

Latrobe nevertheless advised the home agent, Ira Easter, to accept Ritchie's men only if they were willing to leave. The society's future, in his mind, would be immensely injured were it said that emigrants were kept in jail until they agreed to leave the country or were taken straight from prison to the ship.[17]

The problem of interpreting and carrying out the 1832 law was a persistent one. A few conscientious sheriffs inquired what they should do with manumitted slaves who insisted upon remaining in their home areas, but the law was largely ignored or evaded, primarily because of problems in moving blacks out of the state. Furthermore, the forced removal element of the act gave so much offense to pious citizens that in actual practice it was null and void. The leniency of Orphans' Courts in granting permits to newly freed Negroes also explains why the compulsory feature of the legislation was dead in application. Moreover, Colonization Society officers and state fund managers did not attempt to enforce the law because it could be done only by employing so many agents that the appropriation itself would be eaten up thereby.[18]

A notable example of manumitted slaves who refused to leave the state concerned a group of thirty-three blacks belonging to a Charles County family. In January, 1835, George D. Parnham released sixteen hands and his brother-in-law, Henry B. Goodwin, freed seventeen. The two ex-owners notified the state managers that these persons were at the disposal of the state. McKenney, sent to persuade the group to emigrate, was impressed with their physical appearance but found that they had only the most rudimentary idea of what freedom meant. He believed that were they given the choice to move to Pennsylvania or to re-

---

17 *Ibid.*, vol. III, John Goldsborough to McKenney, Easton, Mar. 14, 1835; Goldsborough to Latrobe, Easton, Mar. 31, 1835; McKenney to Latrobe, Baltimore, May 13, 1835; vol. VII, Albert Ritchie to Easter, Frederick, Oct. 23, Nov. 2, 1837; *Latrobe Letter Books,* vol. II, Latrobe to Easter, Baltimore, Oct. 30, 1837.

18 MSCS MSS, *Miscellaneous Letters & Minutes, Collection of 75 Letters from William McKenney,* McKenney to Bishop Andrew, Baltimore, Mar. 10, 1834; *Latrobe Letter Books,* vol. II, Latrobe to William Handy, Baltimore, Oct. 20, 1837.

main in endless servitude upon Parnham's broken-up and worn-out lands, they would choose the latter. His best efforts produced no more than such replies as "If I must—I must—If Master says I must I cannot help it." McKenney finally resorted to warning the Negroes that they were now under the law. If they refused to go to Maryland in Liberia, the sheriff would be forced to take them to Pennsylvania where, in all probability, they would either starve, be sent to the penitentiary, or be hanged. The Negroes still refused to emigrate.

In the succeeding months, harassed by Goodwin and Parnham, a few did sail to Africa, but the bulk remained, refusing to go anywhere. The state fund managers at length decided to hire the able-bodied adults back to their former owners in return for the upkeep of the whole group. Reluctantly, Goodwin and Parnham accepted the arrangement until word could be received from those who had emigrated. One of those remaining behind ran off and worked for himself, whereupon the state managers instructed the sheriff to capture him and to remove him from the state. Once more, interpretation of the law became an issue, with the county officer insisting that he must himself decide the matter. The ex-slave was ultimately released in the District of Columbia. However, the majority of Goodwin and Parnham's former bondsmen remained in their homes. Although forming a chain around their old owners' necks, they proved better workers in their new situation than before having been manumitted. Nevertheless, they could not be persuaded to emigrate. Even Goodwin, who wanted them off his hands, conceded that they had good reasons for resisting. He spoke of the difficulty of reaching a race in whose character a sense of injustice was written, who had seen actual instances of professed kindness become the means of betrayal, and who had for generations received such treatment from whites as to make the concept of benevolence at their hands improbable.

By the summer of 1836 Goodwin had decided to retain the manumitted slaves in his hire. But Parnham claimed that he could no longer maintain those ex-servants who refused to emigrate, and the Charles County sheriff was ordered to transport them out of the state. There is no record of the conclusion of this unhappy episode.[19]

Thus, in actual practice the recruitment of emigrants proved as difficult as the acquisition of gifts to finance operations. Ira Easter, brought into the society's administration to give it greater efficiency and stability, sought the establishment of a system of business operations. He blamed much of the public's lack of confidence in the colonization cause on lackadaisical office procedures. He pointed to the want of public interest as demonstrated by the dearth of both contributions and visitors at society meetings. Contending that it was the Presbyterians who owned and maintained the noble institutions of the country, Easter argued that "it is precisely because Maryland is almost destitute of them, that the contributions of this important enterprise are so inconsiderable. . . . I feel prepared to say that Jehovah himself could not by the ministry of angels collect twenty-five thousand dollars in Maryland for colonization, without working a miracle." He concluded that the great hindrance to the cause was the fact that the bulk of the population was still unaware of the colonization act.

Going upon the assumption that emigration must precede contributions and that both depended upon enlightening the citizenry at large, Easter contended that both problems could be solved if greater efforts were made to inform both whites and blacks of the colonization cause. He held the great defect in previous society operations to have been unwarranted dependency upon faith—one "which was based wholly upon the supreme excellence of the cause itself. Hence they expected that men everywhere would become practical colonizationists without the trouble of preaching and explaining its doctrines. . . ."

19 MSCS MSS, *State Managers Letter Books,* Howard to sheriff of Charles Co., Baltimore, May 4, 1835; Howard to John B. Lawson, Baltimore, July 13, 20, Nov. 2, 1835; McKenney to Henry B. Goodwin, Baltimore, June 8, 1835; *Records,* vol. II, letter to sheriff, n.d. [summer, 1836]; *Letters,* vol. III, McKenney to Latrobe, Nottingham, Apr. 24, 1835; Goodwin to McKenney, Parnham's Retreat, June 30, 1835; Lawson to Howard, Port Tobacco, July 17, 27, Oct. 21, 1835; Goodwin to [McKenney], Parnham's Retreat, Oct. 27, Nov. 5, 1835; vol. IV, George D. Parnham to McKenney, Parnham's Retreat, June 3, 1836.

Easter argued that the society was obligated to hire qualified agents to travel extensively throughout the state organizing branches and awakening general interest in colonization. He suggested that the board immediately secure the services of at least two active agents at set salaries rather than making the latter contingent upon their collections.

Easter was especially critical of the practice of sending society representatives to Annapolis each winter to thwart any efforts to reduce, restrict, or eliminate the colonization fund. The officers themselves on many occasions journeyed to the state capital to stave off repeal of laws upon which their cause depended. Moreover, the society's annual meetings were usually held in the Senate chamber each January in order to indicate that the organization was still active and enjoyed the confidence of many of Maryland's leading men. Easter charged that such procedures were actually detrimental to their cause, for such close scrutiny could only throw suspicion upon the society. He argued that a system of agents at work in every part of the state producing results would convince legislators of the society's efficacy better than any other means.[20]

With Easter's prodding, John Kennard was added to the staff and other men, at intervals, were hired to solicit emigrants and funds. Early in 1837 the society employed the Reverend John C. Cazier of Elkton to seek emigrants from among the emancipated Negroes in his native Cecil County. He was quite unsuited for the job and lasted only two months. He did not persuade a single individual to emigrate and collected only a pitiful $15, all of which went to pay his traveling expenses. The free blacks in his area were, to a man, opposed to the society.

Another agent who proved to be one of the most successful ever in society employ, John M. Roberts, formerly a Maryland State Bible Society representative, was hired in 1838 to visit southern counties, and later went to other areas of the state. During his two-year service for the Colonization Society, he

20 MSCS MSS, *Letters,* vol. IV, Easter to Latrobe, Baltimore, Mar. 17, Apr. 30, 1836; *Miscellaneous Letters & Minutes, Package of Letters to Board of Managers, 1837,* Easter to Latrobe, Baltimore, May 18, 31, 1836; *Records,* vol. II, meeting of the Board of Managers, Jan. 15, 1836.

raised substantial sums of money and secured many *Journal* subscriptions. His experience generally corroborated Easter's view that people gave more willingly and liberally when they saw Negroes from their own neighborhoods moving to Africa. Roberts also found that many whites in southern Maryland wanted the free Negroes removed by force if necessary, and that some desired all Negroes, free and slave, to be driven out of the community. Conversely, on a visit to the Eastern Shore he found that the citizens of Kent County who did not own slaves were opposed to colonization because they feared the loss of their laborers.[21]

While temporary efforts were put forth by Cazier, Roberts, and others, John Kennard continued in his duties as official Maryland society traveling agent. He realized, as Easter did after better acquaintance with that body's operations, that the state appropriation was not sufficient to hire enough representatives adequately to cover the state. However desirable the employment of a full-time representative in each county might be, it was financially impossible.

Kennard consequently pursued a policy of attempting to establish through voluntary efforts an active auxiliary to the state society in each Maryland county. His plan was a direct reflection of Easter's view that success would come not so much from public addresses as by door-to-door visitation among Negro and white community leaders and by the judicious use of reports and journals. Firmly convinced that independent county action was the method most likely to awaken the greatest amount of interest, Kennard addressed letters of inquiry to prominent whites known to favor colonization in each of Maryland's counties.

A lesser man would have quit immediately, for replies from all parts of the state declared that 1837 was an inopportune time to form a society, that Negroes were universally opposed to go-

---

21 MSCS MSS, *Corresponding Secretary Books,* vol. III, Franklin Anderson to John C. Cazier, Baltimore, Apr. 8, 1837; *Records,* vol. II, meeting of the Board of Managers, Mar. 26, 1838; *Agent's Books,* vol. II, Easter to the clergy of Maryland, Baltimore, May 21, 1838; *Letters,* vol. VI, Cazier to Easter, North East, June 26, July 5, Aug. 23, 1837; vol. VIII, John M. Roberts to Easter, Leonardtown, June 12, 26, 1838; vol. X, Roberts to Easter, Still Pond Crossroads, May 9, 1839.

ing to Africa, and that contributions could not be procured. The reasons were standard: that Negroes were suspicious of the society's "philanthropic intention," that many blacks believed abolitionist propaganda declaring slaveholders to be behind the colonization movement in order to keep the price of slaves high, and that many white slaveholders simply refused to free their hands.[22]

Abolitionist work, which was so detrimental to the movement of Negroes to Liberia and hence to voluntary contributions by white citizens, had become intense in the state by 1837. Originally, whites and free Negroes who called for the destruction of slavery rather than colonization resided largely in Baltimore and other cities. But now, five years later, all parts of the state were under the mounting influence of abolitionist sentiment. Kennard lamented that Maryland's black population had been organized by outside agitators and was working in direct concert with the "madmen" of the nation. He reported that the antislavery doctrine was clearly discernible in each of the fifteen counties he had visited. The free Negroes in Baltimore, staunch abolitionists, operated a network of contacts throughout the state to circulate their views. One doctrine spread among the colored people by abolitionists was that, by remaining in the state, they would ultimately get "their rights," meaning full social and political equality. Persons who emigrated were stigmatized as traitors to their race.[23]

To meet this situation, Kennard traveled extensively, putting his independent county action plan into effect. If local leaders could not establish an auxiliary by their own efforts, Kennard visited them, gained their cooperation, and then called for a public meeting. As a consequence, state society branches were founded in numerous counties during 1837, and Kennard was

22 MSCS MSS, *Letters,* vol. IV, Easter to Latrobe, Woodlands, Apr. 14, 1836; for a sampling of the responses, see vols. VI and VII, John L. Hawkins to Kennard, Port Tobacco, Apr. 5, 1837; David Vance to Kennard, Salisbury, Mar. 18, 1837; Hollingsworth to John Fonerden and Kennard, Elkton, May 1, 1837; and A. C. Thompson to Kennard, Cambridge, Aug. 30, 1837.

23 *Seventh Annual Report of the Board of Managers of the Maryland State Colonization Society* (Baltimore: John D. Toy, 1839), p. 10.

certain that the most successful means of acquiring emigrants and funds had finally been hit upon. He was sadly mistaken.[24]

Conventional methods of recruiting emigrants were found to be increasingly unsuccessful. The Maryland society was consequently often willing to utilize likely suggestions from varied sources. One idea popping up periodically was that of sending a male Negro who was respected in his home community to Africa to inspect the settlements there and then to return to tell his friends of the actual situation. Although the managers had declined to follow this suggestion earlier, they were by 1836 willing to finance such reconnaissance trips. In April the board agreed to permit a representative each from Kent and Queen Annes counties to sail to the colony free of cost. However, friends in this country were to bear return expenses. Occasionally, an auxiliary somewhere in the state paid the homeward fare for a Negro observer after having supported his dependents during his absence. That these inspectors ever affected more than a few of their friends is doubtful.[25]

A far more productive means of winning emigrants, and probably the most successful method of all those ever employed, was the use of colonists returned to this country for business or pleasure to accompany the society's agents in trips about the state. An early example of this operation had involved Jacob Prout, so largely responsible for the sizable company aboard the *Lafayette*.

Another case was that of Alexander Hance, an early settler of Maryland in Liberia. He returned to Calvert County in the fall of 1837 to purchase his children who had remained in slavery. The owner asked almost $900 for the three girls. While the Board of Managers maintained its policy of noninvolvement in such affairs, it saw in the situation a means of aiding both Hance and the colonization cause. In return for a sum not exceeding $500, Hance was asked to assist Kennard in the preparations for

24 MSCS MSS, *Letters*, vol. VI, Kennard to Fonerden, Baltimore, June 29, 1837.
25 MSCS MSS, *Records*, vol. II, meeting of the Board of Managers, Apr. 12, 1836; *Letters*, vol. IV, Thomas C. Browne to Latrobe, Centreville, June 14, 1836.

the fall expedition. The two men visited all parts of Calvert County as well as other sections of the state, and the consequence, largely due to Hance's presence, was the departure of eighty-five emigrants on the *Niobe* in November. Ironically enough, Hance's final success in purchasing his children had an unexpected twist. Rather than viewing the accomplishment as something meritorious, critical Marylanders looked upon it as proof that Hance was in league with Kennard and that both were slave traders.

The following fall another visiting colonist, Thomas Jackson, was hired to tour Maryland with Kennard. His influence again resulted in a larger number of Negroes than usual sailing that fall, although many withdrew after colonization opponents visited them. In Calvert County alone nine families totaling forty-nine members decided to remain.[26]

Not infrequently, departees sailing for Maryland in Liberia came from other states. In such cases the benefactor freed his slaves and paid for their passage to Cape Palmas, or some charitable organization, usually a local independent colonization society, assumed the cost of transporting free blacks to the colony. The most notable example of this practice concerned the forty-eight slaves of Richard Tubman of Augusta, Georgia, who were recipients of $10,000 and freedom in Africa upon his death early in 1837. His widow was anxious that those individuals willing to move to Africa select a site where their agricultural abilities could be put to good use. Being partial to the Maryland State Colonization Society because many of the slaves had originally come from her husband's former home in Charles County, she opened negotiations with Latrobe.

The prospect of receiving a large complement of well-disciplined Negroes characterized by their mistress as honest, industrious, and temperate stirred the Maryland society to speedy

---

26 MSCS MSS, *Records,* vol. II, meeting of the Board of Managers, Sept. 29, 1837; vol. III, meeting of the Board of Managers, Sept. 11, 1838; *Letters,* vol. VII, Hance to Easter, Calvert Co., Sept. 11, 1837; Kennard to Easter, Friendship, Sept. 25, 1837; Kennard to Easter, Steamboat, Oct. 8, 1837; Kennard to Easter, Elkton, Oct. 17, 1837; vol. VIII, Kennard to Latrobe, Baltimore, Apr. 30, 1838; vol. IX, Kennard to Easter, Friendship, Oct. 9, 1838; Kennard to Easter, Prince Frederick, Nov. 7, 1838.

action. After a brief correspondence, arrangements were completed for forty-two Tubman Negroes to sail from Charleston to Baltimore where a brig was readied for their embarkation to Affrica. With these emigrants went four others from the Augusta area who had been freed by their owners so that they might accompany their mates among the Tubmans.[27]

Maryland society success in persuading Mrs. Tubman to send the blacks to Cape Palmas also illustrated the continuing rivalry with the American Colonization Society. Ralph Gurley, touring the southeastern states, was infuriated to find that he had arrived in Augusta just three days after the Tubman group had set out for Charleston. Aware before he left Washington that Mrs. Tubman owned some slaves destined for Africa, Gurley had failed to appreciate the urgency of the case and the existence of a contest with the Maryland society in securing the widow's confidence.

Gurley was further incensed by the financial loss connected with this missed opportunity. Besides passage to Baltimore, Mrs. Tubman paid $50 per head for the Negroes' conveyance to Africa and supplied each liberally with everything thought necessary. Gurley was as angry with himself as he was with the Marylanders. He impugned the latters' good faith and honor, asserting that this active state organization intended to destroy the parent institution.[28]

An additional source of tension between the two societies attended the collection of funds in Maryland. On numerous occasions agents from Baltimore discovered American Colonization Society representatives operating within the bounds of the Old Line State. In each case complaint was lodged with the parent board. In effect, Maryland colonizationists sought to deny access to financial sources in the state to all other parties, while they themselves scavenged any likely spot outside their

27 MSCS mss, Letters, vol. VI, Emily H. Tubman to Latrobe, Augusta, Ga., Apr. 9, May 4, 1837; vol. VIII, Tubman to Latrobe, Augusta, May 3, 1838.
28 ACS mss, Letters Received, vol. LXVII, pt. 1 (1837), Gurley to Gales, Augusta, May 7, 1837.

bounds and even instructed agents to canvass areas adjoining the state as well as distant locales.[29]

In spite of such disagreements it became apparent, as the American-planted colonies along the African coast took root, that close cooperation among colonization societies in the United States was desirable. As early as 1835 Latrobe had suggested the establishment of uniform currency and legal systems in the several settlements. The American society had, however, viewed this sensible proposal as additional evidence that the Maryland organization aimed at destruction of the national movement. Two years later agent Ira Easter called for a friendly conference on general colonial interests on the ground that current independent proceedings were prejudicial to the advancement of settlement.

Still, no move toward cooperation took place until 1838, when the parent society, nearly bankrupt but infused with new leadership, agreed to convene in Philadelphia with delegates from New York, Pennsylvania, and Maryland. The topic of discussion was amalgamation of the American Colonization Society's colonies with those of the three state auxiliaries. Heated and lengthy debates resulted only in the adoption of Latrobe's resolution that delegates meet again to consider a plan for commercial cooperation among the different colonies. The Maryland representatives thereupon withdrew. On succeeding days New York and Pennsylvania society spokesmen wrung from Gurley and his associates promises to work for the adoption of a new constitution which would substantially alter the parent group's relationship to the state branches and provide for greater unity of action in Africa.

Explanation for the action of the Maryland delegates in first advocating discussion of joint activity among the African settlements and then boycotting the conference after passage of an empty resolution lies in their appraisal of the American Colo-

29 MSCS MSS, *Agent's Books,* vol. I, McKenney to Gurley, Baltimore, Nov. 10, 1835; vol. II, Kennard to Samuel Wilkeson, Baltimore, Jan. 9, 1840; *Letters,* vol. VI, Kennard to William Matchett, Cambridge, June 13, 1837.

nization Society. The Marylanders were willing to meet with colonizationists from other states and with representatives of the parent society as long as all respected each other as peers. What coordination might result in Africa was expected to emerge from annual conferences of delegates and to involve only such limited measures as tariff and coinage. The New Yorkers and Pennsylvanians had never advocated independent state action as adamantly as the Maryland colonizationists and, intent upon securing domestic changes within the parent society, they were interested in compromising. They were thus willing to back a plan whereby a governor-general, under parent board supervision, carried out the laws passed by a general annual convention if reforms within the American Colonization Society were effected.

Maryland's secession for the national movement came basically because it considered cooperation detrimental to its own projects. After reflection on the governor-general plan, the Baltimoreans asserted that such an official would be of little value to the colonies because of the distances between them. In short, such an arrangement was premature. A final compelling factor involved John Russwurm. For two years this black had served satisfactorily as governor of Maryland in Liberia. To appoint a white governor-general, however limited his powers, would seem to depreciate the earlier trust placed in the competency of Negro leadership.[30]

The political climate in Maryland remained a concern for colonizationists throughout the 1830's. Mindful that only the continued beneficence of the General Assembly kept their movement alive, they forever courted favor in Annapolis. Until colonization became a political expedient, legislative matters bearing upon the state's Negro population were handled in a haphazard manner. Early in 1833, however, the House of Delegates estab-

---

30 ACS MSS, *Letters Received,* vol. LXII, pt. 1 (1835), Gurley to Fendall, Baltimore, Nov. 27, 1835; vol. LXVII, pt. 1 (1837), Easter to Gurley, Baltimore, Aug. 2, 1837; MSCS MSS, *Letters,* vol. IX, meeting of committees from societies having colonies on the coast of Africa, Philadelphia, Sept. 25, 1838; Thomas Buchanan to Latrobe, Philadelphia, Oct. 1, 1838; *Latrobe Letter Books,* vol. II, Latrobe to Finley, Baltimore, Sept. 18, 1838; *Seventh Annual Report of the Board of Managers,* pp. 11–12.

lished a standing committee, known as the Committee on the Coloured Population, to consider Negro affairs throughout the state. Since it also had responsibility for Colonization Society proceedings and expenditure of the state appropriation, members were targets for the society's lobbying activities. The committee proved to be generally amenable to colonizationist wishes, but occasionally it submitted an unfavorable report, suggested passage of laws detrimental to colonization, or questioned the value of continuing the state appropriation. At these times, friends of the cause in the Senate could be counted on to veto any major obstructive action of the lower house.[31]

Nevertheless, successive laws were passed which in effect counteracted the society's aim to alter the racial balance in Maryland. The very first year after passage of the 1832 laws affecting the black population, their intent was violated. The chief purpose of such legislation had been to restrict the introduction of additional slaves into Maryland. Now, in 1833, by a new provision, owners of blacks who had hired them out in any adjoining state, district, or territory, or who wished to do so, could return them to Maryland at their convenience. This alteration reflected the growing reluctance of Maryland legislators to hinder slave interests in the state.[32]

The colonizationist aim to reduce the number of Negroes in the state was again undermined at the following General Assembly session. The Committee on the Coloured Population, directed by skeptical delegates to inquire into the expediency of repealing, revising, or remodeling the acts of 1831–1832 bearing upon blacks, came out with a recommendation to repeal those sections prohibiting the introduction of new slaves into the state. The original law was now supplemented to permit old and new residents of Maryland to bring slaves into the state upon payment of $15 per head on all between the ages of fifteen and forty-five and $5 per person on those under or over these limits. Such fees were to go to the Colonization Society

---

31 Maryland, *Journal of Proceedings of the House of Delegates of the State of Maryland* (December Session, 1832), Jan. 5, 1833; MSCS MSS, *Letters*, vol. III, McKenney to [Latrobe], Annapolis, Jan. 16, 1835.
32 Maryland, *Laws of Maryland* (1832), Chapter 40.

and the newly introduced bondsmen were to remain slaves for life.[33]

In addition to this detrimental legislation, the delegates severely criticized colonizationists for the method in which they had administered the state appropriation. Finding in the report of the state fund managers admission that the society had received $8,000 in 1833 to establish a settlement at Cape Palmas, the delegates branded the loan an unwarrantable extension of the enabling legislation. In spite of its serious accusation, the Committee on the Coloured Population made no move to restrict the state managers.[34]

With each succeeding year, legal threats to colonization became more serious. Early in 1835 a resolution limiting the state appropriation to meeting costs of removing blacks free at the time the first legislation passed was offered in the House of Delegates. Another resolution called for the repeal in toto of all legislation aiding colonization. In 1836 the usual proposition calling for repeal was submitted. A second petition sought consideration of the expediency of forcing all Maryland free blacks to leave the state within a specified period. The Committee on the Coloured Population, to which these measures were referred, hastened to defend the society as philanthropic and the cause as on the frontier of success. The committee expressed abhorrence at the unrealistic proposal to exile free blacks. It declared that such a law would be riddled with injustice, would be contrary to the U.S. Bill of Rights, and would be an expression of a selfishness seeking immediate local benefit at the rest of the country's expense.[35]

---

33 MSCS MSS, *Letters*, vol. II, M. Haynes to McKenney, Annapolis, Jan. 24, 1834; Maryland, *Laws of Maryland* (1833), Chapter 87.
34 Maryland, *Maryland Public Documents* (December Session, 1833), "Report of the Committee on the Coloured Population to which was referred the Report of the Managers of the Colonization Society."
35 MSCS MSS, *Letters*, vol. III, McKenney to Latrobe, Annapolis, Jan. 16, 1835; Maryland, *Maryland Public Documents* (December Session, 1834), "Report of the Committee on the Colored [*sic*] Population"; *Report on the Order Directing an Enquiry as to the Expediency of Repealing the Law of 1831–32, Relating to the Coloured Population* (Annapolis: Committee on the Coloured Population, 1836); *Report of the Committee upon the Coloured Population, to Which Was Referred an Order of This House,*

A constructive measure winning the General Assembly's assent in 1835 concerned collection of the colonization tax. In the three years since passage of the appropriation bill, most counties had failed to meet their assessment regularly. Indeed, Baltimore City and Montgomery and Saint Marys counties did not levy the tax at all during this period. Altogether the counties were over $19,000 in arrears—only a third of the stipulated monies due had been sent in.

To remedy this situation, the General Assembly set July 1, 1836, as the deadline for counties in arrears to settle their accounts and fixed July 1 of each succeeding year as the date for payment of the previous year's tax. It then prescribed rules for more effective collection of the annual assessments. Officials in each county and Baltimore's mayor were made responsible for levying the amounts due upon their respective districts. Within one month a certificate of the amount levied was to be sent to the treasurer of the Western Shore. Each county or city failing to report was to suffer an equivalent reduction in its portion of the Free School Fund until the sum due colonization was paid. When a default was settled, the area involved was to be reimbursed any money due it from the education reserve. While the new measures afforded improved administration, the treasurer still found collection difficult and frequently had to sue collectors to secure payments. Even this was not entirely successful. In 1839, for example, more than $7,000 was still in arrears. Moreover, compliance with the law gave Maryland citizens the feeling that they were doing their share to help colonization when they paid their property taxes and most bristled at requests from the society for voluntary contributions.[36]

Directing Them to Enquire into the Expediency "of forcing all the Free People of Colour to leave this State within a certain period of time" (Annapolis, 1836).

36 Maryland, *Maryland Public Documents,* "Report of the Treasurer of the Western Shore concerning the Tax for Colonization, in obedience to an order of the House of Delegates, of 24th January, 1835"; *Laws of Maryland* (1834), Chapters 160, 197; MSCS MSS, *Miscellaneous Letters & Minutes, Package of Letters to Board of Managers, 1837,* Easter to Board of Managers, [Baltimore], Oct. 10, 1837; *Letters,* vol. X, George Mackubin to Franklin Anderson, Annapolis, May 24, 1839.

The continued reiteration of confidence in colonization by the
House Committee on the Coloured Population and by other
elected representatives in Annapolis and the improvement of
laws directly related to it staved off active opponents but did
little to convince ordinary citizens of its value. Furthermore,
legislative approbation did little to open Maryland pocketbooks.
In the late 1830's the society continued to struggle along with
meager voluntary contributions and subscriptions to the *Maryland Colonization Journal.* It sought to survive by stretching the
$50-per-emigrant allowance from the state fund. This could be
done by supplying future colonists with fewer and less expensive
articles. It also studied its books to see where savings might be
effected.

One of the most expensive features of its operations was the
cost of chartering vessels to carry emigrants and supplies out to
the colony. At any time, it was a game of chance depending
upon prompt departure and a full load of passengers and freight,
but as abolitionist opposition made it an even more speculative
business, the society sustained serious losses. After a particularly
heavy loss late in 1836, the society launched a study to determine the feasibility of purchasing or building a schooner suitable for its needs. Among beneficial results expected from ownership were increased correspondence between colonists and
their friends in America, the encouragement of small capitalists
in both countries to engage in trade, and destruction of the suspicion that emigrants were really being sold to southern markets. Finding that a brig of 150 tons could be built for $10,000,
the society enthusiastically embarked upon raising the requisite
sum. Results were so insignificant that the society did not publicize them. Finally, in 1839, entangled in manifold debts,
officers dropped all idea of constructing or purchasing a vessel.[37]

Another proposal for reducing the society's expenses involved

37 MSCS MSS, *Letters,* vol. V, Easter to Board of Managers, MSCS Rooms,
Nov. 7, 1836; *Miscellaneous Letters & Minutes, Package of Letters to
Board of Managers, 1837,* William Mason to Easter, Baltimore, Oct. 31,
1836; *Records,* vol. II, meeting of the Board of Managers, Jan. 7, 1837.

the colonial doctor. Both humaneness and common sense dictated that a qualified medical person be stationed at Cape Palmas to care for new immigrants during their period of acclimation and for all colonists while they lived at the settlement. The presence of Doctor Hall, a physician as well as a businessman and administrator, obviated the necessity of appointing an additional person in that capacity. While Doctor Holmes was merely a dentist, he was sufficiently versed in medical science and the use of drugs to care for the colonists when he himself was well. His departure late in 1836 left the colony without medical aid and the Maryland society scurried about seeking a physician. Its first choice was to hire Thomas Savage, an Episcopal missionary at Cape Palmas who was also a physician. But his board refused to allow him to give more than emergency treatment to colonists not connected with Cape Palmas mission. Maryland colonizationists well realized that such a plan would prove unsatisfactory, but there was no alternative. They were willing to accept this solution as a temporary expedient. Arrangements were then made to send a young colonist to the United States for medical training.

As early as 1833, when Doctor Hall entered Maryland State Colonization Society employ, he recommended that the Board of Managers send a small library of elementary works on medicine to the proposed colony and that it select several young colonists to study under him or a later appointee. He suggested that two well-acclimated citizens take charge in the community after a two-year apprenticeship. Nothing came of the suggestion until 1835 when Samuel Ford McGill, son of George McGill, asked to come to the United States to learn medicine. Moses Sheppard, assigned to correspond with him, painted a dark picture of his probable reception and the labor necessary to earn a medical degree. He was warned that he could not associate with whites other than as a servant, that he should never expect to hear the term "Mr. McGill" from a white man, and that "studying medicine is not strolling through College Halls, reading an hour and whiling away an hour." If McGill could accept such conditions, would put in three hard years of study, and agree to return to the colony, he would be welcome to come. To his great credit, McGill chose this course of action.[38]

Arriving in Baltimore in the fall of 1836, McGill found the way paved for entrance into the Washington Medical College of that city. The society's Board of Managers had hesitated to send him to a northern school because it feared both the climatic effects and the abolitionist influence upon their protégé. A month after his instruction began, white classmates protested to the faculty that "this Boy has gone far beyond the limited space granted him, and has encroached as far upon the privilege enjoyed by the students, as to wound their feelings, [and] disgust them by his action. . . ." Asking that he be dismissed, they argued that prejudicial publicity resulting from McGill's attendance would endanger the institution and jeopardize their own professional prospects.

Pleas by colonizationists to faculty and students to allow McGill to remain in any capacity so long as he could receive instruction were to no avail. He thereupon withdrew from the college and went to Windsor, Vermont, to study with and remain under the supervision of Doctor Edward Elisha Phelps, an old friend of Hall. McGill made a splendid impression upon his mentor and was received with an unusual degree of respect and attention by the townspeople. He became particularly fond of surgery and, after witnessing three or four operations, declared that he would not hesitate to undertake the amputation of an arm or a leg.

When Doctor Phelps returned to private practice, McGill transferred to Dartmouth College in Hanover, New Hampshire. A kindly faculty member introduced him as a native African, McGill explained away his fluency in English to quizzical students, and he was readily admitted into the classes. Unwilling merely to earn achievement certificates for accomplishments in medical study, McGill made the earning of a degree his goal.

38 MSCS mss, *Agent's Books*, vol. II, Easter to R. Anderson, Baltimore, Sept. 3, 1838; *Letters*, vol. I, Hall to Board of Managers, Oct. 12, 1833; vol. IV, Sheppard to Samuel Ford McGill, Baltimore, Jan. 12, 1836; vol. V, Hall to Easter, Hot Springs, [Va.], Aug. 28, 1836.

Maryland in Liberia (painting by John H. B. Latrobe)

Dr. James Hall (1802–1889)

John H. B. Latrobe (1803–1891)

In October, 1838, he earned the M.D. and returned to Baltimore, hoping for a brief period of clinical experience.

The young physician ingenuously argued that some practical application of his learning before leaving the United States would be valuable to him even though lives might be sacrificed in the process. Indeed, he declared that speeding some of Baltimore's colored population out of this world would not be so great a crime, for if unprepared, their circumstances could not be much worse while if ready, his mistakes might prove a blessing to them. But the society declined to let McGill stay longer in this country. Fearing that attractions here or conversion to abolitionism might result in his refusal to return to Cape Palmas, it sent Doctor McGill to the colony aboard the *Oberon* on November 22, 1838. Accompanying him was the newly appointed colonial physician, Doctor Robert Macdowall, formerly the colonial physician at Bassa Cove, Liberia, under whom McGill was to be apprenticed for a year.[39]

Raising money for a vessel and for McGill's education was supposed to reduce society expenditures, but neither accomplished the desired purpose. The idea of owning a vessel had to be abandoned for want of support, and McGill's medical training cost more than $700, and while he was destined to have a long, useful career, he still required a regular salary.

Debt still overwhelmed the society and it lived from hand to mouth, depending upon the state appropriation to meet sundry notes as these fell due. Fortunately, state managers had become more lenient in accepting responsibility for colony costs by

---

39 MSCS MSS, *Letters,* vol. V, N. Z. Chapline and Richard E. Harrison to faculty of Washington Medical College, [Baltimore], n.d. [Dec., 1836]; students to faculty of Washington Medical College, [Baltimore], n.d. [Dec., 1836]; George R. Vickers to Chapline and Harrison, Baltimore, Dec. 15, 1836; Easter to S. K. Jennings, Baltimore, Dec. 17, 1836; H. D. McCulloch and others to Easter, Baltimore, Dec. 26, 1836; vol. VI, Edward E. Phelps to Latrobe, Windsor, Vt., Feb. 27, 1837; vol. VII, S. F. McGill to Easter, Windsor, July 17, 1837; S. F. McGill to Easter, Hanover, N.H., Aug. 17, 1837; vol. IX, S. F. McGill to Easter, Hanover, Aug. 11, Oct. 16, 1838; Phelps to Easter, Windsor, Oct. 29, 1838; *Records,* vol. III, meeting of the Board of Managers, Sept. 11, 1838; *Agent's Books,* vol. II. Easter to Anderson, Baltimore, Sept. 3, 1838.

1838, perhaps because the settlement was now gaining in population and strength. In fact, they began drawing more than $10,000 from the treasury, pointing out that the initial legislation did not specifically set that sum as the yearly financial limit. They requested and received payment of $15,000 for 1839 only to find that it had actually already been spent by the end of 1838.

This startling revelation caused the society's Board of Managers to review finances. It found that the body's total liabilities were more than $11,000. Since voluntary contributions would yield but little, the board cancelled its regular spring expedition and called for rigid economy. Thirty-two emigrants went to Cape Palmas in the fall but there was otherwise little activity during 1839.

Ira Easter, the home agent, died in January, 1840, and John Latrobe, society president since 1837, saw an opportunity to reduce expenses through administrative reorganization. John Kennard now assumed the home agent duties in addition to his former task of soliciting contributions throughout the state. An office clerk, Mr. Knighton, had his responsibilities enlarged to include canvassing Baltimore City for funds. John Roberts was released because his collections did not warrant his retention. In this way salaries decreased from an annual $3,050 to $1,300. The *Colonization Journal,* edited by Easter during most of his service, was turned back to a board committee.[40]

In addition to reducing expenditures, the society sought means of wiping out existing debts. Although several courses of action were recommended, including appeals to clergymen for a special Fourth of July collection and a September fair, little occurred during the year. No emigrants went out but the society still collected $10,000 of the state fund.

Meanwhile, the board also undertook retrenchment in colonial activities. It abolished various paid positions, closed one of the two public farms, and urged Governor Russwurm to keep

---

40 MSCS MSS, *Records,* vol. III, special meeting of the Board of Managers, Mar. 2, 1839; *Letters,* vol. X, Mackubin to Anderson, Annapolis, May 24, 1839.

down his expenditures, especially those involving gifts to the African kings ("the dash account") and care of the poor, sick, and invalid.[41]

Society affairs stood as follows at the end of 1840: the body had collected $79,353 from the state (including the appropriation and the per capita tax placed upon slaves introduced into Maryland) since its creation; voluntary contributions totaled $15,682; expenditures had reached almost $128,000; 624 emigrants had been sent to Capes Mesurado and Palmas in a total of fourteen expeditions; Maryland in Liberia's population stood at 424, of whom 194 were males and 230 were females, with approximately half of the citizens adults.[42] To society officers who had espoused independent state action, the heavy expenditure on the small success attending their efforts must have been doubly painful. Nevertheless, they spoke confidently of the future and laid careful plans for more efficient operations in both the United States and Africa.

41 MSCS MSS, *Records,* vol. III, meetings of the Board of Managers, Jan. 20, May 1, Oct. 17, 1840.
42 *Ninth Annual Report of the Board of Managers of the Maryland State Colonization Society* (Baltimore: John D. Toy, 1841), p. 13; *Eleventh Annual Report of the Board of Managers of the Maryland State Colonization Society* (Baltimore: John D. Toy, 1843), Appendix, p. 25; MSCS MSS, *Letters,* vol. XI, census of Maryland in Liberia, 1840.

V

Growth
of the Colony

John Brown Russwurm, a native
of Jamaica and an 1826 graduate of Bowdoin College, was thirty-
seven years old when he became governor of Maryland in Liberia. His emigration to Monrovia in 1829 ended a brief career
in the United States as co-editor of *Freedom's Journal,* the first
Negro newspaper in the country. Until his move to Harper, he
published the *Liberia Herald* and was a leading citizen in the
first American settlement. Russwurm's appointment came as a
surprise both to himself and to inhabitants of all the American-
founded colonies along the west coast of Africa. It signified a
new era in the history of the Negro and was a departure from
ago-old beliefs. In Monrovia and in Harper, at least at first,
the idea of a Negro governor was popular. J. Leighton Wilson,
the ABCFM missionary at Fair Hope, considered the appointment judicious, though a revolution in affairs. Thomas Jackson,
a colonial magistrate, asserted that Russwurm's nomination came
at the right time and at the right place.

Visiting Americans, however, tended to be skeptical of the Maryland society's new course. Captain Joseph J. Nicholson, commander of the U.S.S. *Potomac,* on a cruise off Africa late in 1836, was favorably impressed with the colony's steady growth, but urged the society to have white agents at the settlement. He contended that Africans respected whites more than their own kind and that the colonists themselves paid a more cheerful obedience to the government of a white man.[1]

At the outset of Russwurm's administration, his employers in Baltimore determined to give the governor firm direction and to correct certain colonial problems. The Board of Managers reiterated the need for fiscal stringency, its emphasis upon the agricultural nature of the colony, and its desire for the ultimate civilization of the Africans. It hoped that the indigenous blacks would be spared the tragic fate accorded most aborigines and, instead, would slowly be brought under the colony's laws. Russwurm was advised to expand the settlement in a continuous line along Maryland Avenue and in each direction from it as more land was needed. The public farm was to receive special attention because of its threefold function as a provider of food for the indigent, a source of hard labor for criminal offenders, and a model farm for experimentation. The board refused to absolve colonists of debts owed at the colonial store for fear that they would thereby be less inclined toward diligence and thrift. The new governor was encouraged to cooperate with other settlements along the African coast and to accord special solicitude to the missionary group residing at Cape Palmas. Russwurm was advised to "avoid all interference with them in their spiritual effort and allow them no interference in your temporal affairs. Promote their interests in all things. . . ."

Intending to strengthen the new governor's hand in managing the colony, the board reaffirmed the original constitution,

---

1 Philip J. Staudenraus, *The African Colonization Movement, 1816–1865* (New York: Columbia University Press, 1961), pp. 167, 191; MSCS MSS, *Letters,* vol. VII, John Russwurm to John Latrobe, Monrovia, Sept. 28, 1836; Thomas Jackson to Franklin Anderson, Harper, July 6, 1837; *Miscellaneous Letters & Minutes, Package of Letters to Board of Managers, 1837,* Joseph J. Nicholson to Latrobe, U.S.S. *Potomac,* Hampton Roads, Mar. 3, 1837.

adopted additional ordinances, and clarified business procedures. The constitution, with several supplemental ordinances, the most notable concerning legal procedures and the application of jurisprudence, was printed, bound, and distributed in the settlement. An appendix provided the colonial magistrates, at that time three men appointed by the governor, with examples of legal papers and forms to be used. In order to straighten out the bookkeeping chaos of the Hall and Holmes administrations, a system of accounts was drawn up for the colony. By the use of a bills receivable account, a day book, and ledgers, debts, business transactions, and financial matters were to be recorded. All accounts were to be balanced and closed semiannually and detailed statements submitted to the managerial body at home.

An innovation introduced was the adoption of decimals for use in all mercantile transactions. Instead of pricing goods at 6¼, 12½, 18¾, and so forth per yard or pound, items now cost 5, 10, 20 cents and up in like fashion. A paper currency was created, receivable at the government store in payment for goods purchased there, to facilitate such commercial arrangements. Such bills aimed at improving and increasing exchanges both among the colonists and with the Africans. For the benefit of the illiterate, notes were printed with pictures distinguishing the several denominations. A head of tobacco, then worth about 5 cents, appeared on the 5-cent note. The 10-cent note carried the picture of a chicken, and so on. While the new circulating medium was not designed to supersede cotton as legal tender, its appearance attests to the failure of the previous ordinance in conquering barter problems. In reality, cotton was just another commodity calling for barter and did not improve commercial intercourse or serve as an incentive for the colonists.[2]

The currency system and legal code proved to be beneficial

2 MSCS MSS, *Corresponding Secretary Books,* vol. II, Latrobe to Russwurm, Baltimore, June 30, 1836; *Constitution and Laws of Maryland in Liberia; with an Appendix of Precedents,* 2nd ed. (Baltimore: John D. Toy, 1847); MSCS MSS, *Records,* vol. II, meetings of the Board of Managers, Sept. 29, Oct. 10, 1837; *Latrobe Letter Books,* vol. II, Latrobe to Russwurm, Baltimore, Oct. 24, 1837.

and well accepted by the citizens. There was general approbation at having standards to follow in administering justice, although some facets of the judicial procedure were novel to the
colonists. The delineation of judges' powers was an especially
wise aspect of the code, in light of the generally ignorant, hence
defenseless, population. Paper currency was popular among colonists, Africans, and civil officials alike. Colonists and Africans
soon came to ask that at least a portion of their earnings from
work for the authorities or from produce sold at the agency
store be paid in such bills. Some immigrants even began to set
aside savings. The new arrangement tended to draw all business
to the society's store, the source of most goods and the point at
which currency circulation began.[3]

In spite of these measures aimed at the domestic development and stability of the colony, the major factor bearing upon
the community's tranquillity was its relations with surrounding
tribes. Doctor Hall was fortunate in governing when the indigenes were generally peaceful. Much of his success, of course,
depended upon his frequent use of "dash" and his knack at
palaver. Oliver Holmes, Jr., maintained harmony during his
brief administration by distributing at the outset presents sent
by the Board of Managers. But Russwurm soon found that the
greatest challenge to his ability and authority lay in handling
the ever-increasing conflicts between colonists and Africans. At
the beginning of his administration, he saw the colony's existence threatened with possible war. In straightening out his
predecessors' business records, he found that much of the confusion stemmed from thefts by Africans who used unauthorized
keys to enter the store. Even with a watchman inside every
night, whole pieces of cloth and other goods were regularly
stolen. Russwurm determined to put additional locks on the
doors, to install iron bars on all windows, and to erect a guard
house outside the store.

As soon as the Africans got word of such plans, the Cape
Palmas people, living closest to Harper, staged a raid on the

3 MSCS MSS, *Letters,* vol. VIII, Russwurm to Latrobe, Harper, Apr. 26,
1838.

store, stealing about 500 yards of cloth, forty or fifty pounds of tobacco, and other articles. King Freeman's failure to return the goods and punish the culprits induced colony officials to launch their own search. Turning up the loot and the instigator in Cape Town, they jailed the guilty party, whereupon his fellow countrymen converged upon the lockup with guns and sundry other weapons and released the prisoner. The bulk of colonists were away from Harper attending their farms beyond Cape Town. Not half a dozen men remained to defend the settlement should the mob attack them. In addition, those citizens tending their crops found the path home blocked and were forced to spend the night at Fair Hope, the ABCFM mission station. All during the night the two groups of colonists, separated by Cape Town, shuddered at the continual drum beat and the blowing of the war horn. The next morning, a great palaver took place between Russwurm and King Freeman. Surrounded by 400 or 500 Africans, most of whom were armed, the two principals and their chief advisers took seats at opposite sides of a great circle. King Freeman enumerated grievances and Russwurm answered. Resuming the palaver later in the day, the changed attitude among the Cape Palmas people was evident by the lack of weapons. The controversy ended when the king accepted Russwurm's argument that, were the stealing stopped, all difficulties would disappear. Later, he presented Russwurm with a black heifer as an offering for his abusive language during the palaver. The Africans' conduct stemmed from their disappointment at not having received gifts from the new agent and in their conviction that colonial magistrates had abused their power in punishing the thieves.[4]

This experience demonstrated the necessity of drilling and parading the militia regularly, servicing firearms, and protecting the well-oiled cannon. It showed the need for a second stockade at the other end of the colony, now about four miles into the interior. Although farms belonging only to Harper cit-

4 *Ibid.,* vol. VI, Russwurm to Latrobe, Harper, Jan. 12, 1837; J. Leighton Wilson to Latrobe, Fair Hope, June 6, 1837; Yellow Will to Latrobe, Harper, June 8, 1837.

izens lay in that direction then, the large group of Tubmans from Georgia arrived at Cape Palmas some months later and settled permanently in that remote area, thereafter called Mount Tubman.

Another major confrontation between colonists and Africans occurred in 1838. Late on July 25 the large native town on Cape Palmas accidentally caught fire and most of it burned to the ground. At the request of King Freeman, colonists were posted as guards around the ruins to prevent neighboring tribes from looting, as was the custom of the country. Early the next morning a group from Barraway, ostensibly en route to view the village's charred remains, attacked Ebin Parker, a colonist, in his home and murdered him along with three children. Declaring the Parkers innocent victims of savagery, a posse of their neighbors, led by Charles Snetter, undertook immediately to capture the murderers. Unfortunately, a small band of Cape Palmas Africans was mistakenly attacked with several wounded and one killed. Investigation revealed that Parker had daily threatened local Africans, pointing his gun at them, and that the Barraway townsfolk had murdered him to avenge the wounding of a companion several days before.

King Freeman sought no revenge for his men but cooperated with the colonists in placing an effective embargo upon goods sold to the Barraways. The blockade soon brought them to a willingness to negotiate, but several years of truce passed before differences were settled. Assuming that the colony was surrounded by enemies, despite the goodwill pledged by neighboring tribes, the governor stationed guards in various sections of the settlement and maintained regular night watchmen. His more militant posture at least halted thievery at the agency store.

As for the posse, a court of inquiry consisting of civil officers and others met in Harper during August, 1838, heard voluminous evidence, and concluded that: (1) Snetter had acted without authority in ordering the shooting of the Africans, (2) circumstances in the colony at the time mitigated his offense, and (3) the case should be turned over to the governor for a final decision. Convinced that the peace and welfare of the community necessitated stringent measures, Russwurm ordered Snetter to resign his civil and military offices, gave him thirty days to settle his personal affairs, and ordered him to leave the colony forever by the first means after that time.

The Snetter affair unfortunately created further domestic difficulties. Many citizens were incensed that Snetter should be banished. They charged that the court of inquiry was illegal, that the governor favored Africans over colonists in disputes, and that Snetter's actions were justified. Snetter, with two other prominent citizens, Alexander Hance and Anthony Wood, subsequently petitioned the Board of Managers to overrule the governor. They charged Russwurm with being unfair, vindictive, and aloof. But the board sustained him in his action and accorded him additional executive power with which to handle civil disturbances. It also created a small uniformed police unit, paid by the civil authority and under the immediate supervision of a governor-appointed officer. The expulsion of Snetter, a controversial figure since he had been hired as colonial secretary, had a generally soothing effect on the colony.[5]

Deteriorating relations with the Africans showed most conclusively the need for an enlarged military structure. Daily contact between colonists and Africans was steadily erasing that aura of strength upon which the American settlement had heretofore depended. Indeed, the colonists with their few fieldpieces, small number of rifles, and two stockades appeared easy prey. Wilson, observing the situation from Fair Hope, believed that plunder alone would be sufficient motive to bring the colony's extermination. He judged that in forty-eight hours 12,000 Africans, well furnished with arms and ammunition, could be gathered for the venture.

A good supply of weapons to replace and supplement those already in the colony went out aboard the brig *Oberon,* which

---

5 *Ibid.,* vol. IX, Russwurm to Latrobe, Harper, Aug. 6, 21, 1838; vol. X, Russwurm to Latrobe, Harper, Dec. 8, 1839; S. F. McGill to Latrobe, Harper, Apr. 20, 1839; memorial of citizens of the colony of Maryland in Liberia, Sept. 12, 1838; memorial of colonists to Board of Managers, Cape Palmas, Jan. 8, 1839; vol. VIII, proceedings of court of inquiry held Aug. 18 and 20, 1838; governor's decision, Harper, Aug. 26, 1838; vol. XI, Russwurm to Latrobe, Harper, Jan. 18, 1840; *Latrobe Letter Books,* vol. II, Latrobe to Russwurm, Baltimore, Nov. 21, 1839.

also carried Doctors Robert Macdowall and Samuel F. McGill, late in 1838. Doctor Macdowall's arrival coincided with reception of the news that Josiah F. C. Finley, brother of Robert and governor of the infant colony founded between Capes Mesurado and Palmas by Mississippi colonizationists, had been the victim of a murderous attack by neighboring Africans. The new colonial physician urged the Board of Managers to send out more arms, particularly cannon and large shot. He recommended that American warships visit the coast frequently to prevent attacks upon the colonies and upon Americans traveling along the coast. Africans, he contended, saw the Star-Spangled Banner flying at the mastheads of slave vessels so often that they no longer respected either the American flag or United States citizens.[6]

Several small cannon which could be mounted in boats or large canoes were subsequently sent to Harper. The colonists held frequent drills and parades to impress the Africans that any aggression on their part would be repelled. In spite of efforts to keep the community compact, it now spread four miles along Maryland Avenue from Harper to Mount Tubman. Four African towns containing nearly 3,000 people were in the midst of the township. Their existence posed the greatest threat to the colony's safety and future.[7]

It took the combined efforts of all colonization societies in the United States to persuade the Navy Department that regular voyages along Africa's western coast were essential. Heretofore, only an occasional vessel, such as the frigate *Potomac,* had stopped at the various settlements. Success came when overwhelming evidence demonstrated that the slave trade was still in progress despite increased numbers of British cruisers. Thomas Buchanan, one-time governor of Bassa Cove, the Pennsylvania settlement, asserted that nine-tenths of all slave vessels on the

---

6 Houghton Library, ABCFM Papers, *Correspondence, Letters from Missionaries to . . . Africa,* vol. II (West Africa, 1838–1844), Wilson to Rufus Anderson, Fair Hope, Aug. 16, 1837; MSCS MSS, *Latrobe Letter Books,* vol. II, Latrobe to Russwurm, Baltimore, Nov. 20, 1838; *Letters,* vol. X, Robert Macdowall to Ira A. Easter, Mount Vaughan, Jan. 15, 1839.

7 MSCS MSS, *Letters,* vol. X, Macdowall to Latrobe, Cape Palmas, Apr. 9, 1839; *Latrobe Letter Books,* vol. II, Latrobe to Russwurm, Baltimore, Dec. 11, 1839.

West African coast were built in the United States, that most
sailed under American colors, and that, consequently, British
efforts were ineffective. Information from Buchanan, Russwurm,
and Macdowall on slave operations near Cape Palmas was used
in applying directly to President Van Buren to station a man-of-
war permanently on the African coast. The Maryland society
also sought two heavy cannon for harbor defense and two
smaller fieldpieces for the Mount Tubman stockade. Early in
1840 the United States government dispatched two vessels to
Africa and stationed them at Monrovia, which received a large
donation of military equipment. Starting in 1841, the African
Squadron regularly visited Cape Palmas, although that colony
received no surplus armaments.[8]

In seeking to give Maryland in Liberia the necessary military
complexion to thwart outside aggression, the Board of Managers and its paid representatives in the colony came into serious conflict with the local missionary establishment. The board
had recognized the value of linking Christianity and colonization from the outset. Under its direct encouragement, Presbyterians (under ABCFM auspices), Episcopalians, and Methodists had founded stations called, respectively, Fair Hope, Mount
Vaughan, and Mount Emory. The Methodists directed their efforts at the colonists; the other two groups worked primarily
among the heathen.

Because of the African riots soon after he took office, Russwurm found himself confronted with the question of the missionaries' proper function in the colony. More delicate was the
issue of military service by colonists or educated Africans in
mission employ. The constitution specified that "all males between the ages of sixteen and sixty, residing in the territory,
shall be enrolled in the general militia, and be liable to be called
upon, at the discretion of the agent, under officers appointed by
him, in defence of the territory." Russwurm believed that only

---

8 National Archives, *African Squadron Letters*, vol. IV, Thomas Buchanan
to James K. Paulding, Washington, Dec. 15, 1838; MSCS MSS, *Latrobe
Letter Books*, vol. II, Latrobe to Martin Van Buren, Baltimore, May 9,
1839; *Letters*, vol. XI, Russwurm to Latrobe, Cape Palmas, Apr. 7, July
27, 1840.

black persons sent out by missionary societies at home expressly to be preachers or teachers were thus exempt from military training and duty. When, however, he sought to impress all able-bodied men into service, he found that Wilson at Fair Hope objected to having his three Negro assistants called upon for military or civic obligations. One young man, John Banks, had come to Cape Palmas with the original expedition and received bed, board, and education through Wilson's benevolence. Another, John Dorsey, had arrived in Africa only months before, but was under Wilson's tutelage and was expected to become a mission teacher.[9]

During the next year—mid-1837 to mid-1838—an initially friendly disagreement over interpretation of the constitution turned into a bitter personal feud between Russwurm and Wilson. It was complicated by the fact that Wilson, a South Carolinian, had taken a dislike to Russwurm soon after the governor assumed office. He believed that the progress of colonization had steadily declined ever since the selection of a Negro leader. In letters to the American board in Boston, Wilson accused Russwurm of abetting the slave trade by allowing reputed slave vessels to enter Cape Palmas harbor for repairs and crew members to lodge and trade in the colony. He called the governor timid, cowardly, incompetent, and lacking in wisdom. Wilson held a dim view of the colonists as well, particularly as they influenced surrounding Africans. Privately he admitted that mission work would not suffer if deprived of locally hired assistants, for, he claimed, most colonists possessed a superficial piety and had no interest in the Africans. He advised the ABCFM that the colonization scheme should be patronized as a plan of benevolence for American blacks rather than on the score of missionary operations for the heathen. He wrote his brother-in-law in Savannah, however, that anything was preferable to colonization.[10]

9 *Constitution and Laws of Maryland in Liberia,* p. 21; MSCS MSS, *Letters,* vol. VI, Russwurm to Latrobe, Monrovia, June 22, 1837; vol. VII, Wilson to Latrobe, Fair Hope, July 6, 1837.
10 Houghton Library, ABCFM Papers, *Correspondence, Letters from Missionaries,* Wilson to Anderson, Fair Hope, Apr. 16, July 5, Aug. 16, 1837; MSCS MSS, *Letters,* vol. IX, N. J. Bayard to Easter, Savannah, Ga., July 10, 1838.

Seeking to enforce the law as he interpreted it, Russwurm insisted that Banks and Dorsey train with the militia when they were in Harper. The third mission helper, Mr. James, was exempted on grounds that he had been sent out from Boston under ABCFM employ as a printer. When Banks and Dorsey failed to comply, the governor imposed fines. Wilson was so incensed by his course and by a militia officer's effort to collect that he returned the deed for land cleared by Banks and claimed exemption from further military duty for the young colonist. Dorsey subsequently opened a mission at Rocktown, in the interior, and removed himself from controversy by being declared nonresident.

Russwurm was sadly perplexed. Almost every able young man was employed by the missionaries as soon as he arrived in the colony, with the result that the civil administration suffered from a dearth of competent persons to fill the different offices. More important, the tenuous relationship with neighboring Africans necessitated universal military conscription. If missionaries won their way, increasing numbers of able-bodied men would be useless in affording the settlement protection.[11]

With such divergent opinions at Cape Palmas and matters complicated by Wilson's antipathy toward Russwurm, the issue had to be resolved at home. The Colonization Society took the position that public safety necessitated that all able-bodied men participate in the colony's protection just as a passenger aboard a ship might help to prevent its sinking. Except in emergencies, only missionaries, white or black, operating solely in their religious capacity while residing in the colony, were exempt from civic responsibilities. They were likened to foreigners who came to the United States for a temporary period—aliens, yet still answerable for debt, breaches of the peace, and the commission of crimes. But colonists who went to Africa at state society expense or signed the settlement constitution, as Banks and Dorsey

11 MSCS MSS, *Letters*, vol. VI, Russwurm to Latrobe, Monrovia, June 22, 1837; vol. VIII, Russwurm to Latrobe, Harper, Apr. 28, 1838; Wilson to Russwurm, [Fair Hope], Apr. 16, 1838; Houghton Library, ABCFM Papers, *Correspondence, Letters from Missionaries*, Wilson to Anderson, Fair Hope, Apr. 18, Sept. 25, 1838.

had, were in another class. If they entered into mission service, they were still responsible for the performance of all duties expected of other citizens, including military. The primary difference between the two categories was citizenship. Missionaries sent out by their boards in the United States were foreign visitors while their employees were citizens of the colony and permanent residents.

The American board expected to send to Cape Palmas as many black missionaries and assistants as possible because of the climate. It had pretty well accepted Wilson's opinion that American settlements and white Americans along the coast tended to corrupt Africans. Hence the farther the mission from the coast and the less the association with other foreigners, the more promising the religious results. For these reasons, ABCFM missionaries were reluctant to admit any connection with Maryland in Liberia. Echoing them, Secretary Rufus Anderson could hardly imagine circumstances under which spreaders of the Gospel tidings would be justified in participating in military activity against the Africans.

Negotiations between the two benevolent bodies in America were harmonious. Unwittingly, however, Secretary Anderson and President Latrobe reached different conclusions from their correspondence. Latrobe believed that the American board acknowledged full missionary subservience to colonial authorities and accepted his delineation of the two classes of mission workers. Anderson, on the other hand, happily noted that ABCFM missionaries and assistant missionaries, white or colored, sent from the United States or reared from tribes not subject to the colonial government, were to be regarded as foreigners when in the colony. Their interpretations were altogether different and Anderson even added a new class of mission employee—Christianized Africans. Each conveyed his version of the parley to representatives at Cape Palmas.[12]

12 MSCS MSS, *Latrobe Letter Books,* vol. II, Latrobe to Russwurm, Baltimore, Oct. 24, 1837; Latrobe to R. Anderson, Baltimore, July 2, 1838; Latrobe to Russwurm, Baltimore, Nov. 20, 1838; *Foreign Letter Books,* vol. II, Anderson to Latrobe, Boston, June 25, 1838; *Letters,* vol. IX, Anderson to Latrobe, Boston, July 11, 1838.

How far apart their views actually were became apparent only three years later, in 1841, when the mission groups teaching and Christianizing the Africans were again embroiled in the military obligation controversy. This time Wilson came into conflict with Russwurm by claiming exemption for all the young men in his employ. Some were recruits from Sierra Leone and Cape Coast; others were passengers aboard visiting ships who decided to remain at Cape Palmas when they found employment available; still others were native Africans who had acquired enough education to become teachers. All were accorded the title "assistant missionary" by Wilson and were considered exempt from the militia. Doctor Thomas Savage of Mount Vaughan, the Episcopal mission, had adopted the same practice there.

Again Russwurm and Wilson appealed to their respective home boards. It soon became apparent that colonization and missionary views were irreconcilable. The Maryland society defined missionaries as noncolonists who were regularly ordained as ministers of the Gospel through appropriate religious channels and who were in the actual employment of some American or European missionary society. As foreigners, these alone were exempt from civic responsibilities. Any other policy would grant individuals unconnected with the Colonization Society the power to declare who should reside in the colony and be protected by its laws while not being liable to defend the community. Under pressure to be even more explicit, the society finally stipulated that only white mission employees registered with it would thereafter be exempt. This meant that even African pupils from local or distant tribes were expected to undergo military training when they entered mission schools.

The American board believed that members of their mission sent out from the United States, persons hired from other African colonies or from tribes not under colonial jurisdiction, and boarding-school pupils who came from distant tribes were not subject to military obligations. It was actually adding two new classes, African teachers and pupils, to the excepted categories. ABCFM's Prudential Committee questioned the wisdom of training Africans in the use of weapons and the conduct of war.

Paper currency used in the colony in 1837

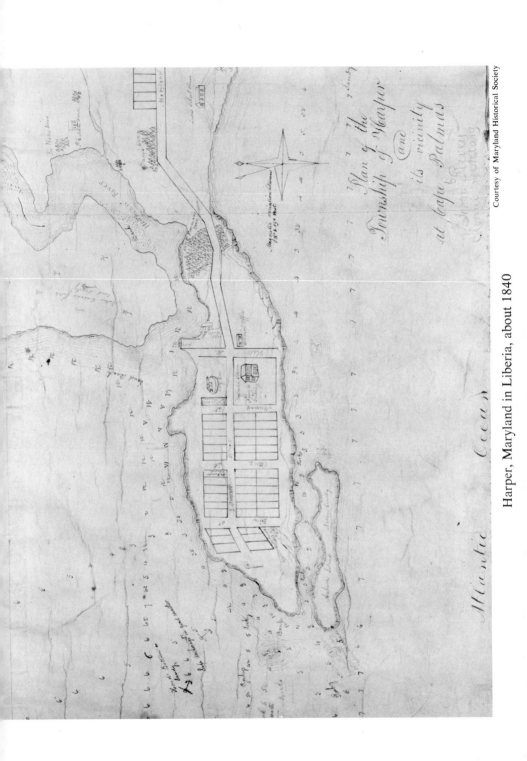

Harper, Maryland in Liberia, about 1840

It called the effort to compel African helpers and pupils from independent tribes to perform military duty oppressive to the mission.

Meanwhile, Episcopal missionaries at Maryland in Liberia were experiencing the same pressure from Governor Russwurm. Like other mission personnel who worked almost exclusively with the indigenes, they faced the dilemma of whether or not to submit to colonial laws respecting military training. Their board in New York had heretofore assumed a spectator position in the discussions, perhaps because, with the fewest black workers at the cape, it was less directly affected. Now, late in 1841, when the Maryland Board of Managers declared that only white missionaries and assistants from the United States registered with it would be freed from militia activities, the Episcopal board protested. The religious character and objects of the mission station, it declared, necessitated that no person connected with its operations and in residence there appear under arms. It asked full exemption for its post personnel and for those under its care in the colony. Since the Episcopal mission had been ambitious in educating and hiring local as well as more distant Africans, consent to its request would have nullified colonizationist objectives.[13]

Throughout 1842 the question of the Maryland society's policy relative to military duties was bandied about in America and Africa. The Reverend John B. Pinney, an ordained Presbyterian minister in American Colonization Society employ, warned Marylanders that driving missionary establishments from the colony would be fatal to its future. He declared that current policy was so contrary to the usual custom for students, so opposed to the spirit of missions, and so unnecessary for the colony's strength as to make it appear designed to force the re-

13 MSCS MSS, *Letters*, vol. XII, Russwurm to Latrobe, Cape Palmas, June 24, 1841; Anderson to Latrobe, Boston, Nov. 3, Dec. 9, 1841; John A. Vaughan to Latrobe, New York, Dec. 16, 28, 1841; *Records*, vol. III, meetings of the Board of Managers, Oct. 1, Nov. 12, Dec. 13, 1841, Jan. 4, 1842; *Latrobe Letter Books*, vol. II, Latrobe to Anderson, Baltimore, Nov. 23, 1841; Latrobe to Vaughan, Baltimore, Jan. 5, 1842; Houghton Library, ABCFM Papers, *Correspondence, Letters from Missionaries*, Wilson to Anderson, Fair Hope, June 26, 1841.

moval of the mission stations. Ralph Gurley, on a visit to the
Northeast in the summer, reported the ABCFM and the Episcopal board anxious to reach an amicable settlement. He cautioned that if the influence of all the missionary boards were
thrown against colonization, it would be difficult to sustain the
cause. Even the society's general agent, Doctor James Hall, dis-
sented from his employers' views in the matter of requiring African pupils in mission schools to do military duty. Nevertheless,
the Board of Managers stood firm.[14]

Two incidents served to exacerbate relations between colonizationists and missionaries during that year. The first was the
arrival in the United States of a round robin signed by agents
of the various denominations at Cape Palmas and sent to their
home boards. They charged that most colonists set a vicious and
immoral example for Africans which discouraged their efforts.
Immigrants, removed from restraints in America, had adopted
vices which unfavorably influenced local blacks. They lamented
that while it was fashionable in the colony to be a church member and to participate in frenzied revival meetings, signs of true
devotion, such as honesty and trustworthiness, were absent. They
accused the settlers of a hatred for Africans so strong as to desire the annihilation of those living in their vicinity. The missionaries declared that the colonial government continually presented serious obstacles in their path by way of regulations and
import duties. Terming the colony's fate uncertain, they appealed for removal from Cape Palmas.

Simultaneously, on the opposite side of the Atlantic the American board decided to reduce its operations at Fair Hope. As
early as 1838 Wilson, the cantankerous central figure in the dispute, had suggested the Gold Coast, Ashantee, or along the
Niger River as new missionary grounds. He ruled out locations
to the windward toward Monrovia on the basis that, should the
American colonies survive, they ultimately would control all ter-

14 MSCS MSS, *Letters*, vol. XIII, J. B. Pinney to James Hall, Philadelphia,
Jan. 4, 1842; R. R. Gurley to Hall, Boston, Apr. 13, 1842; *Agent's Books*,
vol. II, Hall to Gurley, Baltimore, Aug. 25, 1842; Hall to Pinney, Baltimore, Nov. 12, 1842.

ritory between Capes Mesurado and Palmas, hence again holding jurisdiction over the ABCFM mission.[15]

The second 1842 conflict involved the theft of bullocks, cloth, copper rods, and other items valued at about $150, a substantial sum locally at that time, from the Fair Hope mission. Wilson had already abandoned the station for a post on the Gabon River and a Mr. Griswold was now in control at Cape Palmas. Rather than appealing to colonial authorities for redress against King Freeman's people, the culprits, Griswold waited for the arrival of the *Vandalia,* an American warship. Its officers twice went ashore to force restitution, the second time threatening to burn King Freeman's towns and holding two hostages until he complied. Such an obvious usurpation of colonial jurisdiction signaled the final rupture in relations between the colony and the ABCFM station. In Baltimore Latrobe issued an ultimatum to the American board that it give its missionaries explicit instructions to conform to the colony's laws and prevent the recurrence of such episodes or to leave Maryland in Liberia immediately. This demand, coupled with Chancellor Wolworth's recommendation to the ABCFM in September that its mission be removed from the Maryland colony and with financial difficulties of the Boston-based mission board, settled the question. Fair Hope was gradually evacuated, and in early 1844 the area reverted to the Colonization Society. The Episcopal, Methodist, and Baptist stations continued in operation.[16]

The ABCFM's decision to withdraw altogether from Cape

---

15 Houghton Library, ABCFM Papers, *Correspondence, Letters from Missionaries,* Thomas Savage, Wilson, and others to Prudential Committee of ABCFM, [Cape Palmas], Jan. 1, 1842; Wilson to Anderson, Cape Palmas, Dec. 24, 1838, Sept. 22, 1841; *Letters: Foreign* (Copy Book Series, vol. X), Anderson to mission in West Africa, Boston, Dec. 30, 1841.

16 MSCS MSS, *Letters,* vol. XIII, Russwurm to Hall, Cape Palmas, Sept. 26, 1842; vol. XIV, Russwurm to Latrobe, Cape Palmas, June 26, 1843; vol. XV, Russwurm to Latrobe, Cape Palmas, Feb. 13, 1844; *Latrobe Letter Books,* vol. II, Latrobe to Russwurm, Baltimore, Dec. 8, 1842; Latrobe to Anderson, Baltimore, Dec. 8, 1842; *Eleventh Annual Report of the Board of Managers of the Maryland State Colonization Society* (Baltimore: John D. Toy, 1843), Appendix; Joseph Tracy, *History of the American Board of Commissioners for Foreign Missions,* 2nd ed. rev. (New York: M. W. Dodd, 1842), pp. 431–33.

Palmas was influenced by the arrival of Roman Catholic missionaries at Cape Palmas. For more than ten years the hierarchy
in Rome and in the United States, mindful of some Catholics
among the colonists, had contemplated Liberia as a mission
field. In 1841 Father Edward Barron, vicar-general of Philadelphia, and Father John Kelly, pastor of St. John's Church in
Albany, New York, volunteered for the assignment. Assured by
the Maryland society that they would be welcome in Harper, the
two priests and a white lay assistant sailed aboard the *Harriet*
for Africa on December 20, 1841. They were disappointed to
find few Catholics among the ex-Americans in Monrovia and
only eighteen at Cape Palmas. They therefore decided to focus
their efforts on nearby African villages. On the first Sunday in the
colony the two priests, dressed in vestments, preceded by a
cross bearer, and reciting the litany, marched into Cape Town
to meet King Freeman. Later, Father Barron, addressing the
Grebos through an interpreter, found them attentive and respect-
ful until he explained the Trinity and Hell, whereupon they began to laugh.

The three Catholic missionaries passed through the acclimation period with little difficulty and proceeded to launch operations upon lots near the Presbyterians at Fair Hope. Although
Colonization Society officers, colonists, and Africans were generally pleased with this new Roman Church venture, the Protestant missionaries were not. They treated their Catholic brethren
with bare civility and complained that the liberal use of money
and bribes by their competitors put them at a disadvantage.

Catholic success, however, was short-lived. Almost immediately after his arrival in Africa, Father Barron was named bishop
of a new vicariate of the two Guineas and Sierra Leone. Realizing that he needed far more workers for that vast territory, Barron left Cape Palmas in April, 1842, for the United States and,
afterwards, Europe. Reinforcements, in the form of seven inex-
perienced priests and three uneducated laymen, all French, arrived at the settlement late that year. Their inability to communicate with Father Kelly, who subsequently left the colony
following a bitter controversy with a colonist, or anyone else

and their rapid demise from fever brought about Bishop Barron's decision to abandon Cape Palmas for Assinia, Bassam, and Gabon where French government support seemed to assure their success. As it happened, the Barron expedition met disaster at the other stations as well and the bishop resigned, returning to parish work in the United States.[17]

Roman Catholic missionary efforts came under suspicion by the simultaneously increased activity of French vessels along the West African coast in the 1840's. At Maryland in Liberia rumor had it in 1842 that a French squadron of three warships had visited Garroway, some fifteen miles north of Cape Palmas, and had purchased the surrounding country for a coaling station. Indeed, the following year, a French man-of-war stationed itself off Garroway and its crew marked out two sites for occupation, one for a stockade and the other for a town.

Garroway seemed a tragic loss for farsighted colonizationists and settlers who dreamed of making the several-hundred-mile coast between Cape Palmas and Cape Mesurado one long expanse of American control. Governor Russwurm hurriedly purchased Fishtown, once the home of a leading English trader, the late Captain Spence, for about $300. Only ten miles windward from Harper, Fishtown was noted for its fine harbor and bay. Latrobe, in an obvious play to halt French expansion, requested the American Secretary of the Navy, David Henshaw, to have the newly purchased harbor surveyed and charted by the African Squadron. Several months later Commodore Matthew C. Perry, heading the American fleet off that coast, raised the flag over Fishtown and fired a twelve-gun salute. His favorable im-

---

17 MSCS MSS, *Records,* vol. III, meeting of the Board of Managers, Sept. 27, 1841; *Letters,* vol. XIII, Russwurm to Latrobe, Cape Palmas, Feb. 12, May 24, 1842; vol. XV, Russwurm to Hall, Cape Palmas, Jan. 12, 1844; Henry J. Koren, *The Spiritans: A History of the Congregation of the Holy Ghost* (Pittsburgh: Duquesne University, 1958), pp. 78–86; Martin J. Bane, *The Catholic Story of Liberia* (New York: Declan X. McMullen Co., 1950); Houghton Library, ABCFM Papers, *Correspondence from Missionaries,* Wilson to Anderson, Fair Hope, Feb. 1, Apr. 7, 1842; U.S. Catholic Historical Society, "The Mission to Liberia: Diary of the Rev. John Kelly," *Historical Records and Studies,* XIV (1920), 120–53.

pression of the American settlements led to increased naval activity and watchfulness in that part of the globe.[18]

The French purchase at Garroway and the arrival of ten French missionaries at Cape Palmas appeared no accident to apprehensive citizens in the American settlements. The *Liberia Herald,* published in Monrovia, reported, from information obtained through a supposedly reliable source, that the Catholic mission had authority to control the movements of one French man-of-war. This weekly noted that one vessel did indeed constantly hover about Cape Palmas and termed this fact mysterious and ominous. In Harper rumor that responsibility for the Catholic station was to be transferred from the United States to a society in France raised speculation about ultimate foreign designs upon that colony. The subsequent Catholic withdrawal from Cape Palmas and the French failure to develop Garroway eased fears that a foreign government would establish itself along that coastal stretch.[19]

A contributing factor to the generally strained relations between colonizationists and missionaries from 1838 on was the latter's reports to American supporters. Wilson's indiscreet letters to his Savannah brother-in-law and other relatives, the round robin to mission boards, an Episcopal missionary's protest against the Roman Catholic workers which appeared in a leading church periodical—these and other semipublic criticisms reflected badly upon the Maryland settlement. Colonizationists were sensitive precisely because many charges against colonists were accurate. Accounts of laziness among them, of uncivil treatment toward Africans, of immoral behavior in the community, and of a host of other shortcomings were just as true now

18 MSCS MSS, *Letters,* vol. XII, Russwurm to Latrobe, Cape Palmas, Sept. 27, 1840; vol. XIII, Russwurm to Latrobe, Cape Palmas, Feb. 12, 1842; vol. XIV, Russwurm to Latrobe, Cape Palmas, June 26, July 31, 1843; vol. XV, Russwurm to Latrobe, Cape Palmas, Feb. 13, 1844; *Latrobe Letter Books,* vol. II, Latrobe to David Henshaw, Baltimore, Oct. 7, 1843; National Archives, *African Squadron Letters: Cruise of Matthew C. Perry, April 10, 1843 to April 29, 1845,* M. C. Perry to Henshaw, frigate *Macedonia,* Monrovia, Jan. 4, 1844.

19 *Liberia Herald,* Mar. 30, 1844, p. 3; MSCS MSS, *Letters,* vol. XV, Russwurm to Hall, Cape Palmas, Jan. 12, 1844; vol. XVI, Russwurm to Latrobe, Cape Palmas, Jan. 16, 1845.

under the administration of a capable Negro governor as they had been earlier at the Monrovian settlements and during the infancy of Maryland in Liberia.

One of Governor Russwurm's first reports to his employers after taking over at Cape Palmas dealt with an agricultural situation which, with few exceptions, prevailed year after year. He complained that the colonists had planted little on their farms even though it was common knowledge that sustained effort upon a small lot would support a family. They were prone to easy discouragement and were daily becoming more convinced that they could not make a living by cultivation. Rather than farming, they went into the swamps to cut the shingles, plank, and scantling in demand by mission stations and the colonial government. At this time, early 1837, the colony possessed only four teams of oxen and did most tilling with hoes. Russwurm secured some ploughs and yokes, attached them to the oxen, and, to set an example, ploughed about three acres of one public farm. It was a novel procedure to the Africans and to many colonists as well and forever afterward there was a great clamor in the colony for jacks and jennies. However, Russwurm's purpose was defeated. Rather than using such work animals for agricultural projects, the colonists generally put them to hauling timber.

Shortly after this, the visits of three warships, two American and one British, which bought large quantities of fresh produce and kept the women busy doing sailors' laundry, paying in specie in both instances, encouraged many settlers to tackle their farm work with greater enthusiasm in hope of establishing regular commerce with passing ships. Their new resolve was soon abandoned. The following harvest season the cry throughout the colony was of hard times. Russwurm had given out no garden seeds during the last planting because none had come recently from the United States, but he had offered seed for peas, beans, corn, cotton, and coffee. Colonists accepted these and no more was heard from them until they complained of scarcity. While sympathizing somewhat with the people, the governor concluded that nothing short of famine would drive them to agriculture. He noted that in the previous year many colonists had made promises to be more enterprising, but, except for the Tubmans, renowned for their effort and success, they had done little.[20]

The agent was not alone in deploring the lack of industry among the colonists. Alexander Hance, returning to Cape Palmas early in 1838 after a visit to the United States, informed Latrobe that the situation in the colony was definitely less encouraging than when he had left it the year before. Food was scarce, even for the Africans, and, since colonists depended largely upon them, prices were whatever they wanted to charge. Moreover, the Africans had obtained so much tobacco in barter that they no longer accepted it as payment for provisions. Hance complained that prices had doubled during his absence. A young colonist who taught school periodically, O. A. Chambers, held that the settlers badly neglected their fields. The prospect of cash payment for carpentry work led them to turn their backs on farming. Like Russwurm, he was of the opinion that a little hardship would provide the proper antidote for such shortsightedness.[21]

Sheer lack of food did actually turn many colonists back to tillage as their most worthwhile occupation. Acreage under cultivation doubled the next season. A new species of potato, larger and more productive, was introduced from the public farm, and night guards were stationed throughout the colony to prevent plunder by Africans. The following spring was one of unusual plenty in the colony. To maintain settlers' interest in their farms, the colonial government offered prizes to owners of farm lands in the best and most permanent state of cultivation. The highest premium, $30, went to Joshua Cornish, and two other citizens shared the second award, $20. A survey made late in 1839 showed a large variety of produce being grown. Corn, potatoes, okra, watermelons, cabbages, yams, tomatoes, and many other vegetables and fruits were being cultivated on private farms. The

20 MSCS MSS, *Letters,* vol. VI, Russwurm to Latrobe, Harper, Feb. 12, 1837; George R. McGill to Latrobe, Harper, May 13, 1837; vol. VIII, Russwurm to Latrobe, Harper, Apr. 26, 1838.
21 *Ibid.,* vol. VIII, Alexander Hance to Latrobe, Cape Palmas, Apr. 7, 1838; vol. IX, O. A. Chambers to Easter, Cape Palmas, July 10, 1838.

agency experimental station at Mount Tubman then embraced forty-one acres and that at Harper thirty-two.[22]

The colonists not only displayed a marked aversion to cultivating their own land but they sedulously avoided work on the public farms as well. Whereas the Colonization Society and its agent considered these as a means of helping settlers work off their debts, providing food for colonists during periods of personal difficulty, punishing lawbreakers, and experimenting with crops likely to prove suitable for that climate, the citizens generally ignored them. They seldom expressed interest in meeting their obligations. They expected handouts from the agency store during hard times and seldom took notice of the progress of the various plants which the governor watched so closely for indications of success.

The item in which most hope was placed was cotton. The first attempt at its cultivation with seeds sent from the United States was a complete failure. Russwurm conjectured that the seed must have been defective or that perhaps it had been damaged by sea water en route. A second trial with American seeds was likewise unsuccessful and Russwurm concluded that only African seed, yielding an inferior grade of cotton, could ever be used. Although the plants springing up from African seeds grew well, small boring insects often ruined their pods. Russwurm then turned to sugar as a potential export crop. This venture, too, was never more than moderately successful and colonial authorities then laid more stress on coffee-growing. However, unless small trees were planted, the harvesting of coffee beans was a long-term project. Two trees which Russwurm planted on the public farm took some two and a half years to blossom. He later established part of the farm as a nursery for nurturing coffee seeds into young plants for distribution among the colonists. Within two years 4,000 coffee trees had been set out, half of them on the public farm.[23]

---

22 *Ibid.,* vol. IX, Russwurm to Latrobe, Harper, Nov. 1, 1838; vol. XI, report of the Committee on Agriculture to Russwurm, [Maryland in Liberia, Jan. 1, 1840]; agricultural survey of Maryland in Liberia, [Jan. 1], 1840.
23 *Ibid.,* vol. VI, Russwurm to Latrobe, Harper, Feb. 12, 1837; vol. IX, Russ-

An important factor in the colony's agricultural backward-
ness was the poor ratio between male and female colonists. Although at first, as with most new communities, the imbalance
had been the other way, as the colony matured the number of
able-bodied men decreased in proportion to the number of dependent women and children. Early in his administration Governor Russwurm complained of the women with children who
arrived in the colony unaccompanied by husbands. He queried
how they could be self-supporting after the initial six months.
He pleaded, "We want men; we want families with a suitable
head. Your colony is not strong enough yet, to receive any but
able bodied men, without a great expense to the Society." His
advice went unheeded. The next expedition, which left Baltimore in May, 1838, brought very few men to the colony. Russwurm again protested, warning the Colonization Society that unless it wished the settlement overrun with female paupers and
orphans, it must correct such imbalance.

One can only speculate on reasons for appreciably more female volunteers than male. A prominent factor undoubtedly
was the slave owners' calculation of the relative worth of male
and female labor. To manumit a slave woman with children
possibly relieved the owner of financial liability and at the same
time soothed his conscience. If he were disposed to sell his
slaves, his females were generally worth 25 per cent less than
his males, an even greater incentive to free the women. A male
slave given his freedom had many more opportunities for employment at home than did women and thus had less motivation
to move to a far-off land where his future was more doubtful
than if he remained in the United States.

An observation by Samuel Ford McGill, the colonial physician, suggests an additional explanation for the mounting re-
dundancy of females. In his annual report covering colonial
births and deaths he noted that from November, 1839, to November, 1840, there were seventeen babies born to the colonists.
Of these, thirteen were female and four male. He reported further that, from his experience, this disproportion in favor of fe-

wurm to Latrobe, Harper, Nov. 1, 1838, Jan. 18, June 10, 1840; vol. XIII,
Russwurm to Latrobe, Cape Palmas, Apr. 7, 1842.

male children was generally true in Africa, especially among the indigenes.[24]

Occasionally there arrived at Cape Palmas an expedition which consisted of almost unmanageable immigrants. One such gang came aboard the *Niobe,* which embarked from Baltimore in November, 1837, with eighty-five blacks. Upon landing in the colony, for the first two weeks before fever brought them low, the greater part of them acted like madmen. The women abandoned their modesty and some men did likewise. Russwurm declared that "they were a scandal to our quiet town. . . ." In the first two months they caused more trouble than all the rest of the citizens combined. Besides their general loose morality, many demanded the best food available, so much so that the governor remarked that one would have thought them brought up in a parlor. For years afterward the *Niobe* affair was a subject of reproachful, but interesting, comment.[25]

When Maryland colonizationists established their colony, they made much of the settlement's agricultural basis, contrasting it with the American Colonization Society's Monrovia. Most of the latter's deficiencies were attributed to the development of trade and the consequent agricultural neglect. With experience, however, came greater understanding of the need for combined agrarian and commercial enterprise at Cape Palmas. The real problem was not to exclude commerce but to foster a wise balance between the two sources of livelihood. In 1838 famine revived the idea of the colony possessing a boat which would enable civil authorities to seek food from a larger number of tribes and reduce their dependence upon local Africans. Russwurm suggested the purchase of a small coaster of ten or twelve tons with a light draft which could be used to visit nearby points where food was more abundant than at the cape. Later that year the Snetter incident, which brought the colony to the brink of war, impressed Russwurm, as it had Hall before him, with the importance of being less dependent upon the Palmas Af-

---

24 *Ibid.,* vol. VIII, Russwurm to Latrobe, Harper, Apr. 26, 1838; vol. IX, Russwurm to Latrobe, Harper, July 7, 1838; vol. XII, S. F. McGill to Latrobe, Harper, Apr. 9, 1841.

25 *Ibid.,* vol. VIII, Russwurm to Latrobe, Harper, Apr. 26, 1838.

ricans. Moreover, placement of a light-weight cannon in the boat would deter African riots.[26]

At the very time Russwurm was reintroducing the subject of a colony boat, the Colonization Society at home was seeking means of paying its debts. The managers began to look at colonial trade as a potential source of profit but acknowledged that formal separation of the society's political and commercial functions was necessary to preserve its image as a purely benevolent organization. Domestic problems delayed action, but Russwurm was issued a standing order to keep all commerce in agency hands. Unfortunately, the missionaries in the settlement were already competing with the society store. They replenished their stock by every vessel which called, whereas Russwurm had to depend upon the two or three yearly voyages from Baltimore. The missionaries consequently had better goods, which they purchased with specie from home, and avoided dealing with the agency store, while colonists were forbidden to trade with passing merchants. To improve Russwurm's position vis-à-vis the missionaries, he was authorized to spend up to $2,000 a year for articles from the visiting traders, thus giving him a wider range of items to offer purchasers. But the Maryland group took no further action to foster the colony's commercial development. As debts at home compelled the society to reduce its commitments, Russwurm turned to bartering palm oil in exchange for trade goods.[27]

In the spring of 1840 Russwurm, encouraged by a few successful business ventures, purchased a small craft of some six tons. It could carry only sixteen barrels of palm oil and he soon became dissatisfied with its capacity as he dreamed of the profits which could be realized for the colony with a large schooner. He urged Latrobe not to abandon the idea of a commercial agency, for the palm oil trade was steadily increasing. Moreover, the death of Captain Spence, whose factory lay at Fishtown, left a

26 *Ibid.*, vol. VIII, Russwurm to Latrobe, Harper, Apr. 28, 1838; vol. IX, Russwurm to Latrobe, Harper, Aug. 6, 1838.

27 MSCS MSS, *Latrobe Letter Books*, vol. II, Latrobe to Russwurm, Baltimore, Mar. 26, May 7, Nov. 20, 1838; *Letters*, vol. VIII, Russwurm to Latrobe, Harper, Apr. 28, 1838.

vacuum which Russwurm wished to fill for the colony's benefit.

The following winter he was able to acquire a forty-ton vessel from the Spence estate. Naming it the *Latrobe,* he first had to send it to Monrovia for what he estimated would be $200 worth of repairs. But the work done there was so poor that it had to be overhauled again at Harper by carpenters who knew nothing of ship-building. Russwurm discovered, moreover, that he lacked sufficient men to sail both the *Latrobe* and the *Doctor,* as he called the smaller boat. He consequently sold the *Doctor* to two colonists for 1,140 gallons of palm oil on credit of six months. Later, without a master for the *Latrobe,* he felt obligated to sell it as well.

In the short time that the colony owned one or both of the bottoms, business ventures varied in success. Other visitors to the coast recognized, as did Russwurm, the money to be made in palm oil and camwood. But both were in abundant supply and export prices were soon driven down, making the business less lucrative. Moreover, other traders had an advantage over Russwurm in securing palm oil and camwood in that they could offer rum and other items of wider appeal than the governor had at his disposal. During this brief span the colony enjoyed unprecedented prosperity and peace, with the colonists experiencing success on their farms and living in relative harmony with the Africans. But all in all, while it was a sound idea, vessel ownership at that particular time was not especially beneficial to the colony. The managers, preoccupied at home with trying to keep the colonization movement alive and avoiding the necessity of transferring the settlement to some other authority, watched the vagaries of colonial trade with scarcely an idea of how to develop the community's commercial potential. It was at this time, the fall of 1840, that society officials hired Doctor James Hall as their general agent in Baltimore. Engaged successfully in trade along the African coast since the close of his service in the Maryland colony in 1836, he was commonly regarded as the one man capable of redeeming colonization.[28]

28 MSCS MSS, *Letters,* vol. XI, Russwurm to Latrobe, Harper, June 10, 1840; vol. XII, Russwurm to Latrobe, Cape Palmas, Mar. 12, May 31, Sept. 22, 1841; *Records,* vol. III, meeting of the Board of Managers, Sept. 12, 1840.

VI

Emerging
Colonial Independence

The gradual loosening of ties with the founding institution was the major colonial course of the 1840's. Ordinances and laws were increasingly designed to force the settlement to attain greater self-sufficiency and mounting responsibility. Not only were colonists conditioned to expect greater self-government; colonization supporters back home found the society's *Annual Reports* speaking increasingly of the colony's future. Thus, for instance, in 1842 they were told, "The Board believe that the colony in a few years will be wholly independent of aid from this country,—capable to defray the cost of its civil list—military defences, and internal improvements. . . ." [1]

Impetus for steps in the direction of autonomy actually came from sources outside society control. By 1840 American griev-

1 *Tenth Annual Report of the Board of Managers to the Maryland State Colonization Society* (Baltimore: John D. Toy, 1842), p. 11.

150

ances against Great Britain threatened to break into war. At issue were the Maine boundary, control of the Oregon country, and the right of British cruisers to search American vessels off the West African coast for slaves. Fearing hostilities, the Board of Managers adopted "A Declaratory Ordinance, touching the sovereignty of Maryland in Liberia," clarifying the relationship between society and colony. Claiming that the colonial government was as legitimate, sovereign, and independent as any other in the world, the board designated it free of all authority not provided for in its 1833 constitution. The residents owed allegiance to that administration and not to the United States or any other nation.

The fear which produced this declaration was that, in any war between Britain and America, the British would seize the West African settlements on the pretext that they were American colonies. In the belief that the British were anxious to acquire as much of that coast as possible in order to multiply markets for their manufactures, society action served notice of the neutral character of all the American-founded enclaves.[2]

Fortunately, these several Anglo-American disputes were all settled amicably. The "Declaratory Ordinance," nevertheless, was the beginning of the nationhood process. Luckily, too, the settlement possessed in Governor Russwurm a man well suited to lead it toward eventual independence. His generally judicious and tactful manner, as well as his even-natured administration, won approbation from most colonists, from visitors along the coast, and from colonizationists at home who were anxious for the success of a Negro agent. In keeping with their determination to wean their offspring, Maryland society managers gradually extended to the colony greater political, economic, and judicial authority and responsibility.

Politically, the governor gained more control over immigrants and others entering the colony. The growing number of vessels putting in at Cape Palmas, the influx of missionaries, and the

---

2 MSCS MSS, *Records*, vol. III, meeting of the Board of Managers, Feb. 2, 1841; *Latrobe Letter Books*, vol. II, John Latrobe to T. S. Alexander, State Colonization Rooms, Apr. 24, 1841.

increasing population of Maryland in Liberia made it imperative that the governor have greater authority and discretion. The
trip between Baltimore and Africa was still about six weeks' sail
in either direction. Experience taught both Russwurm and the
Board of Managers that they could no longer allow such intervals to lapse in the adjustment of colonial conflicts. Hence, the
managers adopted "An Ordinance for the Better Maintenance
of the Authority of the Government of Maryland in Liberia."
All white persons over fourteen years of age, save those connected with visiting military or commercial vessels not remaining at Cape Palmas over ten days, were to register with the
colonial secretary and to pledge allegiance to the colony's constitution and laws. They were to promise to conduct themselves
"respectfully towards the said Government, and peaceably towards the citizens and inhabitants of said territory." Violators
were subject to arrest and then banishment from the colony on
the first available ship. All arriving black persons who expected
to remain at the settlement more than a month, except children
under fourteen, were to register that intention with the colonial
secretary and to subscribe to local laws. Failure to do so would
result in deportation. The cost of removing either class of law-
breaker was to come from the seizure and sale of his property.
The new ordinance strengthened the governor's hand in applying other laws. It was the first major step in according the colony political independence.[3]

Financial embarrassment at home and the possibility that at
any time the colony might be thrown upon its own resources
necessitated encouragement of gradual economic independence
as well. Russwurm was continually urged to economize; the
board reminded him that the American Pilgrims had no one
at home to pay their officials and to send supplies. The development of an export staple was his first attempt to build financial solvency, but cotton, coffee, and sugar in turn failed to
materialize as money-making crops. The palm oil and camwood
market was too undependable. Nevertheless, trade in a number

3 MSCS MSS, *Records,* vol. III, meeting of the Board of Managers, Jan. 24,
   1843.

of agricultural products did bring small incomes to many colonists, and missionaries paid for the citizens' labor with manufactured articles brought from home or purchased from visiting ships with coin.

In reality, it was commercial activity by the missionary establishments which helped move the colony toward economic autonomy. The missions provided the most profitable immediate source of livelihood because of their need for plank and other building supplies which colonists could haul from the jungle with less effort than their farms demanded. Missionaries paid for the labor with a wide assortment of trade articles. But this was a sore point because they set even higher values upon their goods than did the agency store whose inflated prices often evoked complaint from the colonists. In July, 1841, the colony's governor and council, prompted by a citizen petition, took matters into their own hands and passed an act restricting trade within the settlement. With certain exceptions, only citizens were thereafter allowed to buy, sell, or exchange articles as a business or in return for labor rendered. Missionaries were authorized to barter trade goods with Africans for provisions, to pay the regular salaries of persons connected with their establishments in goods or in provisions sent out from the United States, and to receive from the colonists goods or money in payment of mission services.

The missionaries naturally protested, for the legislation deprived them of the right of paying colonists in goods, as they were accustomed. The Board of Managers in Baltimore, about to give serious consideration to permanent commercial regulations, vetoed the recent enactment. Noting that a citizen could remedy the undesirable payment system by refusing to work for any person with whom he could not arrange mutually agreeable terms, the board considered the new measures a hindrance to the establishment of more comprehensive codes. But an anchorage duty for ships visiting Cape Palmas remained in force.[4]

4 MSCS MSS, *Letters,* vol. XII, John A. Vaughan to Latrobe, New York, Dec. 16, 1841; Russwurm to Latrobe, Harper, Sept. 22, 1841; *Records,* vol. III, meeting of the Board of Managers, Dec. 13, 1841.

Nearly two years elapsed before the board adopted a revenue ordinance. An *ad hoc* committee chaired by George W. Dobbins, a society manager, looked into means whereby the colony could contribute toward payment of its own civil list and its operating expenses. A basic assumption was that the time had come for the colonists to assist with colonial costs. The easiest method of teaching them how to accept responsibility for their own welfare was the imposition of light import duties. The Dobbins committee suggested a uniform 10 per cent *ad valorem* rate for all goods landed in the colony. Since merchandise was priced at least 100 per cent higher in Africa than at its point of origin, the true *ad valorem* rate would be only 5 per cent. Licensing fees were recommended at a level aimed at discouraging colonists from becoming merchants rather than agriculturalists. The committee advised that a lighthouse duty of 8 cents per ton on vessels stopping at the cape replace the anchorage duty.

All committee recommendations—the lighthouse duty, the 10 per cent tax on the invoice prices of goods imported, save for the property of immigrants from the United States and supplies sent out by the Colonization Society, and substantial license fees for all persons trading in the colony—were adopted. A revenue collector, appointed by the governor and compensated by a 2 to 5 per cent commission on receipts, was given broad powers to enforce the regulations and to impose stiff fines for attempted evasions. The governor was directed to erect a customs house and, with the council, to work out whatever additional rules might prove necessary. The Maryland society recognized that the ordinance was perhaps not altogether suitable or permanent, but considered it a first step in finding a beneficial system for raising government revenue.[5]

Announcement in the colony of the board's revenue ordinance prompted a wave of protest. Russwurm maintained that the area's commerce was so inconsiderable that it needed every

5 MSCS mss, *Records,* vol. III, meeting of the Board of Managers, Nov. 2, 1843; *Agent's Books,* vol. II, James Hall to Russwurm, Baltimore, Feb. 22, 1844.

encouragement possible to induce trading vessels to stop while sailing along the coast. The new legislation seemed contrary to that goal. He contended, moreover, that the collector could never know if he were levying the correct amounts upon goods, for it was a practice of sea captains to carry two and even three different invoices for the same cargo. Both the 10 per cent *ad valorem* and the 8-cent-per-ton lighthouse duty were assailed as being detrimental to the welfare of the colonists to whom the additional cost would be passed. The governor, admitting doubt as to the kind of money to be received in payment for duties, asked for specific instructions.

The managers were plainly irked by the colonial attitude. They considered the import tax simple to apply and a small price to pay for advantages enjoyed at the settlement. Latrobe asked, "Are not freedom and their present rights worth this much to the colonists?" As for complaints that ships' masters submitted false invoices, the board averred that such dishonesty could not hurt the colonists, for the lower the invoices, the lower the ultimate cost of items. Russwurm was directed to use his own discretion in receiving duty payments.

Nonetheless, the board bowed to colonial protest. In what was to be the first of several revisions, the managers suspended the revenue ordinance until January 1, 1850, and set up a schedule for gradually increased rates. The *ad valorem* duty was to be 5 per cent until January 1, 1847, and 7½ per cent until January 1, 1850. The lighthouse duty was reduced from 8 cents per ton to 4, with the colonial administration given authority to raise it at any time.[6]

The following summer both the governor and the colonial physician reported that the revenue laws were working tolerably well. Both complained, however, that a better system of payment was necessary. Whereas only gold specie and camwood were accepted for duty fees, most citizens offered palm oil for

6 MSCS MSS, *Letters,* vol. XV, Russwurm to Latrobe, Cape Palmas, Aug. 24, 1844; *Latrobe Letter Books,* vol. II, Latrobe to Russwurm, Baltimore, Nov. 12, 1844; *Records,* vol. III, meeting of the Board of Managers, Nov. 13, 1844.

goods. The agency store rejected palm oil because of its over-abundance at that time. Obviously, trade was curtailed, for visiting merchants no more wanted palm oil than did the cape government. Russwurm suggested that the colony now needed a paper currency redeemable in gold and camwood for circulation.

The revised law was just as unpopular as the original legislation and the majority of colonists opposed it. Even more disconcerting was the lack of consensus regarding its application. Some traders, taking into consideration the 100 per cent mark-up, insisted that the 5 per cent *ad valorem* duty meant that the collector received but 2½ per cent on gross sales. This interpretation, in effect, converted the *ad valorem* tax into an excise duty. In the controversy Russwurm found that nine-tenths of the masters refused to provide invoice prices, and for two months no duties were collected at all. Russwurm finally ordered his collector to demand a fixed sum for each of the many trade articles entering the colony. For example, every 100 pounds of gunpowder carried with it a duty of 50 cents and every new gun was subject to a tax of 10 cents. Once more Russwurm appealed to the board at home to remedy the situation. He suggested a fixed duty equivalent to about 5 per cent *ad valorem* placed upon staples as the only means of restoring peace in the colony.[7]

Taking up the thorny problem, the society in November, 1846, came out with a second revision of the original revenue law passed three years before. Concurring fully with Russwurm's views, the board now imposed specific duties amounting to about 5 per cent of their value upon a wide range of articles and gave the colonial agent and council authority to establish rates on items not enumerated in the new schedule. As before, the belongings of arriving immigrants and cargo sent by the Colonization Society were exempt. With the promulgation of this third revenue decree, colonial clamor over the matter died down. The citizenry retracted a petition about to be sent to the

7 MSCS MSS, *Letters,* vol. XVI, Russwurm to Hall, Cape Palmas, June 9, 1845; Samuel F. McGill to Hall, Harper, June 8, 1845; Russwurm to Latrobe, Harper, Mar. 7, 1845; vol. XVII, Russwurm to Latrobe, Cape Palmas, May 13, 1846.

board and turned its attention to another object of irritation, medical care.[8]

Heretofore, all colonists had received free medical services and medicines without restriction. In November, 1846, the board, hoping to promote economic self-dependency in the settlement, declared that henceforth new immigrants would receive gratuitous services only during their first year at the cape. All other persons who could afford to pay were now obliged to become private patients of the colonial physicians, McGill and another young man, Demsey Fletcher, who had been trained in the United States under McGill's late mentor, Doctor Edward E. Phelps. To obtain free advice and medicine, older settlers had now to secure orders from their selectmen or governor.

Not surprisingly, new furor raged through the colony. Russwurm characterized the protesters as spoiled children and Demsey Fletcher likewise reported the immature reaction toward the measure. With the advice of several leading men, he had most medicine priced at 10 cents a dose and the physician's fee at from 5 to 75 cents per visit, according to the patient's financial circumstances. On the average, ailing citizens got medicine at a quarter its cost, yet they circulated a petition which declared that such prices would impoverish them.

Unwittingly, the timing of the medical issue was inauspicious. During 1846 unprecedented illness affected man and beast. Nearly all livestock perished from distemper and mortality among colonists and Africans was higher than at any previous period of the settlement's history. The 1847 summer, too, was a period of great sickness at Cape Palmas. Fletcher estimated that almost three-fourths of the colonists were seriously affected, although mortality was slight. He attributed the difference in the death rate to a deficiency of medicine the previous year. He diligently visited from home to home, supplying medicine without hope of compensation. The general food scarcity in the settlement at that time prompted him to beg the board for an

8 MSCS MSS, *Records,* vol. III, meeting of the Board of Managers, Nov. 28, 1846; *Letters,* vol. XVIII, Russwurm to Latrobe, Cape Palmas, Jan. 23, 1847.

arrangement whereby the colonists, whom he characterized as positively too poor to pay for medicine, could receive free treatment. The board took no action. The following spring McGill, returning after a visit to the United States, complained that he, too, was unable to get colonists to pay a cent for medicines or professional services. This state of affairs continued for ten years, with the physicians being reimbursed from public funds.[9]

The third major effort of the Maryland society during the 1840's was the development of a respected colonial judiciary which would become the court of last appeal, heretofore a function exercised by the Board of Managers. By the "Ordinance for Temporary Government," the governor and two justices of the peace comprised the Court of Monthly Sessions. All major civil and criminal cases fell within their jurisdiction. But experience showed that unpopular decisions such as those in the Snetter affair and the revenue controversy diminished the colonists' respect, not only for the men as judges but of the governor as the society's paid administrator. Fully aware of this phenomenon, Russwurm requested to be relieved of his responsibility as a presiding judge, holding that governors ought never to sit in that capacity if there were qualified individuals in the colony for these posts.

In May, 1847, the Board of Managers voted to separate the office of judge of the Court of Monthly Sessions from that of governor. The new ordinance created the post of chief justice and transferred the judicial duties of the governor to the incumbent of that office. He was to be appointed by the Colonization Society and was to hold office as long as he served with integrity. The chief justice was to preside not only over the regularly held court sessions but also over a newly created Orphans' Court which received jurisdiction in all matters pertaining to ad-

9 MSCS MSS, *Latrobe Letter Books,* vol. II, Latrobe to Russwurm, Baltimore, Nov. 30, 1846; *Letters,* vol. XVIII, Russwurm to Hall, Cape Palmas, Mar. 1, 1847; Demsey Fletcher to [Board of Managers], Harper, Mar. 3, Oct. 5, 1847; S. F. McGill to Hall, Cape Palmas, Mar. 28, 1848; vol. XVII, S. F. McGill to Latrobe, Harper, July 12, 1846; Russwurm to Hall, Cape Palmas, July 11, 1846.

ministrators, guardians, and the assignees of insolvent debtors.

During preparation of the ordinance, the board debated the selection of the chief justice. Deciding that no one then at the cape was suitable, they chose a Baltimorean, William Cassell. He was well known for his integrity and common sense, and although he possessed no legal training, he was considered a better appointment than certain experienced men in the colony who were also known as rascals. In May, 1848, Cassell, who had gone to Africa first in 1833 to help found the Maryland colony but had returned home after his wife's death, arrived at Cape Palmas and successfully passed the acclimating period. In November he received formal appointment as the colony's chief justice.[10]

One of the numerous reasons that the Maryland society began loosening ties with the colony in the 1840's was the increased attention which the United States Navy was paying Africa. When the several colonization groups at length convinced the Van Buren administration of the wisdom of dispatching more than an occasional vessel to the coast, the navy began to take that command more seriously. For years before this, complaints about the use of the American flag and forged papers by assorted foreign slavers to avoid search by British cruisers, and periodic claims that the British, in their zeal to end the infamous traffic in blacks, had infringed upon the rights of American merchants doing legitimate business along the coast, had created tension between Britain and the United States. Finally, in August, 1842, the two governments signed the Webster-Ashburton Treaty, originally known as the Treaty of Washington. Resolving a number of the serious issues between the two nations, several articles dealt with mutual efforts to suppress the slave trade. Each nation agreed to prepare, equip, and maintain

10 *Constitution and Laws of Maryland in Liberia; with an Appendix of Precedents,* 2nd ed. (Baltimore: John D. Toy, 1847), pp. 148–51; MSCS MSS, *Records,* vol. III, meeting of the Board of Managers, May 18, 1847; *Agent's Books,* vol. III, Hall to Russwurm, Baltimore, Feb. 1, 1848; *Letters,* vol. XVIII, Russwurm to Hall, Cape Palmas, Mar. 1, 1847; S. F. McGill to Hall, Cape Palmas, Mar. 28, 1848; William Cassell to Hall, Cape Palmas, May 5, 1848; Cassell to Latrobe, Harper, Nov. 23, 1848.

in service on the African coast a sufficient and adequate squadron carrying not less than eighty guns to enforce already existing
laws against what had for years been an international crime.[11]

Americans interested in Africa favored the presence of their
navy off the western coast. Matthew C. Perry, commodore of
the African Squadron from April, 1843, until April, 1845, was
impressed with the continent's legitimate trade potential and
lamented that, thus far, Americans had not assumed a leading
role in developing it. He held that the value of legal African
commerce was far greater than commonly believed since traders
netted huge profits by exchanging goods of inferior quality for
such commodities as gold dust, ivory, and timber which brought
high prices in European and American markets. Perry attributed
the pre-eminent position enjoyed by British and French captains
to the more frequent appearance of their men-of-war off the west
coast. He expected his small fleet of three ships to provide the
same favorable circumstances for the heretofore unprotected
American traders operating in the area.

The first task of the recently enlarged American African
Squadron was the punishment of Africans at Berrily and Sinoe
for the massacre of the master and crew of the *Mary Carver*,
a vessel out of Boston, and the murder of a mate aboard the
Edward Barley. Perry soon found that in most cases in which
Africans purportedly committed some outrage against American
and other vessels, the Africans had been at least as much sinned
against as sinning. To Secretary Abel Upshur, Perry confided
that home folk heard only one side of the story. What they did
not know was that visiting captains commonly mistreated the
Africans, firing into towns and fishing boats and creating other
mischief. The *Mary Carver* episode was a genuine case of African assault upon a well-stocked ship but, in the death of the
Edward Barley mate at Sinoe, the American had initiated the
quarrel.[12]

---

11 United States, *Treaties and Other International Acts of the United States
   of America*, ed. Hunter Miller, 6 vols. (Washington: U.S. Government
   Printing Office, 1934), IV, 369.
12 National Archives, *African Squadron Letters: Cruise of Matthew C. Perry,
   April 10, 1843 to April 29, 1845*, Perry to Abel Upshur, U.S.S. *Saratoga*,

Perry's arrival upon the African scene and provisions of the Webster-Ashburton Treaty which assured that regular navy patrol between the American-founded settlements would continue through the foreseeable future prompted Russwurm's happy claim that a new era had opened for the colony. He noted a striking new vigor in the citizenry and hoped for an all-around improvement. The squadron's value had been attested to only two months previously, for its arrival probably saved the Maryland colony from near extinction.

In November, 1843, King Freeman, the difficult but usually placable chieftain closest to Harper, called together all the kings and headmen from Fishtown, on the windward, to the Cavally River, on the leeward, for a palaver ostensibly to settle old problems bearing upon their Grebo country. A fortnight later representatives converged upon Russwurm for a trade palaver. At issue was the African desire to raise current prices on rice and palm oil. Russwurm's refusal to meet their demands brought an embargo on all trade between the two parties and an order by Freeman prohibiting contact with any African working for, siding with, or assisting the colonists. Citizens armed themselves and prepared for an attack by combined African forces from miles around.

Russwurm notified the king that the nonintercourse order was equivalent to a declaration of war. The situation remained tense for several days and then Commodore Perry's squadron, visiting the various settlements on its way to Berrily, unexpectedly appeared upon the horizon. After firing a thirteen-gun salute, Perry staged a palaver with the Grebos. Impressing upon them that they could ask what prices they pleased for their produce but that there must be no further embargo and nonintercourse measures, the commodore cautioned them not to be so foolish as to create a threatening situation again.

Although Perry had saved the colony from attack, his cannon salute had the unexpected result of initiating intertribal war.

Porto Grande, Sept. 5, 1843; Perry to David Henshaw, frigate *Macedonia*, Mesurado Roads, Nov. 22, 1843; Perry to Henshaw, frigate *Macedonia*, at sea, Jan. 29, 1844.

Some bush residents, hearing the firing, supposed that hostilities had opened. A party of some forty armed men appeared at Mount Tubman several hours later, evidently on the way to plunder Cape Town, King Freeman's residence. For refusing to lay down their arms as they passed the colony's stockade, they were fired upon by the colonists and two men were killed. The king acted as mediator for Russwurm and, although he prevented retaliation by the bush people, war broke out between the Grahways and the Half Cavallys who, besides having long-standing grievances between them, disagreed over Freeman's proceedings. Strife between these two interior groups continued off and on for five years, sometimes impeding Russwurm's travel inland and often interfering with trade.[13]

Perry, having settled one controversy and inadvertently begun another, proceeded on down the coast to Berrily, forty-odd miles below Cape Palmas. He there executed several men connected with the *Mary Carver* murders and ransacking, and burned five African towns. His tour of all the American-established colonies left him with a favorable impression of their goals and actual accomplishments. He noted that at all settlements along the coast, regardless of the nation backing them, citizens were more inclined to commerce and small trade than to agricultural pursuits. He concluded that the experiment of establishing free black people from the United States upon the African coast had succeeded beyond the expectations of the most optimistic colonizationists. Characterizing Joseph J. Roberts, the new Negro governor of Liberia, and Russwurm as intelligent and valuable men, Perry put them forth as proof that blacks were capable of self-government. This conviction and the expectation that the U.S. Navy would provide a protective wing over the colony had already motivated Colonization Society officials in Baltimore to give it a greater degree of independence.[14]

13 MSCS MSS, *Letters*, vol. XIV, Russwurm to Latrobe, Cape Palmas, Dec. 23, 1843; vol. XV, Russwurm to Latrobe, Cape Palmas, Jan. 12, 1844; vol. XVI, Russwurm to Latrobe, Harper, Mar. 7, 1845; vol. XVIII, Russwurm to Latrobe, Cape Palmas, Apr. 26, 1849.

14 *Ibid.*, vol. XIV, Russwurm to Latrobe, Cape Palmas, Dec. 23, 1843; National Archives, *African Squadron Letters: Perry*, Perry to Henshaw, frigate *Macedonia*, Monrovia, Jan. 4, 1844.

The actions of Maryland society managers in extending to the colony greater political, economic, and judicial authority and responsibility nonetheless failed to call forth greater efforts from the colonists to prove themselves worthy of this additional trust. Except following periods of famine, colonists persisted in their aversion to agricultural enterprise. They remained chronic complainers who made life thoroughly miserable for Governor Russwurm and seldom hesitated to protest over his head to the Baltimore board. A typical petition of grievances was drawn up in October, 1844. A chief point of contention was the number of citizens employed by the colonial government. Residents complained that no more than a third of them could work for the agency and that the soil was too poor to support the rest. They insisted that they had tried to cultivate the soil to the best of their ability, but that they could not grow enough to feed and clothe themselves. Even when they did have produce to market, there was seldom anyone to purchase it. Charging that the Colonization Society had the responsibility of ameliorating their suffering, the petitioners asked, "What would be the state of your flourishing country today if it hadnt been for the labor of the colored man[?]" Asserting that inducements offered upon emigration were deceiving, they queried, "What is liberty without bread or something in place of it[?]—its a very distressing & grieveous situation to place a parcel of people in a poor desolate land far from the land which gave us birth & say to us it is the land of our forefathers. Had we being sent to the land of our forefathers with what we have earn[ed] for many of you Gentlemen[,] only small sum of it or a part of it[,] we would be better able to contend with deprivation, & suffering of this country. . . ."

In actual fact, individuals who had lived in the community for ten years expected employment from the society just as much as the newcomers. The older residents even considered that they had been deprived of their rights where they were not accorded government employment. It was true that visiting vessels remained in port for such a short time that inhabitants had little chance to supply them with fresh produce or to do their laundry. Russwurm lamented, "We begin almost to despair with such colonists as the majority of ours are—depending wholly on what the society can do for them." [15]

Nearly five years later a more comprehensive petition reached the board. On the face of it, the contents appeared markedly different from the earlier one, but underlying the colonists' requests was the same preference for nonagricultural work. First, the citizenry sought cancellation of more than $1,100 debt incurred by their recent construction of a new treasury office and jail. Second, it asked that the annual license fees for importers and retailers be reduced. Terming the charges exorbitant and a chief impediment to their welfare, petitioners claimed that they suffered from the consequent monopoly of trade enjoyed by a few. They likewise believed that increased trade and the consequent additional revenues would counteract the decreased sum coming from less expensive licenses. The third subject concerned their paper currency. Issued first in 1837 by the colonial government, it had fallen into disfavor because newly arrived Cape Palmas merchants refused to accept it in payment for goods. Only the agency store, often carrying inferior and less attractive wares, received it. The existing currency was an artificially created one which had lost value through the years. Colonists asked for a new issue based upon such permanent articles as palm oil, ivory, or camwood.

As usual, some complaints were justified but most were not. The agent and council had voted to construct the two new buildings at the colony's expense. When costs exceeded estimates and Russwurm used society funds to cover the balance, the citizens accused the agent of running the settlement into debt without consulting them. Their appeal for cancellation of the $1,100 debt reflected an unwillingness to assume full responsibility for their own welfare and, at the next election, they turned out of office every man connected with it. The colonists' request that licenses be reduced to $20 and $10, respectively, from the society's annual rate of $100 and $25, expressed their desire to

<hr />

15 MSCS mss, *Letters,* vol. XVI, "A Petition to the Md. St. Col. Society," Cape Palmas, Oct. 24, 1844; Russwurm to Hall, Cape Palmas, Oct. 27, 1844.

participate in business ventures. Their aversion to farming was perennial. On this score, the governor believed that "the wrong ideas which they imbibe about 'liberty' is a hindrance to their engaging *vigorously* in any undertaking in which patience and perseverance are necessary." All persons at Cape Palmas, from the governor down, agreed that a better currency system was needed.[16]

The Board of Managers, studying this latest petition closely, stood firm for the time being on the debt repayment but agreed to submit the license and currency matters to a referendum at the next colonial election. If colonists voted against existing rates in a clear majority, the governor and council were to set up new reduced fees. If they voted against the currency, Russwurm was to cease issuing it and to redeem it as it was paid into the agency store.

Russwurm was further directed to begin circumscribing society operations. Relief and employment were to be curtailed as much as possible. The governor was advised that the time had come for the colonists to stand alone. The board, in fact, took their latest petition as evidence of the citizens' ability to be more self-supporting and, since it had yielded on two issues, it wished to step more to the background in colonial government. Speaking for the board, Latrobe stated that it desired in this respect to imitate the American Colonization Society which, having granted total independence to Liberia in 1847, now did little more than forward emigrants there.

The board's conciliatory reply wilted the colonists' sturdy protest and put them into a state of remorse. Samuel Ford McGill, grown arrogant with success and wealthy from his commercial ventures, reported that there was a general backing out on the part of the sixty-six signers: "The blockheads seem to imagine that they have acted criminally in signing it. 'Tis impossible for them to stand up and boldly request what they deem to be for their benefit without apprehensions of the disapprobation of the

16 *Ibid.*, vol. XVIII, "The Citizens of Md. in Liberia, West Africa, to the Hon. Bd. of Mgrs. of the Md. State Col. Soc.," [Harper], Apr., 1849; Russwurm to Latrobe, Cape Palmas, Apr. 17, 26, 1849.

Board. It is perhaps well enough in this instance as their complaints were childish." The penitent citizens later confessed that they had signed it hastily and imprudently. Applauding the managers' wisdom, they now requested that their petition be ignored.[17]

Education in Maryland in Liberia was a haphazard affair from the time the settlement had been established. By the "Ordinance for Temporary Government," all children "of a fit age" were to attend public schools until they could read, write, and "cast accounts." Other sections of the law made a fair degree of education essential for participation in colonial government. For example, to be a juryman required good repute and the ability to read and write. Incidentally, school teachers and other semipublic and government officials were automatically exempt from jury duty. Until 1835, when the colony was laid out and somewhat built up, not much was done by way of attaining the educational goals. The first school the colonists' children attended was run principally for African children by Mrs. J. Leighton Wilson at Fair Hope. Mrs. James Thompson, a citizen's wife, opened another one, chiefly for immigrant children. Late in 1835 a Margaret McAlister opened a third school in the settlement.

Miss McAlister, a white woman and a member of a Methodist church in Baltimore, applied to the Board of Managers to sail aboard the *Harmony* in June, 1835, for the purpose of devoting her life to the education of colonist and African children at the cape. She expected her school to be supported by contributions from sympathetic Christians in Maryland. Upon this basis the board agreed to provide her free passage. James Hall found that she unhappily possessed few of the necessities called for by her new life and had no means for obtaining them. Although her work was to be voluntary and in no way connected with the society, she had to be furnished supplies from the agency store. She lived briefly with the Wilsons and then in a room rented for

17 *Ibid.*, S. F. McGill to Hall, Cape Palmas, Oct. 20, 1849; Russwurm to Hall, Cape Palmas, Nov. 19, 1849; vol. XIX, petition of citizens to the Board of Managers, Harper, Jan. 14, 1850; *Latrobe Letter Books,* vol. II, Latrobe to Russwurm, Baltimore, July 31, 1849.

her by Hall. Her presence in the colony caused even more consternation when it developed that she was totally unable to
teach anything. She could scarcely read and then only the
printed word, was unable to spell correctly words of only one
syllable, could not write script, and did not even know the alpha-
bet. Moreover, she was too ill from the outset to conduct classes
and died in less than a year. The board later learned that she had
volunteered for African service after her physician suggested that
new environment as the only hope for the restoration of her
already delicate health. Wilson in a confidential letter to Latrobe
urged the board to prevent any unprotected white woman from
coming to the colony again. Such, he said, were the difficulties
encountered in the colony that a woman had her influence con-
travened in ways and by means which neither she nor her friends
would ever anticipate.[18]

In an effort to make good its promise of education to the
immigrant children, the society finally appealed to Maryland
women to form female colonization auxiliaries which would
raise the several hundred dollars per annum needed for colonial
schools. The society even envisioned a college at Cape Palmas.
The consequence was the founding in 1837 of the Ladies' Society for the Promotion of Education in Africa. A Baltimore
group, it agreed to employ a qualified teacher to take charge of
the proposed stone schoolhouse in Harper. The salary was to be
$300 per annum and, in addition, the teacher was to receive a
grant of $200 the first year for the purchase of appropriate per-
sonal belongings. The money came principally from the congregations of city churches and from life memberships in the
new organization. The Ladies' Society engaged Benjamin Alleyne, a West Indian, and his wife, and they sailed aboard the
brig *Niobe* late in 1837. The Alleynes successfully acclimated
themselves to the coast but were disappointed to find the promised school not yet under construction. Governor Russwurm

18 "An Ordinance for the Temporary Government," *Constitution and Laws
of Maryland in Liberia,* Sections 29, 31; MSCS MSS, *Records,* vol. II,
meeting of the Board of Managers, June 23, 1835; *Letters,* vol. III,
Hall to Latrobe, Harper, Aug. 26, 1835; vol. IV, J. Leighton Wilson to
Latrobe, Fair Hope, June 25, 1836.

furnished them a vacant house on a lot in Harper and Alleyne converted it into a temporary school. Space was so limited that only thirty or thirty-five "Schollars" could be enrolled. The following February, 1839, after successfully operating his school nine months, Alleyne died of fever. His widow, considering herself unqualified to continue his work, moved to Fair Hope to assist the Wilsons, and a few of Alleyne's students transferred there.

Alleyne's successor was George R. McGill, the Baltimorean who had emigrated to Monrovia in 1827 and then to Harper in 1834. He began his work in the new schoolhouse on January 1, 1841. He taught all the usual subjects to forty-five students and, with additional space and help, could have admitted another twenty for instruction. His teaching career came to an abrupt end two years later when he was expelled from the Methodist Church for marrying an African woman. The Colonization Society thereupon withdrew its recommendation of him and he was summarily dismissed. The Ladies' Society now became dormant, no teachers were hired to staff the colony's one official school, and missionaries largely took over the educational function.[19]

A subject which greatly concerned the Board of Managers, especially as it granted the colony greater rights, was citizen morality. Theoretically sending only applicants of industry and good character to the settlement, the society considered its laws and its emphasis upon missionary effort sufficient encouragement for the continuation of exemplary conduct. Such behavior never characterized many colonists and, as they grew in number, vice and crime increased. Moreover, the longer the colonists lived

19 *Fifth Annual Report of the Board of Managers of the Maryland State Colonization Society* (Baltimore: John D. Toy, 1837), p. 14; MSCS MSS, *Letters,* vol. VII, report of the Executive Committee [of the Ladies' Society] to the Board of Managers, [Baltimore], Nov. 21, 1837; vol. IX, Benjamin Alleyne to Ira A. Easter, Cape Palmas, July 10, 1838; vol. X, Wilson to Ann Turnbull, Fair Hope, Feb. 18, 1839; vol. XII, George R. McGill to the Board of Managers, Ladies Academy, Cape Palmas, Sept. 24, 1841; vol. XVI, Russwurm to Hall, Cape Palmas, July 28, 1845; vol. XVIII, J. Payne to Latrobe, Cape Palmas, Nov. 22, 1848; *Records,* vol. III, meetings of the Board of Managers, Aug. 29, 1843, Sept. 6, 1848.

in Africa, the less they were restrained by the admonitions of their old masters "to walk in the way of the Lord." The presence of barbarous peoples in and around the community contributed materially to a loosening of civilized inhibitions.

One of the first indications of a general lowering of colonial morals was the James Thompson case in 1837. Although acquitted for lack of evidence of charges that he seduced colonial and African girls, he was popularly considered guilty. Two years later Governor Russwurm lamented that several instances of bastardy had recently occurred and that some law was needed to stop this evil. Colonists frequently struck up liaisons with African females, though few went as far as George McGill.

From the emphasis in its *Annual Reports* upon continuing the principle of abstinence, the board appeared more interested in the liquor question than in other deviations from the straight and narrow path. In 1846 letters from the settlement began divulging actions taken by the agent and council against persons breaking the abstinence vow. Two men who had been trading in spirits were brought to trial on three counts and fined $100 in each case. In December, 1847, Samuel Ford McGill complained that W. A. Prout, a tippler, had been reappointed the colonial secretary by Russwurm. McGill contended that retaining Prout was hardly consistent with the temperance ideals activating colony founders. Unknown to him, persons in even higher administrative echelons than Prout were likewise enjoying intoxicants.

In 1848 Russwurm made a brief trip to the United States. His health had been failing for several years and on several occasions hope had been lost for his recovery. Wanting to visit the homeland, he was granted a leave of absence with full pay and free passage. Doctor McGill became acting governor. Russwurm, who had known Hall from his previous visits and residences on the African coast, developed a rapport with Hall during his Baltimore stay. The governor's first communication to the United States following his return to Africa requested the general agent to send him a variety of alcoholic beverages. In a letter marked "private," Russwurm expressed a desire for cheap wine and brandy for the medical department and ten boxes of good claret and twenty boxes of ale for his cupboard. This request was more than met by the good doctor.[20]

The only event of interest occurring during Russwurm's absence was talk among citizens of the governor's administration. Joshua H. Stewart, a prominent and vociferous man, took the opportunity to protest the length of Russwurm's appointment. Claiming that the inhabitants had long desired a change in leadership, Stewart demanded to know whether the Board of Managers contemplated keeping the colony under one man for life. Denying any incompetency on Russwurm's part, Stewart asserted that after twelve years any man would lose all sympathy for those he governed and would inevitably become a petty tyrant. He argued that such a long term in office violated the rules of republicanism and he affected a fear that the colony might next have a king over it. Doctor McGill also came under attack. Reporting rumors that the latter would be the next governor, Stewart warned the board that such action would not sit well with the colonists because they considered him too young and too closely related to Russwurm's administration. In fact, McGill was almost forty—he had served as colonial physician for nearly a decade. He was, however, Russwurm's brother-in-law and, although their opinions on colonial direction were so divergent that the two scarcely spoke to each other, their differences did not overcome the colonists' suspicion of nepotism.[21]

Life's uncertainties were soon to remove the chief object of complaint. Russwurm's health deteriorated steadily after his return from the United States and he died on June 9, 1851. McGill, assistant agent for the preceding two years, took over until instructions could arrive from Baltimore. He had already purchased a home in Monrovia, planned to move there with his family, and had no desire to fill the vacancy.

In many respects Russwurm's death closed one era and marked

20 MSCS mss, *Letters,* vol. X, Russwurm to Latrobe, Harper, June 24, 1839; vol. XVII, Russwurm to Latrobe, Cape Palmas, July 11, 1846; vol. XVIII, S. F. McGill to Hall, Harper, Dec. 17, 1847; Russwurm to Hall, Cape Palmas, Nov. 22, 1848; *Records,* vol. III, meeting of the Board of Managers, Apr. 7, 1848.
21 MSCS mss, *Letters,* vol. XVIII, J. H. Stewart to ?, Cape Palmas, June 12, 1848.

the beginning of another. Under his administration a colony of former American slaves achieved a large degree of self-government. A Negro leader nudged unwilling compatriots through the intricacies of legal, political, and economic development. A black man proved capable of handling the difficulties imposed by like-skinned Africans and white missionaries. For all his skill, however, things were far from perfect. Nine months before he died, Russwurm complained that the existing generation of colonists was still too unenlightened to accomplish much; better things would come only from their children. McGill at the same time fretted that the colony was at a dead standstill. Noting that the people were unfit to carry out any plan on their own, he insisted that the governor would have to suggest something afresh to move the settlement from its state of torpidity.

In September, 1851, McGill summed up the condition of Maryland in Liberia:

> This Colony has increased its numbers only since you [Hall] governed it but I really cannot discover any material increase in intelligence, respectability or self-dependence. The governor must still originate every enterprise, must instruct every one, and perform every thing, there are none from whom he can seek reliable council or advise; if he is successful, he gets no thanks, if he fails through inadequate means or assistance he is d—— d——[.] Ignorance, ingratitude, and malevolence meet him at every point and renders his life miserable.
>
> Ninety out of every hundred of our people are paupers, and would be contented as such during their lives if the Society would give [in]. . . .[22]

Despite McGill's gloominess respecting the citizens, Russwurm left a tangible legacy in the form of territorial expansion. Whereas Doctor Hall had given the agent a handful of paper agreements signifying some vague control over vast interior areas, Russwurm had visited far and wide during his fifteen years of stewardship, adding validity to society claims. Although

---

22 *Ibid.*, vol. XIX, S. F. McGill to Latrobe, Cape Palmas, July 11, 1851; S. F. McGill to Hall, Cape Palmas, Sept. 15, 1850, Sept. 18, 1851; Russwurm to Hall, Cape Palmas, Sept. 16, 1850.

the colonial government still had little voice in inland affairs and could not stop the intertribal warfare which had recently been renewed, it had succeeded in purchasing the coastline from Grand Cess to the River Pedro, a length of 130 miles. The colonial population numbered between 900 and 1,000 while the indigenous population in the immediate Cape Palmas area was estimated at 100,000.[23]

These were Russwurm's achievements and shortcomings. His passing marked the close of the colony's age of innocence, but he had laid sure foundations for a new chapter in the colony's history. By coincidence, Russwurm's death came just at the time when the Maryland legislature's twenty-year appropriation was running out. Colonizationists were already marshaling facts and figures by which to win approval for a continuation of state grants. The major topic under discussion in Africa was the settlement's future. The citizens had already divided into groups, some of which favored merger with the new Republic of Liberia and others which stood for independent nationhood. On both sides of the Atlantic, then, issues of major consequence to the colony were soon to be decided. Russwurm had pushed his people ahead, as Moses, to whom the black governor occasionally likened himself, had driven the Israelites, and in the crucial year, 1851, he died.

23 "Report of the Board of Managers of the Maryland State Colonization Society," *Maryland Colonization Journal*, n.s., VI, no. 9 (Feb., 1852), 130.

VII

Attempts to Maintain Home Support 1840-1850

While the colony at Cape Palmas struggled through gradual, though sometimes imperceptible, improvement toward political independence, efforts in Maryland to sustain the colonization cause foundered. The death of Ira Easter, the home agent, in January, 1840, and society officials' realization that at least $12,000 would be needed to meet debts and new expenses resulted in a careful reappraisal of organizational activities. Paid employees both in Baltimore and in Harper were reduced in number and colonial expenses were lowered. No emigrants were sent to the colony that year. The few positive moves which the Board of Managers took to bolster its lagging position proved inconsequential.

Much of the society's failure to arouse public interest during 1840 can be attributed to the keen attention paid to politics and the depression. State and presidential elections as well as money matters occupied men's minds to an unusual degree. The Democratic national convention, held in Baltimore in May, renominated President Martin Van Buren as its candidate against the Whig, William Henry Harrison. The contest was one of the most heated and animated in United States history, with Van Buren's opponents characterizing him as an aristocratic sissy and picturing Harrison as a lover of the simple pleasures close to the common man's heart. John Latrobe, society president, complained that until the state election in October and the national election in November were both over, nothing could get the public attention: "Drums, banners and transparencies make night hideous and forbid all meetings but political ones— Even the Theatre is closed and 'till after the Election' everything is at a stand." Harrison's election and subsequent death brought a vice-president to the highest office for the first time in history. Unfortunately, John Tyler lacked ability to meet the domestic crises of the day and his administration was a rather ineffectual one.[1]

While the Colonization Society trod water financially, it sought to engage a general agent to operate its affairs in this country and in Africa. Doctor James Hall, then pursuing private business along the West African coast, was at length persuaded to accept the post for an annual salary of $1,000, annual leaves during July and August, and permission to continue trading on his own account. His early connection with the society and his years in Africa made him highly effective. He stood second only to the American Colonization Society's Ralph Gurley as an authority on the movement. The prestige Hall brought to the Maryland society was undoubtedly important in its subsequent success in averting bankruptcy and meeting opposition forces in the state.[2]

The reinvigorated organization's first task was to publicize its continued existence and its efforts to send more blacks to Africa, while still maintaining Maryland in Liberia. John Kennard,

---

1 MSCS MSS, *Latrobe Letter Books,* vol. II, John Latrobe to John Russwurm, Baltimore, Aug. 1, Oct. 6, 1840.
2 MSCS MSS, *Records,* vol. III, meetings of the Board of Managers, Sept. 12, 1840, Jan. 15, 1841.

stationed in the Baltimore office since Easter's death, now re-
sumed his earlier role as a fund-raising traveling agent. Touring
around the head of the bay and down the Eastern Shore,
Kennard found that while audiences varied in size and interest,
the amount of money raised at such gatherings was fairly even—
scarcely a cent! He was distressed to learn that many persons
he met considered the society a troublesome begging concern.
Besides seeking contributions, Kennard publicized the forthcoming colonization convention and aided auxiliaries in the
selection of their delegates.[3]

The idea of holding a statewide colonization convention in
Baltimore seems to have originated with Hall. The first Thurs-
day of June, 1841, was set for the meeting and the attendance
goal was thirty delegates from each county. The financial goal
was to raise $10,000 to cancel liabilities, to meet current ex-
penses, and to cover solicitation costs in seeking contributions
for a Baltimore–to–Cape Palmas packet. The other conference
objective was to consider the merits of African colonization,
not yet generally accepted as a workable solution, and its beneficial effect upon the state's white and black populations. In a
circular to the public the society pointed out that, excluding
Baltimore City, Maryland's white population had diminished
in the past ten years while there had been an increase of 17 per
cent in the free Negro population. Including Baltimore City,
white citizens had increased but 8½ per cent. It noted further
that the black population's character was changing from predominantly slave to free. Predicting that traditional harmonious
relations between the races would cease as whites, bolstered by
arriving European immigrants, pre-empted the labor market,
the broadside argued that Negro removal was inevitable and that
colonization was the only means of facilitating transfer without
conflict. To Baltimore citizens, the society distributed flyers with
even more dire warnings of the blacks' impending fate. Again,
colonization was offered as a rational, peaceful solution.[4]

3 MSCS MSS, *Letters,* vol. XII, John Kennard to James Hall, Havre de
 Grace, Feb. 4, Chestertown, Feb. 17, Cambridge, Mar. 15, 1841.
4 MSCS MSS, *Records,* vol. III, meetings of the Board of Managers, Feb.
 2, Mar. 13, 1841.

While delegates were to be white, Hall thought it politic to solicit an expression of approbation from Baltimore's free black community. Addressing the Reverend William Walkins, a well-known local pastor, he asked that the colored population memorialize the convention upon the colonization subject. The candor of Hall's letter suggested his naiveté with regard to Baltimore Negroes. Walkins' reply, while a gracious refusal, stated his opinion that "colonizationists, *in general,* are so hostile to our remaining in the land of our birth[,] so intent upon the prosecution of their scheme," that outside views were of secondary importance. Further, anything but a declaration favoring colonization would result in more virulent prejudice and an increased impetus to persecution and proscription.[5]

The convention met on June 3 and 4 at the Methodist Church on Light Street. More than 200 delegates were registered, though not all attended. Aside from Baltimore, which listed sixty-nine, Harford and Washington counties sent the largest number of representatives, thirty and thirty-two respectively, while Somerset and Worcester counties had none present. There was no relationship between the number of delegates and the proportion of free blacks and slaves to whites in the counties. The colonization convention adopted the following resolutions: (1) removal of the free colored people and manumitted slaves to Africa, with their consent, was a legitimate object of the colonization system; (2) "the idea that the coloured people will ever obtain social and political equality in this State is wild and mischievous . . ."; (3) if the free black population remained in Maryland in the hope of enjoying equal social and political rights with the whites, they would inevitably, in time, be forcibly removed; (4) the continuing support of the colony was a sacred and binding obligation; (5) the establishment of direct commercial intercourse between Baltimore and Cape Palmas was a matter of utmost importance and should be quickly arranged; and (6) to keep interest in colonization alive,

5 MSCS MSS, *Agent's Books,* vol. II, William Walkins to Hall, Baltimore, May 24, 1841.

auxiliary associations should be formed in every neighborhood of the state.[6]

Rather than creating genuine interest in colonization or improving the state of society funds, the convention made the position of whites and Negroes more rigid. Even before the Baltimore meeting, an intended delegate from Hagerstown suggested that the Colonization Society canvass the registers of wills in the various counties about the enforcement of laws affecting manumitted slaves. He found that in Washington County the number of newly freed Negroes allowed to remain in the state without permits from the Orphans' Court far exceeded the number which complied with the law in this respect. Hall thereupon contacted county officials and in every case found either total neglect of the law or so little attention to it that it might as well not have existed. Evidence confirmed earlier speculation that manumitted slaves frequently remained unnoticed in the community, keeping the fact of their freedom as quiet as possible and relying upon their own insignificance for exemption from the law.[7]

Reports from about the state in the months following the convention told of increased opposition among whites toward the free black population. John Roberts, rehired as a traveling agent, found that the whites in Charles County were unanimous in demanding the forced removal of all free Negroes. Hall, the society's foremost recipient of correspondence from throughout the state, concluded that whites were determined to order blacks out and that Africa offered the most favorable opening for the victims of this more militant attitude.

The Negro population continued to exhibit at least as much reluctance to African emigration as it had previously. The same reports which spoke of heightened white determination on that score frequently noted the uselessness of endeavoring to persuade the blacks to move. Kennard, for example, complained that it was almost of no avail to free slaves by will to go to Liberia,

6 *Maryland Colonization Journal*, n.s., I, no. 1 (June, 1841), 15.
7 MSCS MSS, *Letters*, vol. XII, Daniel Wiesel to Latrobe, Hagerstown, May 24, 1841; *Latrobe Letter Books*, vol. II, Latrobe to William Coad, Baltimore, Jan. 12, 1841.

since it was to the interest of heirs, to whom they reverted as bondsmen if they failed to depart, to discourage emigration. Roberts, visiting southern Maryland, which was heavily Roman Catholic, relayed the prevailing opinion that the priests had lost their influence among blacks by selling all their own slaves to the number of 200 or 300 into the South. Area blacks told him that they would no more believe the priests than they would him, an accused kidnapper.[8]

Another event detrimental to colonization and reflecting the hardened white attitude was a slaveholders' convention held in Annapolis January 12–14, 1842. In the month or so preceding the gathering, citizens, by election district, met to appoint delegates, a surprising number of whom had attended the colonization convention the previous June. The groups not infrequently formed auxiliary colonization societies and expressed approval of the earlier parley's resolutions. When the slaveholders assembled at the Maryland capital, half of the organization's officers, including the president and two vice-presidents, turned out to be colonizationists. The actual extent of harm done by the apparent close affiliation between the two causes cannot be determined, but for months after the colonization movement was stigmatized.

The slaveholders' purpose clearly was to lobby for legislation which would protect their bondsmen by restricting the number and liberty of free blacks. Their twenty-five-point memorial to the Maryland legislature called for laws to prevent manumission by will, for manumission only upon condition of instant transportation outside the United States at manumitter's expense, for more stringent restraints on free Negro activities, for the strict enforcement of existing laws, and for the prohibition of additional free Negroes moving into the state. Actually, despite Colonization Society officers' and members' abhorrence of the convention, many slaveholders' goals corresponded with their own aims. Their intention was, however, antithetical, for the one

---

8 MSCS MSS, *Letters*, vol. XII, John M. Roberts to Hall, Pikawaxam, Sept. 27, 1841; Roberts to Hall, Leonardtown, Nov. 23, 1841; Kennard to Hall, Bladensburg, Nov. 9, 1841; *Agent's Books*, vol. II, Hall to Russwurm, Baltimore, Dec. 15, 1841.

wished to strengthen slavery while the other hoped for its demise. The society later sought to disassociate itself from the January proceedings but at the same time to capitalize on the assertion that they substantiated white unity behind the colonization movement. This was a rather dubious inference, for the slaveholders made no pronouncement respecting Maryland in Liberia and one delegate was reported to have criticized the cause publicly and to have charged that each immigrant transported had cost the state $5,000.[9]

The slaveholders' convention memorial was referred to the House of Delegates' Committee on the Coloured Population, of whose five members four represented southern Maryland counties. The bill which it subsequently framed incorporated many suggestions and had four objectives: (1) to prevent the escape of slaves from their owners; (2) to make the state's free blacks a more industrious group, thus eliminating the idleness which bred crime; (3) to halt the increase of free Negroes within the state; and (4) to make penalties sufficiently severe to deter criminal activity. The committee bill passed the House by a vote of forty to thirty-one, but by the time it came up for consideration in the Senate, public sentiment had come to demand its defeat.

On the one hand, colonizationists, fearing that further agitation would only harm both the white and Negro populations, sought merely to have existing laws enforced. This, they believed, would be sufficient protection to slave owners and would impose adequate restraint upon the free blacks. But, on the other hand, abolitionists, theoretically antipathetic to colonization views, argued that the bill would inflict new evils upon the state. Citizens held public meetings in numerous cities and counties, memorials opposing the pending legislation descended upon Annapolis, and the upper house finally defeated the measure by more than a two-thirds majority.[10]

---

9 *Niles' National Register,* 5th ser., XI, no. 23 (Feb., 1842), 356–58; MSCS mss, *Letters,* vol. XIII, Kennard to Latrobe, Anne Arundel Co., Jan. 29, 1842.
10 Maryland, *Maryland Public Documents* (December Session, 1841), "Report of the Committee on the Colored [*sic*] Population," Feb. 9, 1842;

Although colonizationists—and abolitionists—had their way with this particular bill, the Maryland legislature in the 1840's was generally less amenable to their wishes and more inquisitive respecting their activities. The Committee on the Coloured Population frequently requested details of society pursuits. Increasingly in the forties an entire county delegation to the legislature formed itself into a select committee of the House to recommend more restrictive legislation for the black population. Early in 1844 representatives from Charles County asked for the removal of all free blacks from that southern area. Although the 1840 census showed only 819 such persons residing there, the petitioners obviously feared their supposed pernicious influence on the 9,000 slaves in the county. The delegation asserted, moreover, that free Negroes should be removed from the entire state since their presence was an unmitigated evil and their condition would nowhere be worse than in Maryland. Finally, it held Maryland in Liberia to be the fitting and proper place for settling the free colored population. But it made no recommendations about effecting this transfer of residence.[11]

Two years later Charles County delegates again raised the issue. They were now far less approving of colonization, which had obviously had little effect in reducing the Negro population, and were more insistent upon driving free blacks from the state. Contending that it would be both humane and legal to force their removal, the representatives revealed their true feelings: "Thus the institution of slavery is a constitutional right and that of the free negro is a legal right, and in a conflict the latter must yield to the former, and the idle existence of the free negro is doing an injury to the slave, the constitutional *property* of the master."

In an effort to muster scientific evidence for its demands, the select committee presented Maryland census returns for the pre-

James M. Wright, *The Free Negro in Maryland, 1634–1860* (New York: Columbia University, 1921), pp. 302–3.
11 Maryland, *Maryland Public Documents* (December Session, 1843–1844), "Report from the Select Committee, to whom was referred the Subject of the Removal of the Free Colored Population from Charles County," Jan. 24, 1844.

vious half century and projected the relative positions of the two groups fifty years and a hundred years hence. It concluded that whereas whites numbered 317,717 and free blacks 62,020 in 1840, a century later Maryland would have 517,717 whites and 3,869,280 free Negroes.[12] The outcome of such a situation, averred its members, would be elimination of the white laborer throughout the state and the emergence of a society composed of white landholders and free Negroes who would do the work, gradually accumulate property, and eventually drive out the white citizens—a reversal of the 1840 situation.

As for colonization, the select committee labeled it an experiment which had not yet proved the Negro's capacity for self-government and improvement. Certain only that Negroes ought to be expelled, it offered no suggestion as to where they were to find refuge.[13]

The legislature declined to act upon either of the two Charles County petitions, in part because of the dearth of constructive ideas in them but, more important, because they offered no new home for free Negroes. The upshot, then, of the various proposals considered by Maryland lawmakers in the 1840's was a great deal of discussion and perplexity but no action. Attempts in the House of Delegates to repeal the colonization tax on account of the smallness of apparent results were successively defeated in the Senate where such staunch colonizationists as Colonel Thomas Emory, himself a substantial slaveholder, quashed them.[14]

One recommendation of the June, 1841, colonization convention was the establishment of regular commercial contact with Maryland in Liberia. The following February the Board of Managers sought to stir up interest and to gain funds. Results were meager. Agent Kennard, traveling on the Eastern Shore, was unable to get anything for the Liberia packet and

12 The actual 1940 population was 1,518,481 whites and 301,931 blacks.
13 Maryland, *Maryland Public Documents* (December Session, 1845), "Report of the Select Committee, consisting of the Delegates of Charles Co., Relative to the Removal of the Free People of Color of Charles County," Jan. 28, 1846.
14 MSCS MSS, *Letters*, vol. XV, Roberts to Hall, Annapolis, Feb. 2, 1844; vol. XVIII, N. B. Worthington to Hall, Annapolis, Jan. 10, 1847.

concluded that the slaveholders' convention had aroused enough colonization opposition to make collection for it impolitic at that time. Nor was he more successful in other parts of the state and the packet idea was, perforce, abandoned.[15]

The effort to open commercial operations between Baltimore and Cape Palmas was renewed in 1845. "A respectable and intelligent coloured man" of Baltimore, never named, began a a movement to form a company and to buy or build a vessel for trade with Africa. Primarily Negroes were to own the concern, but Doctor Hall agreed to be their agent in conducting the business. The Maryland society and the American colonization group combined in guaranteeing passengers and freight sufficient to yield $2,000 a year. To protect shareholders, the enterprise was incorporated by the Maryland legislature as the Chesapeake and Liberia Trading Company in February, 1845. William Crane, James Hall, and John Latrobe, all white Baltimore colonizationists, were authorized to accept subscriptions to the capital stock, which was to consist of no more than a thousand shares priced at $100 each.[16]

The plan was to construct a vessel of 2,500 to 3,000 barrels capacity, furnished especially for carrying emigrants. A black crew from the United States and Liberia was to man the ship and, in the future, to officer it as well. Two voyages a year from Baltimore and Norfolk to Monrovia and Cape Palmas were projected. For adult passengers the steerage fee was to be $30 a person, including meals, and cabin passage, $100. Ordinarily freight was to cost $1.50 a barrel. Homebound rates were to be generally lower to encourage trade.

Although the Liberia packet was to be a predominantly Negro concern, only forty of the 200 shares initially offered were taken up by blacks in this country and Liberia, and Governor Russ-

---

15 MSCS MSS, *Records,* vol. III, meeting of the Board of Managers, Feb. 12, 1842; *Letters,* vol. XIII, Kennard to Hall, Chestertown, Mar. 18, 1842.
16 *Maryland Colonization Journal,* n.s., II, no. 22 (Apr., 1845), 337; MSCS MSS, *Records,* vol. III, meeting of the Board of Managers, Mar. 20, 1845; *Letters,* vol. XVI, William McLain to Hall, Washington, Mar. 25, 1845; Maryland, *Laws of Maryland* (1844), Chapter 195.

wurm bought ten of them. The newly constructed Baltimore vessel cost $19,500. She was capable of carrying 2,000 barrels of cargo in her lower hold and 132 passengers in comfort. The maiden trip began in Baltimore on December 3, 1846, with five cabin passengers, twenty-six adult steerage travelers, twelve children, and a full load of cargo. Returning by way of the Cape de Verdes, it added 5,000 bushels of salt and fourteen United States seamen to the eight cabin passengers and Liberian cargo already aboard. The round trip was made in the good time of four months and five days. In the fall of 1847 the packet made a second journey out, this time taking a full cargo of merchandise and eighty emigrants. At the company's first annual meeting in November, 1847, directors voted a dividend of $6 a share, or 6 per cent interest on the investment.

The venture continued a financial success through several years. At times the company owned more than one vessel, and James Hall, the genius behind the scheme, frequently sent bottoms to Europe to participate in that market or chartered ships to take advantage of especially tempting opportunities to add to company profits. An occasional ship was lost and in 1852, after six years' operation, the firm closed when it found itself without vessels.

In some respects, the Liberia packet enterprise fell short of its goals. Negroes never owned more than a small percentage of the stock. Only occasionally could black officers be found for the ships, although colored crews normally manned them. For various reasons, basically Hall's exuberance in squeezing in as many trips a year as possible, the packet never sailed on a regular schedule. And a vein of skepticism ran through the company's last report: vague anxiety that the undertaking be wound up while it was ahead financially. The loss of the barque *Ralph Cross,* the line's last vessel, although fully insured, seemed a warning that the company's luck had run out. The endeavor was, in reality, a profitable one with an average annual cash dividend of 10 per cent. While the society had the advantage of employing the company as agent for its operations, it did give up the services of its outstanding employee, James Hall, to insure the venture's success. But by 1852 the opportunity to liquidate while still solvent was too inviting to resist.[17]

While the Colonization Society endeavored to pay debts, maintain the colony, stave off attacks in the Maryland legislature, and open trade with Africa, the central object of its existence, the emigration of free Negroes, seemed a secondary concern. Agents traversing the state, particularly the Eastern Shore and southern Maryland, largely despaired of convincing either free blacks or potential slave colonists that their future lay in Africa. In the entire decade of the 1840's only 287 settlers left Baltimore for the colony and 142 of them sailed aboard the *Globe* in December, 1842, after the state's political climate and a poor harvest seemed to preclude any improvement in Negro conditions.

The *Maryland Colonization Journal,* now under the energetic editorship of Doctor Hall, queried, "Why Don't the Coloured People Go to Africa?" It suggested that the universal opposition must be based upon more than an attachment to one's birthplace, to ignorance and indolence, or to the hope that social and political equality with whites was attainable. The January, 1847, issue declared that the main cause was colonizationist language which excited pride among blacks. It pointed out that a basic assumption of African colonization had been that political or social equality between the races was impossible in the United States and that the weaker race must serve or flee. Admitting that this doctrine, however kindly or judiciously announced, was extremely unpalatable to blacks, it argued that the resulting pride steeled their hearts against emigration. The article concluded that the colonizationists would have to await the gradual erosion of that opposition and the slow acceptance by Negroes of the correctness of colonization principles.[18] In actuality, the cure seemed unequal to the illness.

While the tone of colonizationist arguments undoubtedly incensed some Negroes, by far the greatest hostility to the cause

---

17 *Maryland Colonization Journal,* n.s., II, no. 22 (Apr., 1845), 338; IV, no. 5 (Nov., 1847), 72–76; VI, no. 18 (Nov., 1852), 274–77.
18 *Ibid.,* III, no. 19 (Jan., 1847), 290–91.

came from abolitionists, white and black. From the beginning of the society's active existence in 1831, these worthies seized every opportunity to belittle and question its efforts. Colonizationists were pictured as being in league with slaveholders in order to elevate artificially the value of bondsmen. Abolitionists visited prospective settlers and artfully informed them that a painful death in the wilds of Africa would be their lot should they sail. One of the most prevalent practices was slyly to assure emigrating citizens that they would end up as slaves in Georgia. Another common technique was to spread rumors that previous emigrants had met sad fates of one kind or another. The general ignorance and superstition of the black population made it an easy target of detractors.

Abolitionists frequently published their views on colonization. An early tract assailing the Maryland cause was published by the fiery William Lloyd Garrison in 1834. Entitled *The Maryland Scheme of Expatriation Examined,* the pamphlet printed in full the acts relating to free Negroes and slaves passed by the state legislature in March, 1832. Garrison analyzed the laws section by section, adding pungent criticisms in footnotes. He charged that while Americans boasted of theirs as the land of the free, there was actually not another civilized nation on earth which had so many slaves or which tolerated so cruel and debasing a servile regime.[19]

The usual stance of the Colonization Society was stony official silence. Privately, officers and employees deplored attacks and activities, but they seldom did the abolitionists the honor of open reply. In the late 1840's, as emigration stagnated and abolitionists became more adamant, the *Colonization Journal* took to answering charges against society operations. It also began challenging abolitionists openly by reprinting their denunciations and refuting them point by point. The society took the unusual step in 1847 of publishing the proceedings of the 1830 libel trial against Garrison.

In November, 1829, Garrison and Benjamin Lundy, co-

---

19 William Lloyd Garrison, *The Maryland Scheme of Expatriation Examined* (Boston: Garrison and Knapp, 1834).

publishers of a Baltimore paper entitled the *Genius of Universal Emancipation,* had accused Francis Todd of Newburyport, Massachusetts, of engaging in the slave trade between Baltimore and New Orleans. Todd had sued Garrison, whose initial "G." was affixed to the newspaper account, for slander, and the jury had found him guilty. Now, in 1847, Garrison was the well-known editor of the *Liberator* and occasionally alluded to this suit as persecution by slaveholders. The Colonization Society collected the documents, including affidavits that most, if not all, of the jurors opposed slavery, and published the compilation in pamphlet form.[20]

Abolitionist agitation not only dissuaded Negroes from emigrating but discouraged slaveholders from manumitting their servants for passage to the settlement. While some owners, it is true, cared little or nothing for their people's welfare, many had tender feelings and looked upon their slaves almost as members of the family. Correspondence between master and servant frequently continued for years until death severed the relationship. The society archives contain numerous inquiries from former owners who did not keep personal contact with released slaves about their health and fortune. Likewise, colonists regularly besieged newly arriving immigrants for word of home and old master and sent verbal greetings back to the United States with returning citizens or visitors.

For slaveholders who wished the best for their bondsmen, unfavorable reports caused them to hesitate before consigning the unfortunates to a speedy end in Africa. Even if owners themselves did not believe the fantastic rumors, it took a hard heart to insist that the reluctant blacks be off. Apart from abolitionist tales, admitted shortcomings of the colony were enough to dismay kindly disposed masters. Famine and suffering reported in abundance seemed a high price to pay for liberty and self-government. Controversies with missionaries and criticisms aired in religious periodicals caused still more men to adopt a skeptical attitude toward the whole colonization business.

---

20 MSCS, *Proceedings against William Lloyd Garrison for a Libel* (Baltimore: William Wooddy, 1847).

Not only did slaveholders pause in freeing their hands for emigration because of the bad publicity from Liberia—contributors and potential givers became hesitant to support the cause. Such persons generally were city or town dwellers without any bondsmen to free. They were frequently women inspired by the desire to educate and convert the heathen tribesmen dwelling in and around the colony. Reports that colonists treated the Africans like slaves and had a detrimental effect upon them alarmed many a well-disposed humanitarian. Missionary complaints undoubtedly affected the giving element of the community more than they influenced prospective slave benefactors. Whereas voluntary contributions from 1831 to the close of 1840 amounted to $15,682, the total had reached only $29,102 at the end of 1851, indicating a substantially lower rate of giving in the latter period.[21]

The society's chief source of livelihood, the colonization tax, received frequent abuse in the 1840's. Although the lower chamber of the Maryland legislature failed repeatedly in attempting to get a bill repealing the tax past the Senate, the delegates were, in fact, representing their constituents quite faithfully. Society agents found a great deal of opposition to voluntary gifts because payment of the annual grant seemed sufficient support. They also encountered, especially among the well-to-do citizens most affected, decided opposition to the annual levy. Roberts, touring the Eastern Shore, discovered that the more wealthy could tell him to a dime how much their counties paid year to year. The prevailing opinion was that they were not in the least benefited by the system. In central Maryland, around Westminster and Frederick, Roberts found the citizenry even more adamant about the tax. The universal cry was that the law ought to be repealed and that the Negroes could go to the devil. A few years later an agent visiting southern Maryland bewailed the local attitude toward colonization. Residents frequently told him that the number of colonists was so small and that the blacks

---

21 *Ninth Annual Report of the Board of Managers of the Maryland State Colonization Society* (Baltimore: John D. Toy, 1841), p. 13; "Report of the Board of Managers of the Maryland State Colonization Society," *Maryland Colonization Journal,* n.s., VI, no. 9 (Feb., 1852), 132.

were so hostile as to render the movement an impractical scheme, causing them to pour out their money like water but to no avail.[22]

A final reason that Maryland Negroes declined to emigrate can be found in the fact that their situation was reasonably tolerable. Despite the allegations of Charles County lawmakers, the condition of free Negroes and slaves was actually not deplorable if one discounts political and social inequality. There is an abundance of evidence, much already cited, demonstrating that free Negroes had considerable liberty and found ready employment. The numerous petitions to the legislature show *ipso facto* that this was the case. Colonizationists learned that in good times, when harvests were abundant, Negroes lent deaf ears to anything about Africa, considering that they were doing well enough in Maryland.[23]

The efforts to break Negro lethargy and hostility to the idea of returning to their forebears' home encompassed a wide range of techniques. By the 1840's attitudes and opinions were fairly well fixed either in favor of colonization or, more often, opposed to it. One of the more successful methods of obtaining emigrants was to select at least one colonist annually to return to Maryland to visit his old home and to travel with the society agent to other parts of the state. Throughout the body's history probably more volunteers were secured in this manner than in any other, although results were generally modest. Joshua Cornish, from near Frederick, was one of the first men brought back. He had gone to the colony in 1837, and four years later, after several colonizationists, including his former master, had interceded, he was given permission to visit the United States at society expense. His trip dispelled friends' beliefs that his letters had been forged and that his real destination had been Georgia, but he was so discouraged when they refused to accept what he

22 MSCS MSS, *Letters,* vol. XII, Kennard to Hall, Cambridge, Mar. 15, 1841; Kennard to Latrobe, Baltimore Co., June 10, 1841; vol. XIII, Roberts to Hall, near Salisbury, Aug. 6, 1842; vol. XIV, Roberts to Hall, Frederick City, May 23, 1843; vol. XVIII, John W. Wells to Hall, Leonardtown, May 25, 1849.

23 *Ibid.,* vol. XIV, A. C. Thompson to Hall, Cambridge, Oct. 31, 1843.

said about the colony that he wished never to visit his old home again. Nonetheless, colonizationists thought that men like Joshua, who were too ignorant to be disbelieved, were the best cure for apathy, and credited him with securing the thirty-two blacks who went back with him. In succeeding years settlers regularly visited throughout the state, but never after December, 1842, when the *Globe* took the large group of 142, did more than forty-five sail at one time.[24]

Throughout the society's active existence, the foremost means of publicizing its program and aims was the work of traveling agents. In the tradition of Finley and McKenney, other men traversed the state, except for western Maryland which had too few Negroes and too sparse a white population to make the effort seem worthwhile, soliciting funds and recruiting emigrants. Their careers followed a consistent pattern. Usually unassigned ministers, they began their tours enthusiastically and sent optimistic initial reports back to Baltimore. They then became discouraged and ill and talked of resigning. They frequently quarreled with the Board of Managers over salaries. Whereas at first the board usually paid a straight salary, traveling expenses, and a commission on collections over a certain sum, it soon found that agents seldom brought in even as much as the agreed-upon payment. The managers then set salaries at a certain percentage of the contributions raised and said nothing about expenses. John Kennard, who served the society nearly six years, resigned when the new policy was adopted because he considered it impossible for an agent to make a living on the commission basis. He was correct so far as he himself was concerned and it was probably his personal experience which led the board to change its system. During the six years in society employ his salary and traveling expenses came to $7,332 but he actually took in only $2,120, with another $4,212 pledged and of doubtful consequence to the society. Even if all pledges were collected, an utter impossibility, he would still have cost the society a

24 *Ibid.*, vol. XII, George Winthrop to [Hall], East New Market, Sept. 30, 1841; William Newton to Hall, Hicksborough, Nov. 25, 1841; vol. XV, Thompson to Hall, Cambridge, May 16, 1844.

thousand dollars more than he produced. Successive agents were, with few exceptions, no more adept at raising funds than Kennard and generally lasted only a year or so each.[25]

The scarcity of emigrants did not mean that the society resorted to taking all applicants. Continuing a policy of some selectivity, the society refused, for example, to accept convicts. Early in 1843 the Maryland legislature considered a resolution to deport criminals to the colony. Latrobe protested vehemently that to make Cape Palmas another Botany Bay, the British penal colony in Australia, would do irreparable harm to the colonists and lessen the attractiveness of the African settlement for prospective emigrants. He concluded that jailbirds were hardly likely to contribute to the colony that measure of brotherhood necessary for its survival.[26]

A few years later the board turned down the application of Thomas Cooper, in the Baltimore City prison for purchasing a few barrels under false pretenses, who volunteered to emigrate to Africa with his wife if the society would secure his release. The young couple professed a great desire to become colonists and the board was sympathetic to their petition but, after considering all the circumstances, decided that it would be inexpedient and establish a bad precedent to receive them.[27]

The decade of the 1840's witnessed, then, a generally moribund colonization movement. The society got out of debt only by curtailing its activities at home and in the colony enough to accumulate a surplus from the annual $10,000 state appropriation. Less than 300 Negroes, not all of them Marylanders and by no means all headed for Cape Palmas, departed from Baltimore. With decreasing strength, colonizationists averted legislation detrimental to the cause, and in 1850 Maryland lawmakers succeeded in passing a measure contrary to society goals.

25 *Ibid.*, vol. XII, Kennard to Latrobe, Baltimore Co., June 10, 1841; *Latrobe Letter Books*, vol. II, Latrobe to Kennard, Baltimore, May 25, 1842.
26 MSCS MSS, *Latrobe Letter Books*, vol. II, Latrobe to Dr. Graves, n.p., n.d. [1843].
27 MSCS MSS, *Records*, vol. III, meeting of the Board of Managers, Dec. 1, 1846; *Letters*, vol. XVII, J. J. Walcott to Latrobe, Baltimore, Nov. 28, 1846; Henry Cooper to Board of Directors of MSCS, Baltimore, Dec. 1, 1846.

"An Act to repeal all laws prohibiting the Introduction of Slaves into this State" lifted restrictions on the importation of slaves by Maryland citizens and eliminated the per capita tax formerly levied on newly arriving bondsmen. While not a significant source of revenue, the tax had amounted to more than $12,000 since 1832. Its recipient, the Colonization Society, was in such financial straits that every penny had been jealously sought. Aside from the prospective monetary loss, the bill opposed in principle society aims. It had worked for nearly twenty years to reduce the number of slave and free Negroes in the state. It had fought off periodic attacks and had used every means it considered judicious to persuade the black population to choose Africa as a new home. Now its efforts were to be subverted by the abandonment of a concept basic to its operations. Added to society officers' consternation was their knowledge that the $200,000 appropriation would soon run out. They could only wonder if this long-dependable source of income, too, would be cut off. Nonetheless, the Board of Managers adopted resolutions reasserting its faith in colonization and its satisfaction with the colony and pledging continued efforts to sustain the cause. Although it did not convene again for nearly a year, affording some indication of administration energy, a few such men as President Latrobe and agent Hall began a statewide campaign to publicize the society's achievements. With an eye on 1852, they realized that only a strong demonstration of public confidence would save colonization. To produce that support was their immediate objective; to secure a renewal of the state appropriation was their long-range goal.[28]

28 Maryland, *Laws of Maryland* (1849), Chapter 165; "Report of the Board of Managers of the Maryland State Colonization Society," *Maryland Colonization Journal*, n.s., VI, no. 9 (Feb., 1852), 132; MSCS mss, *Records,* vol. III, meeting of the Board of Managers, Apr. 4, 1850.

VIII

Domestic Operations
1850-1857

The comparatively dormant condition of the Maryland State Colonization Society in the 1840's eliminated liabilities and kept the colony alive, but hardly inspired much interest at home. With the exception of certain high points such as the colonization convention in 1841, the *Globe* sailing in 1842, and the Liberia packet enterprise in the last part of the decade, the state's citizens could scarcely have been much aware of society activities.

The large group of prominent Baltimoreans who had founded the organization in 1831 and had actively participated in its early years had dwindled until, by 1850, only a few men directed the movement. Hugh Davey Evans, William Fell Giles, Frederick W. Brune, and John Latrobe, all well-established attorneys, Thomas Wilson, prominent merchant, and Charles Howard, civic leader, were at the front of the organization. Many original founders, including George Hoffman, Doctor Samuel Baker, Peter Hoffman, Solomon Etting, Luke Tiernan, and John

Hoffman, had all died. Such others as Moses Sheppard and Judge Nicholas Brice were elderly and no longer active.

The one man who provided administrative continuity was the general agent, James Hall. While Latrobe developed a lucrative practice which brought him recognition as a masterful railroad and patent attorney, Hall initiated reforms, suggested society projects, directed the traveling agents, advised Russwurm, and outfitted expeditions. He seldom took a vacation, although illness at times restricted his activities. Whereas Latrobe was titular head of the Maryland colonization movement, Hall was its actual dean, and in 1851 and 1852 it was largely Latrobe's name and Hall's work which accomplished renewal of the state grant.

The first task in securing this continuation was to wage a campaign of publicity demonstrating colonization's effectiveness and its indispensability. Taking a more aggressive role, the society began early in 1850 to cultivate Maryland lawmakers and to spread news of its operations beyond state boundaries. The *Annual Report* that spring was mailed to the governor and the treasurer as well as to each member of Maryland's two-house legislature. Five copies went to the historical society and to the governor of every other state in the nation.[1]

A wider audience which, it was hoped, would indirectly influence the legislative process was reached by the *Maryland Colonization Journal*. Although the periodical went only to actual contributors among the general citizenry, it was sent gratuitously to such community voices as pastors. A major obstacle for the society to overcome was the imputation that colonization, having accomplished little, was no longer of interest to Maryland's two races or to other Americans either. The *Journal* assured readers that a rapid change was taking place among the free black people. It attributed the shift to one of two things: either the abandonment of abolitionist opposition or a loss of that influence over people of color. Not presuming to know which was the correct explanation, the paper concluded

1 MSCS MSS, *Records,* vol. III, meeting of the Board of Managers, Jan. 18, 1850.

that it was in the state's interest to continue its aid, particularly since a few years' more support would firmly establish the colony at Cape Palmas.

The *Colonization Journal* quoted papers from around the state to substantiate its assertion that the population was calling for the continuation of state aid. The *Unionist* of Cumberland advised its readers to study the society's proposals, for a more laudable cause could not be brought to their attention. An Upper Marlboro paper, the *Planter,* although annoyed that the society took the official stand that slavery was an evil, nonetheless supported renewal of the state subscription: "*We* believe African slavery to be a *blessing,* and this reflection upon ourselves and our fathers, is badly calculated to enlist us. . . . Notwithstanding this reproach, we are in favor of Colonization for our free blacks. We would send them away because they are no advantage to us or to themselves while here. As to our slaves, we would keep them as they are. Hence, we cannot be expected to advocate any measures for their diminution or removal." Another southern Maryland publication, the *Port Tobacco Times,* called the African colonization scheme the most practical and humane plan yet devised for the benefit of the black race in the United States: "It is the child of Maryland and claims her protection—at least for a little while longer. We hope, then, that this matter will receive the most favorable consideration of the Legislature." Other papers, including the *Baltimore American* and the *Frederick Examiner,* were quoted as favoring the suggested legislation.[2]

Exaggerated claims and unrealistic appraisals, largely generated by the Baltimore colonizers themselves, permeated society reports. In February, 1852, full statistics for twenty years' work were published in the *Colonization Journal* to demonstrate society accomplishments. The Board of Managers forsook humility in praising the establishment of the society in 1831:

> There was wisdom and humanity in what the state of Maryland did, as well as great political forecast. In 1831, few persons deemed that slavery, as a topic of national interest, would cause

2 *Maryland Colonization Journal,* n.s., VI, no. 8 (Jan., 1852), 113–16.

the excitement, which has, until recently, prevailed over the length and breadth of the country. Few persons then anticipated a foreign immigration, amounting to half a million a year, and coming at once into active competition for bread with the free colored people, who had for years been filling stations to which they seemed to have a prescriptive right, and from so many of which we have seen them excluded.

But those, who then had the interests of the State in their keeping, seem to have had a clear perception of coming evil days,— and the Legislature of that period provided against them well and carefully, humanely and honorably. . . . Avowing the policy of Colonization, abolitionism was kept down; and while other States were disturbed and excited, the people of Maryland enjoyed a total exemption from all agitation in regard to it. They have been affected neither by the jealous apprehensions of the South, nor the blind fanaticism of the North.

An audit of funds received and spent and a listing of the number of emigrants sent to Liberia told a far less glowing tale.

The total amount of money received by the society from 1831 to January 1, 1852, was $317,049.18, broken down as follows:

State appropriation	$186,922.16
1827 state grant (belated)	930.00
State colonization tax	12,851.85
Contributions	29,102.77
Profit and loss	76,369.03
Other sources	10,873.37
	$317,049.18

The profit and loss item largely represented colonial trade earnings.

Costs attending the gathering and preparation of prospective colonists were $117,536.08:

Expeditions	$ 69,466.45
Collecting and outfitting emigrants	9,038.20
Supporting emigrants six months in Africa and longer, if necessary	39,031.43
Total cost of collection, outfitting, transportation, and support	$117,536.08

African expenses amounted to nearly $150,000:

Purchase of territory, erection of buildings, public improvements, civil list	$133,876.25
Vessels and boats trading on the coast	10,821.97
Education of immigrants in the public schools	5,216.26
Total expenditures in Africa	$149,914.48

Home expenses recorded were:

Office outlay, including rental of room in the Baltimore Post Office	$ 42,048.13
Printing of *Colonization Journal* and other publications for general distribution	5,050.49
Stock held by the society in the Liberia packet	2,500.00
Total home expenses	$ 49,598.62

To recapitulate:

Total receipts from all sources		$317,049.18
Total expenses of collection, outfitting, transportation, and support of newcomers	$117,536.08	
Total expenditures in Africa	149,914.48	
Total home expenses	49,598.62	$317,049.18

Emigrants sent by the society to Liberia totaled 1,049, of whom 934 came from Maryland, 35 from Virginia, and 80 from Georgia.[3]

The board emphasized that African outlays represented the largest sum and that land had to be acquired, buildings and fortifications erected, and a government organized before a single immigrant could be received. It argued further that African

3 "Report of the Board of Managers of the Maryland State Colonization Society," *ibid.*, no. 9 (Feb., 1852), 132–33, 142.

expenditures had gradually diminished since the founding of the colony and predicted the disappearance of this financial imbalance in the near future. Another point stressed was that the state appropriation would have been inadequate by itself to accomplish what had been done with the organization's added resources. The board noted that society contributions had paid home expenses and were sufficient, in addition, to cover many African costs. It concluded that the connection between the state and the society had enabled the former to execute a plan which the 1832 appropriation by itself could never have effected.

A more difficult task was to convince Maryland legislators that their original appropriation must be renewed in order to reap the real rewards of the first grant. Forecasting independence for Maryland in Liberia within a few years, the Board of Managers argued that continuing emigration, resting substantially upon state assistance, would hasten that day when outside aid would no longer be necessary. A growing population would increase coastal trade and yield greater revenues from import and lighthouse duties. Internal revenue from licenses and other sources would expand as the community swelled. The board pledged that if the state continued aid to the colony "a little longer," its namesake and offspring would become self-paying and independent. To drop the project, however, would be looked upon by colonization enemies as Maryland's defection and their triumph and would even impugn the wisdom of the legislators who had supported the movement over the years.[4]

A delicate issue kept as secret as possible in the period before the legislature met was the fact that independence was a burning issue in the colony. The American Colonization Society's decision to grant its Monrovian settlement control of its own destiny in 1847 and Russwurm's absence in the United States the following year had launched greater political discussion at Cape Palmas. Maryland colonists began to agitate for altered status and before long they had divided into factions advocating different remedies. Most citizens wished a severance of society ties. Many favored affiliation with the Liberian Re-

4 *Ibid.*, pp. 133–37.

public but were divided as to whether it should be a federative arrangement or incorporation as a county. Others pushed for the establishment of the Maryland commonwealth as a republic. Society officers favored independence and later federation with the republic, but expected such political change to require some time, with power and institutions being gradually transferred to the authority of the residents.

The point which they stressed to Russwurm and, after his death in 1851, to Samuel Ford McGill, was that while steps toward independence should be initiated, county annexation must be ruled out because the state appropriation certainly would never be renewed if Maryland in Liberia were submerged within the republic. The colonial officers were given permission to study society plans for independence, but so far as people at home, and particularly the lawmakers, were concerned, they were to be led to believe that no change in relations between colony and society were contemplated.[5]

The most important body within the Maryland legislature to convince of society merits was the House of Delegates' Committee on the Coloured Population. Well supplied with information from the Colonization Society and influenced by its officers sent to Annapolis to lobby for a new appropriation bill, the committee issued a favorable report and called for continuing aid. It cited census figures for preceding decades and emphasized the dire predictions respecting the black population outstripping the white. Declaring its belief that the two races could not permanently live side by side, it claimed that no place on the American continent was suitable as a Negro refuge. It presented Africa, where the white man could not live, as the only place in the world fulfilling the blacks' need for a home. Voicing the opinion that free Negroes were beginning to realize that they must eventually emigrate, the committee suggested that to "stop now, when the object to be accomplished under the act of 1831, is on the eve of completion, would be to deny

---

5 MSCS MSS, *Latrobe Letter Books*, vol. II, John Latrobe to John Russwurm, Baltimore, July 17, 1851; Latrobe to Samuel Ford McGill, Baltimore, Oct., 1851.

the policy of a legislation which circumstances show to have been most wise and just."

To colonization opponents deriding the small number of emigrants actually sent to Africa, the delegates replied that the true standard by which to estimate the success of colonization was the condition and capacity of the colony. If it afforded free blacks a safe and comfortable home in a congenial climate, as they believed it did, the society had done all that could be reasonably required and had fulfilled the purpose of its existence.[6]

The bill which the committee recommended passed the General Assembly in May, 1852, and $10,000 annually was thus again made available to the Colonization Society for six years. The one restriction imposed was that such public funds could benefit only Negroes who had been Maryland residents for five years preceding their application. The legislature did reserve the right to repeal the appropriation at any time. The dearth of comment upon the action suggests lack of both opposition to and interest in the whole matter of colonization. Latrobe was naturally pleased with the renewal and believed that the grant would be continued many years longer, if necessary.[7]

Aside from securing the state's beneficence, the society's central aim in the 1850's was to enroll emigrants. Editorializing in the *Maryland Colonization Journal,* Hall declared that men were Liberia's biggest need: "Give but Liberia these [men], and all other things shall be added unto her. We say this has been the great want of Liberia; but never the *sine qua non,* until now."

The society had not enjoyed the services of a successful traveling agent since John Roberts five years before. In April, 1850, the managers appointed the Reverend John Seys to fill that post. Seys was a white man but had been born and reared in the West Indies. He had established the Methodist Episcopal mission at Cape Mesurado after two earlier failures by others and had la-

6 Maryland, *Maryland Public Documents* (January Session, 1852), "Report of the Committee on the Colored [*sic*] Population to the House of Delegates," Apr. 19, 1852.
7 Maryland, *Laws of Maryland* (1852), Chapter 202; MSCS MSS, *Latrobe Letter Books,* vol. II, Latrobe to Joseph Tracy, Baltimore, May 29, 1852.

bored there successfully for years. James Hall considered him to have done more for colonization in the United States, more for Africa, the colonists, and indigenes than all other missionaries put together. Confident that Seys would attract emigrants and funds, the former being the more important, the society generously granted him a salary of $1,000 annually plus a 10 per cent commission on all collections over $1,000, agreed to pay his traveling expenses while engaged as its agent, and met the cost of moving his family from Connecticut where he then had a pastorate.[8]

The expectations centering around Seys's appointment were fully realized. In his first two and a half years he sent out from Baltimore 192 emigrants, two-thirds the total number that had gone out in the preceding decade. Nonetheless, Seys was personally discouraged with results. Visiting Charles County, for example, he found that he could get neither money nor emigrants and concluded that the area would always be a sterile field for colonization. In Frederick he found a falling off of interest in Africa. To keep him in its employ, the board agreed to pay him an extra $2 per person embarking from Maryland for Cape Palmas but in three remaining years of service Seys could persuade only 102 persons to emigrate.[9]

Early in 1856 he resigned his position in Maryland to accept a corresponding one with the American Colonization Society in Ohio, where two sons had settled. Soon after he accompanied an expedition sent by the parent group to establish an interior settlement in the Liberian Republic.[10] From then on his path did not cross that of the Marylanders.

---

8 *Maryland Colonization Journal*, n.s., V, no. 11 (Apr., 1850), 184; no. 12 (May, 1850), 185; MSCS MSS, *Agent's Books*, vol. II, James Hall to Ralph Gurley, Baltimore, Sept. 30, 1843; *Records*, vol. III, meeting of the Board of Managers, Apr. 4, 1850.

9 MSCS MSS, *Letters*, vol. XIX, John Seys to Hall, n.p. [Charles Co.], n.d. [Apr., 1851]; Seys to Hall, Frederick City, June 5, 1851; *Records*, vol. IV, meeting of the Board of Managers, Jan. 4, 1853; "Report of the Board of Managers of the Maryland State Colonization Society," *Maryland Colonization Journal*, n.s., VIII, no. 9 (Feb., 1856), 135.

10 MSCS MSS, *Letters*, vol. XXII, Seys to Hall, Baltimore, Dec. 24, 1855; William McLain to Hall, Washington, Mar. 22, 1856; Gurley to Hall, Washington, Mar. 24, 1856.

Seys's record was actually an impressive one. In less than six years he recruited 294 Marylanders for Liberia. His salary, commission, bounty, and traveling expenses totaled only $6,875 and his collections totaled $12,276, a sizable increase in the annual rate over the previous years. Net proceeds for the society were thus in excess of $5,000.[11] Such unaccustomed surplus funds added to the treasury constituted a great boon.

In 1854 and 1855 the society received applications from several slave owners in Virginia, Georgia, and Tennessee requesting that their servants be transplanted to Africa. Under Maryland law, state funds could not be employed to transport such nonresidents. The society could, however, use its own funds, and it did. In December, 1854, the brig *General Pierce* carried fifty-three Georgia and nine Tennessee blacks to Africa, and the *Cora* took twenty from Virginia and eight from Tennessee in May, 1855. Transporting these individuals cost more than $5,600 and if one adds the expense of their six months' upkeep, it is obvious that the society was spending some state money in the process. Appropriation overseers protested the expenditure of Maryland money for out-of-state slaves, but the fact that almost all had settled at Cape Palmas served to alleviate their qualms.[12]

Seys's success strengthened society officers' belief that they had only to canvass the state adequately to acquire new colonists and voluntary funds. They of course realized that the current state appropriation would expire in another two years and that a further renewal depended upon signs of active colonization interest coupled with a steady flow of Negroes to Africa. The best means of stepping up both support and emigration was thought to be the appointment of two agents as Seys's replacement. The state was consequently divided into two districts, the Eastern and the Western Shores, and Baltimore City was divided

11 MSCS MSS, *Records,* vol. IV, meeting of the Board of Managers, Mar. 18, 1856.
12 *Ibid.,* meetings of the Board of Managers, Oct. 18, 1854, Apr. 30, 1855.; *Letter Press Books,* vol. I, Hall to Charles Howard, Baltimore, Nov. 19, 1856; Hall to McLain, Baltimore, Mar. 10, 12, 1855; "Report of the Board of Managers of the Maryland State Colonization Society," *Maryland Colonization Journal,* n.s., VIII, no. 9 (Feb., 1856), 137.

north and south along Charles Street. Each man was to receive $1,000 annually plus traveling expenses, all exclusively from his own collections. A 10 per cent commission on receipts over $1,000 and $2 per emigrant bounty were also provided. The individuals selected were the Reverend Philip D. Lipscomb and the Reverend Jeremiah W. Cullum, both of the Methodist Episcopal Church's Baltimore Annual Conference. Lipscomb was assigned the Western Shore and Baltimore from the west side of Charles Street and Cullum the Eastern Shore plus Baltimore from the east side of Charles.[13]

Evidence respecting their activities is slight. Correspondence from them is negligible and their reports are merely accounts of money collected and their expenses, without commentary. For the period April 1, 1856, to February 28, 1858, Lipscomb raised $3,869, of which $2,303 went for salary and expenses, leaving a balance of $1,566 for the society. Cullum at the same time took in $3,347, claimed $2,252 for himself, and left the society with $1,095. From June, 1856, to November, 1857, only thirty-eight Maryland Negroes embarked for Africa and 1858 figures could hardly have been much different. The managers thereupon decided that the number of emigrants recruited, the central goal of their operations, was too small to warrant retention of both agents and released Cullum. Records covering Maryland emigrants after 1857 are incomplete, the colony in that year being annexed to the Liberian Republic and the society thereafter sending out its few emigrants under American Colonization Society auspices.[14]

The general fusing of Maryland operations with those of the parent society in the 1850's signified a number of changes. Over the years, the bitter strife accompanying the first expeditions and the decision to found a separate colony at Cape Palmas had been mollified as the Washington board's predictions on costs

13 MSCS MSS, *Records,* vol. IV, meetings of the Board of Managers, Mar. 18, Apr. 11, 1856; *Letter Press Books,* vol. I, Hall to E. J. Way, Baltimore, Mar. 10, 1856.
14 MSCS MSS, *Records,* vol. IV, meetings of the Board of Managers, Mar. 2, 1858, Jan. 31, 1859; "Report of the Board of Managers of the Maryland State Colonization Society," *Maryland Colonization Journal,* n.s., IX, no. 8 (Jan., 1858), 119.

and difficulties were borne out. During the forties increasing opposition to colonization throughout the country, endless missionary controversies, and establishment of the Liberia packet brought the two groups into closer harmony and some cooperation. The mutual woes of operating colonies with typically indolent and dependent populations created an empathy between the two groups' officers. Perhaps the most important factor in the growth of amity was, however, the selection of John Latrobe as American Colonization Society president early in 1853.

Head of the Maryland movement since 1837, Latrobe now succeeded the late Henry Clay in the national cause. He was much more of a figurehead in the new position than he had been in Baltimore where, time permitting, he had given close scrutiny to the colonizing activities being directed from state headquarters. Assumption of the post coincided with Latrobe's rise to new eminence as an attorney of international repute, affording him even less time for Maryland colonization projects. Not long after this he made a trip to Russia and successfully represented his clients, who had constructed a railroad between St. Petersburg and Moscow, in a claim against Czar Alexander II.

Even as the Washington society was considering Clay's successor, it raised an issue all the more delicate because of attendant circumstances. Late in 1852 the American Colonization Society presented two long-standing bills to the Maryland board for emigrants from that state who had been taken to Africa under the parent group's auspices. One statement requested payment of $3,780, or $30 each, for 126 Marylanders transported to Monrovia. The other sought $660 for twenty-two transported to Cape Palmas. The national group sought immediate payment in order to meet pressing obligations.[15]

At the next board meeting in January, 1853, Latrobe submitted the two claims, stating that he had been totally ignorant of them until the week before. Noting that his name had been mentioned in the newspapers in connection with the American Colonization Society vacancy, he deduced that there was a connection between the approaching election and presentation of

15 MSCS MSS, *Letters,* vol. XIX, McLain to Hall, Washington, Dec. 28, 1852.

the bills. Nonetheless, he thought that the matter should be settled on its own merits before the new national executive officer was selected. The managers thereupon voted to reject the $3,780 claimed for the transportation of Maryland emigrants to Liberia but to pay the $660 for colonists landed at Palmas.[16] The action was indicative of the Maryland group's continuing resolve to employ its funds solely for the improvement of its own colony even if its president were to be denied the honor of leading the national colonization movement.

Despite the Maryland board's action, Latrobe was elected to the national office and resigned his local position for it. Charles Howard, a founder of the rejuvenated state society back in 1831, was unanimously chosen to fill Latrobe's place. A general reshuffling of officers occurred, reflecting more accurately the society's active membership. William Fell Giles, for example, moved from recording to corresponding secretary, and Frederick W. Brune replaced him in the former role.[17] The society was fairly dormant during 1853 notwithstanding its new leadership and guaranteed state funds. No meeting of the managers was recorded between March 22, 1853, and January 7, 1854. Seys's luck in assembling Maryland emigrants ran out at about the same time so that the society finally dispatched ex-slaves from other states to the cape.

In the years following Latrobe's departure from the Maryland administration, the state colonization movement became increasingly dependent upon the national organization for inspiration. Greater cooperation was demonstrated by the national society's action in sending forty-one emigrants to Harper rather than Monrovia in June, 1856.[18]

The effort to build and pay for a vessel to replace the Liberia packet brought further coordination between the two societies. The American Colonization Society had begun such a movement in 1854 with $5,000 and had added pledges of $15,000

---

16 MSCS MSS, *Records*, vol. IV, meeting of the Board of Managers, Jan. 4, 1853.
17 *Ibid.*, meetings of the Board of Managers, Feb. 8, 15, Mar. 22, 1853.
18 MSCS MSS, *Letter Press Books*, vol. II, Hall to Howard, Baltimore, Nov. 19, 1856.

from Maine sympathizers who expected to build the ship in Bath and $5,000 from the Maryland society. But the anticipated cost of the clipper, coppered and fitted for passengers, was $36,000.[19]

At this juncture, a prospective benefactor appeared on the horizon. Sometime in 1854 a John Stevens of Trappe, in Talbot County, Maryland, read that the Washington organization was considering buying a suitable ship to convey colonists to Africa. In September, 1855, through his fellow Eastern Shoreman, John Bozman Kerr, a prominent politician and chargé d'affaires to the Republic of Nicaragua during the Fillmore administration who was then practicing law in Baltimore, Stevens tendered a generous contribution to Latrobe for the project.[20]

In the ensuing months Stevens received so many conflicting reports respecting the proposed vessel that he almost abandoned the notion of according financial assistance. He heard, for example, that the Washington board had relinquished all intention of building or purchasing a steamer in favor of a Maryland-owned, Baltimore-built clipper. More serious, his offer was unaccountably ignored by Latrobe. In time James Hall came to learn of Stevens' interest and, with characteristic aggressiveness and efficiency, set about to secure the donation. Seeming indifference was replaced with energetic steps to assure the potential benefactor that his support would be heartily welcome.[21]

Rather than urging that the gift be given to the Maryland society, as Stevens was then considering, Hall now suggested that Stevens return to his first idea of assisting the national cause. Hall argued that Maryland emigrants and freight were not sufficient to warrant a vessel exclusively for them. He held that the most desirable and economical procedure would be to transport emigrants from several states together. Latrobe, writing as American Colonization Society president, advised Stevens

19 *Ibid.*, vol. I, Hall to John Stevens, Baltimore, Jan. 2, 1856; *Stevens Donation Correspondence and Proceedings,* Hall to Stevens, Baltimore, Jan. 3, 1856.
20 MSCS MSS, *Stevens Donation,* Stevens to John Bozman Kerr, [Trappe], n.d. [Sept., 1855].
21 *Ibid.,* Seys to Stevens, Baltimore, Sept. 26, 1855; *Letters,* vol. XXII, Stevens to Seys, Trappe, Dec. 22, 1855.

not to contribute several thousand dollars, as originally intended, to the proposed Maine-built sailing ship but, rather, to contribute sufficient money to cover the entire cost of a second one. Confessing that he would like to be able to say that a Maryland citizen had himself donated a vessel to the national society, he cast doubt that the first ship would even be built. A month later, reiterating his uncertainty that the Maine project would succeed, Latrobe appealed to the wavering potential donor to make the ship *John Stevens* possible.[22]

Latrobe's salesmanship succeeded. Stevens offered the Washington group two mortgages and a bond held by him, together with over $35,000. A Philadelphia firm, White, Stevens and Company, in which the donor's brother was a partner, owed the bond, valued at $25,000, and interest since November 1, 1855. Daniel Lloyd, a prominent Talbot County man, was indebted to Stevens for nearly $5,000, with the lien on a large property near Easton. General Tench Tilghman, son of the famed Continental Army officer by the same name, owed Stevens $4,000 and interest thereon from January 1, 1856. A valuable farm near Oxford, where the general lived, had been given as collateral for the loan and, although it had fallen due four years previously, Stevens had been content to receive interest on the principal. About to travel to Baltimore for medical attention and apparently impressed by the uncertainties of life, Stevens gave specific information on these claims and stipulated that a committee be appointed to receive the funds and construct the ship. He wanted the Baltimore clipper to be named the *Mary Caroline Stevens* for his surviving daughter. His brother, upon the benefactor's subsequent death that spring, at first insisted that it be christened the *John Stevens of Maryland* but yielded when the daughter declined changing her father's request.[23]

Meanwhile, as Latrobe had predicted, it proved impossible to

---

22 MSCS MSS, *Letter Press Books,* vol. I, Hall to Stevens, Baltimore, Jan. 2, 1856; *Stevens Donation,* Latrobe to Stevens, Baltimore, Jan. 2, Feb. 4, 1856.

23 MSCS MSS, *Stevens Donation,* Stevens to Latrobe, Trappe, Feb. 12, 1856; Latrobe to Elisha Whittlesey, Baltimore, May 3, 1856; James Stevens to Latrobe, Trappe, May 17, 1856.

raise sufficient money to construct the Maine vessel, and the American Colonization Society turned its whole energies to the Stevens project. A trust fund was established for management of the gift and Hall, Elisha Whittlesey, a Washington attorney and government employee, and Latrobe were placed in charge. They set about to garner the money and build the ship. White, Stevens and Company promptly paid its loan which, with interest, totaled $25,750. But both Lloyd and Tilghman pleaded inability to pay their debts immediately. The former proved the more cooperative of the two, agreeing to pay half his obligation on July 1, 1856, and the remaining three months later. The trustees received in cash on January 22, 1859, $5,502.98 on Lloyd's judgments. Whether legal action in his case was necessary is unknown, but in the Tilghman instance the gentleman argued that, although he could not forthwith raise the mortgage amount, he could earn it sooner than it could be collected through court proceedings. Latrobe feared that it would be necessary to foreclose on Tilghman's farm but the general undertook to pay the debt by October 1. In actuality, he paid $2,000 cash on December 4, 1856; $1,125.50 on February 19, 1858; $217.40 interest upon the remaining principal on October 5, 1861; and the final amount of $1,333.27 in May, 1863.[24]

Contracting for construction of the vessel was easily accomplished. The best offer came from John J. Abrahams, a Baltimore ship builder of high repute. For $35 a ton, he agreed to lay down a clipper 140 feet long with a hold 19 feet deep and a 32-foot beam. It was to be built with the best white oak, locust, and cedar top timbers. October 1 was set as the completion date for carpentry. The total cost of the *Mary Caroline Stevens,* including water tanks and all fixtures for emigrants, amounted to $43,612. Frederick Brune donated the tanks, valued at $1,200. A member of the Maryland Board of Managers, Thomas Wilson, furnished the ship with an expensive library. Having a

---

24 *Ibid.,* Latrobe to John Stevens, Baltimore, Feb. 19, 1856; Latrobe to Whittlesey, Baltimore, May 3, 22, 1856; Latrobe to Tench Tilghman, Baltimore, May 3, 1856; Tilghman to Latrobe, Oxford, Apr. 22, 1856; Tilghman to Latrobe, Easton, May 16, 1856; for Tilghman's payments, see accounts on the various dates.

capacity of 713 tons, it could carry some 225 emigrants.

On November 25, 1856, dignitaries from the national colonization movement as well as from northern state societies gathered at Fell's Point in Baltimore to inspect the vessel and to
witness its launching. It carried 217 colonists on the maiden
voyage the following week, but only one came from Baltimore.
The rest were sent by the parent body and represented numerous
northern and southern states. James Hall, granted leave of absence on full salary, led the expedition and returned to Africa
to visit the Liberian Republic and to examine affairs in the
Maryland commonwealth. His arrival on the West African coast
early in 1857 proved of immense importance to the American
settlements.[25]

Construction of the *Mary Caroline Stevens* cost more than
$6,000 in excess of Stevens' donation, of which only $29,250
had been obtained by December 1, 1856, leaving a deficit of
$14,000. To fill the gap, the Maryland society lent fellow
Washington colonizationists, who were officially the ship's back-
ers, $5,000 and its own credit on the books of the defunct
Chesapeake and Liberia Trading Company. Altogether the loan
amounted to $8,750, to be repaid as Maryland emigrants and
freight went out aboard the clipper.[26] The Maryland society
could not afford to lend the money and scarcely could hope
ever to recoup in the manner designated. The first two voyages
of the *M. C. Stevens,* as the trim little ship was known, were
very profitable, but within a few years it became a liability for
want of sufficient emigrants. From 1861 through 1864 a mere
169 sailed, reflecting the unsettled conditions attending the
American Civil War.[27] The Stevens donation trustees at length
sold the craft in 1864 for $30,000 and invested the money in
United States securities. They purchased another ship several

---

25 *Ibid.,* meetings of trustees, Apr. 18, May 16, 1856; Hall to Latrobe and
   Whittlesey, Baltimore, Dec. 4, 1856; *Baltimore American,* quoted in the
   Maryland Colonization Journal, n.s., VIII, no. 18 (Nov., 1856), 273–74;
   no. 19 (Dec., 1856), 290.
26 MSCS MSS, *Stevens Donation,* Hall to Latrobe and Whittlesey, Baltimore,
   Dec. 4, 1856; *Records,* meeting of the Board of Managers, Apr. 11, 1856.
27 Philip J. Staudenraus, *The African Colonization Movement, 1816–1865*
   (New York: Columbia University Press, 1961), p. 251.

years later for $22,000, gave the American Colonization Society full control of it, and paid the remaining money over to the parent treasury.[28]

The Maryland society's financial position failed to improve as the decade advanced. Aside from Seys's collections which partially covered costs of sending out-of-state emigrants to Cape Palmas, the $10,000 annual state gift was the Marylanders' only resource. Late in 1856 before he left for Africa, Hall, as general agent, reviewed the organization's finances for its president, Charles Howard. Expenses for office rent, supplies, printing, and local salaries ran $2,000 yearly and the civil list at Cape Palmas, with two additional years of responsibility anticipated, totaled the same. The society had $4,000 banked. The $5,000 loan to the parent society, although designed to serve Maryland needs, was of little consequence since few Maryland emigrants could be obtained. Because of this situation, the colonizationists had not collected the 1856 state appropriation. Casting up accounts, Hall found that liabilities far exceeded assets and advised that the society should either declare bankruptcy or draw a part of the state fund.[29]

It did neither. Both the 1856 and 1857 appropriations remained in the state treasury. At the end of the latter year liabilities stood at $4,551.[30] The only sure source of income was the state and, by now, the Board of Managers was either too scrupulous or too wary to use grants unless Maryland blacks were actually removed. Moreover, the second state grant ran out at the end of 1857. The board, ever hopeful that free and slave Negroes would choose Africa as their new home, prevailed upon the General Assembly to renew the appropriation for one last time early in 1858. Maryland in Liberia had by then become an integral part of the Liberian Republic, but the board pointed out that the dissolution of political relations with the

28 MSCS MSS, *Stevens Donation,* Hall to Latrobe, Oct. 24, 1864; "Report of the Treasurer to the Trustees," Washington, Jan. 15, 1867.
29 MSCS MSS, *Letter Press Books,* vol. II, Hall to Howard, Baltimore, Nov. 19, 1856.
30 MSCS MSS, *Letters,* vol. XXIV, "Estimate of liabilities of the Society to 1st January 1858."

colony did not affect its power to send emigrants. It asked for an appropriation solely covering emigrant transportation costs, their upkeep for six months, the maintenance of a Baltimore office from which to disseminate information, and the salary of an agent in Africa to oversee the distribution of society provisions.[31]

The legislature's last indulgence to the Maryland colonization movement was a four-year appropriations act. In March, 1858, it allotted the society $5,000 annually and a per capita allowance not to exceed $5,000 in any year. For each emancipated slave or free Negro over ten years old removed to Africa, the society was to receive $70; for all others, the contribution was $35 per head.[32] Thereafter, the society gradually sank into unredeemable moribundity. It fared no better than did the parent organization during the War between the States and, in fact, did not re-emerge following the conflict. Its debts were fully met through a combination of state money and miscellaneous receipts and eventually, in the late 1860's, what little money remained was used to establish a James Hall School Fund in aid of Liberian education. The officers maintained their confidence in colonization to the end and, although disappointed at the dearth of emigrants, experienced keen satisfaction in the establishment of a true home for Maryland's Negro population.

31 "Report of the Board of Managers of the Maryland State Colonization Society," *Maryland Colonization Journal,* n.s., IX, no. 8 (Jan., 1858), 117–19.
32 Maryland, *Laws of Maryland* (1858), Chapter 425.

IX

Independence and Merger with the Republic of Liberia

$\mathbf{T}$wo unrelated events—governmental change in Monrovia and John Russwurm's death—served to arouse political consciousness at Cape Palmas. The American Colonization Society's decision to grant its colony independence in 1847 because of the continual financial drain at Monrovia initiated the cry at Harper also for a different political relationship with the Maryland society. The prestige accruing to the Negro republic, which incorporated all American-founded settlements save Maryland in Liberia, put Cape Palmas citizens at a severe disadvantage in competing for immigrants and commercial links. Russwurm's death in June, 1851, forced them to think more constructively about their future. For some time the governor had been a scapegoat for dissatisfactions in the community, and on at least one occasion a plan to depose him was suggested. His death eliminated him as the target of frustrations and also invited change in the administrative structure. A few months later, however, colonists almost came to civil war as they tried to decide what that new political form should be.

The only point that Cape Palmas inhabitants agreed upon was their dislike of the acting governor, Samuel Ford McGill. As the former colonial physician and, during Russwurm's absence from Harper, the assistant agent in charge of affairs, McGill had earned the disfavor of many fellow citizens. He not infrequently displayed vanity and contemptuousness toward them. He spent most of his time building up a lucrative trade along the coast and the success of that operation caused a great deal of jealousy among his compatriots. Moreover, as Russwurm's brother-in-law, he was inextricably associated with the late governor's policy. Having just bought a home in Monrovia, McGill had no ambition for the top executive office. Nonetheless, citizens held a public meeting the week following Russwurm's death to petition the Maryland board not to appoint him the new governor. Interestingly, they now lauded Russwurm as a statesman, philanthropist, and Christian whose equal could scarcely be found.[1]

Characteristically, most Maryland in Liberia citizens were unable to suggest some viable political system to replace the existing one. They wanted freedom from society restraints, some critics said, in order to wage war against the Africans, but they wanted continuation of society supplies and subsidies. Many undoubtedly concurred with the old colonist who advised John Latrobe that the society was considered a father whose direction was necessary for every step taken. A few residents wished no alteration in the settlement's political status, citing Section 42 of the constitution which stipulated that upon reaching 5,000 male inhabitants in the territory, representative government would be authorized.[2]

1 MSCS mss, *Letters*, vol. XIX, Samuel Ford McGill to John Latrobe, Cape Palmas, July 11, 1851; citizens of Cape Palmas to Maryland board of the Colonization Society, [June 18, 1851]; committee from colony to the Board of Managers, [Cape Palmas], Aug. 2, 1851.
2 *Ibid.*, Boston J. Drayton to Latrobe, Cape Palmas, Apr. 10, 1851; John

The colony's political future was complicated by its geographic proximity and historic ties to the Republic of Liberia. Although some coast between Monrovia and Harper remained to be settled, the republic claimed all territory as far south as Maryland boundaries. Three counties—Mesurado, Grand Bassa, and Sinoe—comprised it, each with representatives to a two-house legislature. Since few Cape Palmas residents believed their community capable of standing alone were it granted independence, some arrangement with the republic appeared mandatory. What that relationship should be became an overriding dispute.

The first indication of severe division within the settlement came in July, 1851, when a party of men met to celebrate the republic's fourth anniversary. Popularly known as annexationists, they believed that the Maryland community should seek admission into the neighboring nation as a county. Rumors that Monrovia's flag would be raised over the gathering brought the remaining inhabitants out to interrupt festivities. McGill effectively used his small police force to prevent a clash and the merrymakers escaped none the worse for the abusive language heaped upon them by opponents.

Subsequently, the annexationists prepared a lengthy address to the Maryland managers detailing their arguments for county affiliation. Assuming that the settlement was too backward and too weak to be accepted into the republic as a confederated state on terms equal with existing parts, they spoke of benefits expected from their proposed course of action. Cape Palmas residents, backed by national military power, could exercise greater authority over coastal trading vessels, at the same time giving greater confidence in business ventures to foreign merchants. An uplifted morale would stimulate agricultural efforts and industriousness. Most of all, the Maryland colony would thereafter share the republic's attractiveness for emigrants and traders. When the county annexationists circulated their petition among the citizenry, it received only fifteen signatures, revealing their minority position. While few residents were positively against

E. Moulton to Latrobe, Cape Palmas, Sept. 22, 1851; Anthony Wood to Latrobe, Harper, Sept. 24, 1851.

some connection with Monrovia, there was little agreement about what that arrangement should be.[3]

The acting agent, McGill, during all the clamor held the reins of power from a sense of responsibility rather than from choice. He believed that the Maryland colony's position on the Liberian border automatically settled its future. In one form or another, it would unite with the larger state. He was certain, however, that the republic would resist even county annexation unless an emergency existed. In short, Cape Palmas had nothing to offer any union. The former American population was sparse, the people were economically dependent upon outside aid, and they were generally an indolent, quarrelsome bunch. McGill nonetheless recommended to his employers that they grant the settlement independence and apply diplomacy and pressure in securing its merger with the republic.[4]

These were the views held at Cape Palmas, but as a people subject to society wishes, residents awaited word from Baltimore. It arrived at last in late 1851. As spokesman for the Board of Managers, President Latrobe advocated a plan of independence and confederation. Noting that the distinction "Republic," enjoyed by those residing at Monrovia, was detrimental to the "colony" with its less favorable connotations, Latrobe instructed Russwurm (whose death was not yet known at home) to publicize board intentions to grant self-determination. County annexation was opposed on the grounds that chances of receiving further state appropriations would be doomed, that it would be abandonment of the independent state action scheme which had secured initial public funds, and that it would be an affront to the colonists if they were handed over as a dependency to the older settlement.[5]

The board's message to Maryland colonists had to be broadcast by McGill, of course. In view of his unpopularity and

3 *Ibid.*, McGill to Latrobe, Harper, Sept. 16, 1851; Drayton to Latrobe, East Harper, Sept. 25, 1851; petition of annexationists, Cape Palmas, Sept. 25, 1851.
4 *Ibid.*, McGill to Latrobe, Harper, Sept. 25, 1851; McGill to James Hall, Harper, Sept. 18, 1851.
5 MSCS MSS, *Latrobe Letter Books*, vol. II, Latrobe to John Russwurm, Baltimore, July 17, 1851.

known affinity for Monrovia, his duty of proclaiming society wishes was unpropitious for their acceptance. At first the colonists refused to believe that the statement had not originated with McGill. Finally, they came to accept it as emanating from only one or two managers and, hence, unauthoritative.

In the months following the board's declaration the citizenry divided itself according to four different opinions respecting the colony's future. One party, considered by McGill to include the most worthless and idle, opposed any change of government and considered the communication the work of the president alone. A second segment of the community, comprising the majority, favored independence and confederation. A third faction advocated county annexation. The fourth and smallest division preferred absolute self-determination—withdrawal from society control and complete autonomy. The acting agent declared that the last group consisted principally of officeholders and political aspirants who saw the development of a self-governing state their best chance for prominence. Reflecting his own bias, McGill claimed that the third alternative held support from the most intelligent sector, but believed that an alliance of groups two and three, encompassing about three-fourths of the population, could effect a suitable political arrangement.[6]

The person who emerged as spokesman for the dominant groups was William A. Prout, long-time resident and colonial secretary. A reasonable and moderate man, widely respected except by some few colonists who abhorred his violation of the no-drinking covenant, Prout prepared a twenty-page memorandum concerning independence. Accepting official opinion that republicanism and confederation were the wisest steps for Cape Palmas, he made specific proposals for the establishment of a self-sufficient state. While he said nothing about the colony's future relationship with Monrovia, his memorandum was a remarkable document, considering the dearth of constructive ideas and the general helplessness displayed by most residents.

Prout admitted, first of all, that things were not what they

6 MSCS MSS, *Letters,* vol. XIX, McGill to Hall, Harper, Dec. 15, 1851; McGill to Latrobe, Harper, Jan. 6, [1852].

ought to be at Cape Palmas. Agriculture had been neglected in spite of the fertile soil, with the result that manufacturing and commercial development had been retarded. He predicted both economic growth and an enhanced treasury if residents concentrated on agricultural pursuits. The colony's new government should be republican in form with a governor, lieutenant governor, secretary of the treasury, secretary of state, and munitions inspector, all elected by majority vote of the citizens. The legislature suggested was a two-house body consisting of a senate and a house of representatives, the former to have two members and the latter four. The judiciary would be headed by a chief justice, with four associate judges and four justices of the peace. Prout recommended that the top justice be appointed by the executive, in consultation with the legislature, receive a fixed salary, and be subject to removal only for malfeasance in office.

An important problem which Prout next attacked was that of money. Estimating that just the civil list would require $2,635 annually, not to mention all other governmental expenditures, he suggested a number of revenue sources. In addition to the usual port fees, import duties, and property taxes, he recommended an annual penalty of 75 cents per acre on citizens owning wild and uncultivated lands on which they made no improvements and, most controversial of all, a duty of 20 cents per gallon for newly legalized liquor. He proposed that the colony's immediate financial needs be met by an annual $4,000 loan from the Maryland society or through it from American merchants, the advance to come in the form of tobacco and gunpowder for trading purposes and to be repaid in installments as the new republic earned profits.

Having set down his ideas for erecting a viable governmental structure, Prout enumerated questions concerning society property and jurisdiction which had to be resolved before a republic could be declared. First, he asked, how much territory will the society hand over to the new nation? In what way will negotiations with the African chiefs for Garroway be settled? What disposition will be made of public buildings such as schoolhouses and offices? Will the society reclaim the coasting boat it supplied the colony? Are the cannon and war materials to be deeded the new government? How will the medical department function and what is to become of the colony's invalid and indigent citizens? Can we depend upon society support for education? Will the society cancel commonwealth and individual debts and liabilities? [7]

Only a man of ability and experience could have drawn up such a comprehensive survey. As important as his systematic approach was the fact that Prout was popular with the citizenry and, consequently, had become leader of the independence drive. A public meeting of colonists endorsed the colonial secretary's views and incorporated them in an address to the Maryland board. They had doubts only about the liquor duty, but these they rationalized away on the supposition that trade in spirits would open up the interior country to their dealings. Prout himself defended the liquor proposition upon the basis that a grogshop, always well stocked, had been in operation in a nearby African town for the past eight months. Not only could colonists purchase as much liquor as they pleased, but lucrative business with inland areas had already attracted a competitor. Predicting that at the present rate the law prohibiting traffic and sale of alcoholic beverages would become inoperative, Prout recommended that the government channel the trade in a manner advantageous to its treasury.

Memorialists also concurred with Prout that once the Maryland colony achieved independence, it should confederate with the republic as a state equal to the existing three parts. They chose a committee of community leaders to negotiate society withdrawal from the colonial management.[8]

McGill, remaining as much in the background as possible, was generally skeptical of the new turn of affairs. He felt little goodwill toward Prout and considered colonists gullible in accepting his leadership. He believed, furthermore, that secret features of the plan provided for Prout to be secretary of the treasury and William Cassell, then chief justice, the governor in

7 *Ibid.*, William Prout to chairman [of public meeting] and fellow citizens, [Harper], Nov. 10, 1851.
8 *Ibid.*, petition of colonists to Board of Managers, Harper, Nov. 15, 1851; Prout to Latrobe, Harper, Jan. 6, 1852.

the new administration. The acting agent remained convinced that the Liberian Republic would not accept the Cape Palmas settlement as a confederate state and doubted that it would receive it even as a county unless pressured.[9]

The only utterance coming from Monrovia at this time was an editorial in the *Liberia Herald*. Acknowledging the inevitability of the Maryland community's application for admission to the republic, the weekly noted that citizens were prepared to look favorably upon the forthcoming petition if it suggested honorable arrangements "in consonance with the present organization of our government." This would preclude, of course, anything other than county annexation.[10]

After Cape Palmas residents submitted their petition to the Maryland society, they heard no more for months. A private correspondence ensued between Latrobe and McGill which made the former appear indeed the author of the board's recommendations, as one colonial faction already believed. Latrobe insisted upon independence followed by confederation and his intransigence frustrated McGill so that the latter became increasingly emphatic in his request for release from official duties. A year later, in November, 1852, a board committee outlined steps to be followed in establishing the new government.

Carefully studying the proceedings between the American Colonization Society and Liberia before independence was declared in 1847, Maryland managers decided that they could do no better than to follow that example. The one modification recommended was that the civil list be subsidized for four years after the new government was organized. Colonists were first to conduct a plebiscite upon the question of a separate and independent government. If the decision was affirmative, they were to call a constitutional convention and to select two commissioners to represent them at subsequent negotiations in Baltimore. The relationship between the newly created Maryland

9 *Ibid.*, McGill to Hall, Harper, Dec. 15, 1851; McGill to Latrobe, Harper, Jan. 6, [1852].
10 *Liberia Herald*, n.s., II, no. 7 (Nov., 1851), 3.

commonwealth and the Liberian Republic was to be settled by the citizens themselves after they were on their own.[11]

McGill, handed the committee report, was given private instructions for its proclamation. Preceding the forthcoming poll, citizens were to be disabused of the notion that the state appropriation's recent renewal meant that things would go on in the same way for another six years. Thereafter, public funds would be used solely for transporting emigrants to Cape Palmas, provisioning them the customary six months, and maintaining a colonization office in Baltimore. The society's contribution toward the civil list would come from voluntary sources. Society officers suggested that once independence was agreed upon and a convention had drafted a constitution, it should be submitted to the board for review. The joint effort would combine the colonists' practical experience with society members' political and legal sagacity, producing a better instrument than either party alone could create. Finally, the board could not resist comment on Prout's advocacy of liquor traffic. Noting that Maine and Massachusetts had recently adopted prohibition, the managers announced their firm opposition to any plan which would freely admit intoxicants to the cape.[12]

Arrival of board instructions coincided with a political crisis in the colony. The citizens, about to declare freedom from the society unilaterally, had petitioned the governor and council to call an election of delegates to a constitutional convention. Society orders extricated the colonial government from an embarrassing position and enabled it to comply with wishes of both managers in Baltimore and residents in Harper.

The polls opened at 6 A.M. on January 31, 1853, and by nightfall, 122 colonists registered approval of independence. Although no opposition ballots were cast, some few voters favoring the status quo remained home. In February another election was held to select nine delegates for the convention. There was

11 MSCS MSS, *Records,* vol. IV, meeting of the Board of Managers, Nov. 20, 1852.
12 *Ibid.,* Board of Managers to McGill, Baltimore, Nov. 20, 1852.

an attitude of haste. McGill concluded that, having finally decided to stand on their own, the citizens now wanted to complete the action before they had time for second thoughts. Representatives chosen were prominent men well known to society officers in Baltimore: W. A. Prout, William Cassell, Boston Drayton, Joseph Gibson, and Anthony Wood, among them. The two commissioners elected to present the proposed constitution to the board were Prout and Cassell.[13]

By the end of March the new constitution and bill of rights had been drafted and had received voter approval. In reality, they were minor mutations of the original documents sent out with Doctor Hall twenty years before. One section, however, was stricken from the proposed bill of rights—the rum clause.

The exclusion of the no-alcohol rule from the statutes was the only objection the Board of Managers held to the convention recommendations. Claiming that "this provision the Society have believed, has tended to promote in the Colony, good order, morality and religion," the managers asked citizens to reconsider their action. The board admitted that the people of Maryland in Liberia were free to adopt whatever laws they deemed wise but recounted efforts in various American localities to check the use and sale of liquor because of the growing conviction that intemperance was the parent of crime and misery. Upon the board's advice, citizens took up the subject of intoxicants again. After a period of heated debate, they voted ninety to three in favor of excluding that trade article and instructed the convention to reinsert the prohibitory clause in the constitution.[14]

Establishing the new government's basic laws was but a small part of the work necessary to sever the political relationship between society and colony. Such issues as the disposition of society buildings and property, continuation of education, public welfare and employment, settlement of private and corporate indebtedness, and reception of new immigrants had to be re-

13 MSCS MSS, *Letters,* vol. XX, McGill to Latrobe, Harper, Jan. 28, Feb. 9, 15, 1853; Joshua Stewart to Latrobe, Harper, Feb. 6, 1853.
14 MSCS MSS, *Records,* vol. IV, meeting of the Board of Managers, Jan. 27, 1854; *Letters,* vol. XXI, McGill to Charles Howard, Harper, May 13, 1854.

solved. Prout and Cassell, the two commissioners selected to
journey to the United States, expected the society to be generous
in its withdrawal from colonial management. They believed that
the government house and warehouse should be deeded to the
new administration, that all military equipment should revert to
it, that society medical aid should be continued to the indigent,
and that all debts due the society by the commonwealth should
be cancelled. They declined to give opinions on the future of
the public farms and the employment thereby provided the destitute, on the disposition of colonists' individual debts to the
society, or on support for education.[15]

Early in January, 1854, the commissioners arrived in Baltimore. For six weeks the two parties held conferences to work
out an amicable arrangement. On February 14 they signed the
Articles of Agreement, which, if ratified within twelve months
by the new government, were to be binding on both bodies. The
terms were as follows:

1) The society agreed to cede all public lands within the
colony to the people and government, upon condition that

a) future immigrants be allowed, out of unoccupied or
unsold land, a ten-acre farm lot or a one-quarter-acre town lot
in any new settlement, or a ten-acre farm lot in the present settlement and a one-eighth-acre town lot; when public lands were
sold, alternate lots, farms, sections, and square miles would be
left as reserves for new arrivals;

b) all sales of public lands would be at public auction to
the highest bidder; parcels unsold in this manner would be sold
privately at a set minimum price;

c) tracts reserved for immigrants could, with the society's
consent, be exchanged for others of equal value, or sold, with
proceeds going to the benefit of education;

d) the new government would appropriate at least 10 per
cent of proceeds from sale of public lands to schools or educational purposes;

15 MSCS MSS, *Letters,* vol. XX, document received from Messrs. Prout and
Cassell, commissioners from the colony, referred to in connection with
questions respecting the commonwealth's future, n.p., n.d. (considered by
Board of Managers, Jan. 14, 1854).

e) the society retained the right of locating future immigrants in any of the present townships or in any new one;

f) the establishment of new settlements was agreed upon jointly by the society and the Maryland republic;

g) lands retained by the society for immigrants would be tax-exempt;

h) Maryland in Liberia consented to allow the society a maximum 100 acres from public lands, still uncommitted to any use, for the settlement of recaptured Africans, should the U.S. government determine to relocate them at Cape Palmas;

i) the society would retain the public store and adjoining wharf, the existing receptacle for new colonists, and half of the public farm; in all future settlements, the society would receive a lot suitable for accommodation of newcomers; society property and improvements would be tax-exempt.

2) The society retained the privilege of landing duty-free all supplies and provisions necessary for the welfare of new colonists; vessels chartered by the society and carrying out emigrants would be exempt from lighthouse and anchorage fees.

3) Recaptured Africans would be admitted into Maryland in Liberia should the U.S. government wish to send them there and provide their support.

4) The society ceded to Maryland in Liberia the government house and public offices, forts and all munitions, and the new warehouse, but retained all other property not specifically transferred.

5) Immigrants hereafter sent to Cape Palmas by the society would be eligible for citizenship upon the same terms as earlier colonists.

6) Should the Maryland State Colonization Society at any future time merge with another such group or should its duties be assumed by state-appointed agents, all provisions of the present agreement would continue mutually binding.

7) These articles could hereafter be altered at any time by the mutual agreement of the respective parties.

8) After the new government was organized and the agreement ratified, the republic would receive a deed confirming, con-

veying, and vesting in it title in fee simple to all said lands, subject only to conditions and reservations already stated.[16]

A number of important questions remained undecided. The society made no commitment concerning a subsidy for the civil list, aid to education, medical attention, public employment and welfare, and settlement of all indebtedness. These matters were purposefully left out of the agreement in order that they could be determined at some later date without the restrictive clauses imposed by a legal document. The managers believed that it was wise to leave broad policy areas unbound by pledge or promise, explicit or implicit.[17]

The commissioners, Prout and Cassell, arrived back at Cape Palmas in May. On the 15th the constitutional convention reconvened to adopt laws, organize the government, and provide for popular elections. Prout missed the first three days' proceedings, having celebrated his return with a drinking spree. Reporting that the man's best friends despaired of his ever becoming sober, McGill judged that Cassell had the best chance of being elected governor. Plans for the new government were soon completed and elections held. On June 8, 1854, the republic of Maryland in Liberia was proclaimed and officials inaugurated.

The governor of the newly independent state was William A. Prout, Cassell having been disqualified because of a constitutional provision requiring the Chief Executive to have lived in the settlement for six years preceding his term of office. Boston J. Drayton became the lieutenant governor and leader of the Senate. Cassell retained his nonelected position as chief justice and Thomas Mason was appointed secretary of state. Four senators and five delegates represented the citizens in the two-house legislature. The following day, June 9, continuing the custom of the country, the governor was presented to the neighboring African chiefs. They received a generous dash consisting of three barrels of gunpowder, 600 pounds of tobacco, two dozen knives, two boxes of pipes, six dozen plates, and a quan-

16 MSCS MSS, *Records*, vol. IV, Articles of Agreement, Feb. 14, 1854.
17 *Ibid.*, Harper to McGill, Baltimore, Feb. 18, 1854; report of committee on the colony, meeting of the Board of Managers, Jan. 27, 1854.

tity of cloth. In July the Senate ratified the Articles of Agreement submitted by the commissioners. The matter of affiliating with the Monrovian government was dropped as both leaders and ordinary citizens reveled in their power. They were well aware that even state confederation, unlikely as it was, would necessitate submission to the better-established parent republic.[18]

Soon after the inauguration and launching of the small state, McGill took up his long-postponed residence at Monrovia. His place as the society's representative was taken by Joseph T. Gibson, then connected with a mission station at Cape Palmas. McGill handed over to him property and buildings appraised at $4,928 and an inventory of merchandise estimated at more than $14,000 in value. Gibson's duties were to superintend the settlement of new immigrants, keep society possessions in good repair, and judiciously represent his employers in any controversy over the terms of agreement.[19]

In the years immediately following independence, Maryland in Liberia took a course similar to that in the period preceding its new status. The Maryland society continued to pay the civil list, provide medicines for all needy citizens, pay half the cost of building homes for new settlers, and grant charity to particularly worthy cases. Gibson was not infrequently given almost contradictory instructions. On the one hand, he was to help the community become self-sufficient while, on the other, he was warned repeatedly that the society could no longer take care of everything and everybody. The agent complained that things were dull and money scarce. Debts owed the society by individual citizens were ignored and considered by many as cancelled now that their own republic governed them.[20]

18 MSCS MSS, *Letters*, vol. XXI, McGill to Hall, Harper, May 17, 1854; McGill to Hall, Monrovia, June 17, 1854; "An Act Ratifying the Treaty Agreed to by Commissioners on the Part of the State of Maryland in Liberia and the Maryland State Colonization Society, passed by the Senate," July 11, 1854.

19 *Ibid.*, receipt for property, Harper, June 1, 1854; letter of instructions, McGill to Joseph T. Gibson, n.p., n.d. [June, 1854].

20 MSCS MSS, *Letter Press Books*, vol. I, Hall to Gibson, Baltimore, Oct. 28, 1855; *Letters*, vol. XXII, Gibson to Hall, Harper, Aug. 22, 1855, Mar. 26, 1856.

Prout's administration was neither stimulating nor bold. Agriculture proceeded at its usual snail's pace and the governor's only suggestion for its encouragement was the levying of a tax on uncultivated fields. Exports remained at their same low level. With scarcity of goods and money, little was imported either, so that the national treasury's chief outside source of revenue was of small consequence. Few improvements and no sales of public lands were made. Contrary to expectation, immigrants did not pour into the tiny republic, a mere 234 arriving at Cape Palmas from 1853 through 1857.[21]

The only subjects of much interest in the settlement were the frequent local wars in the interior and the citizenry's desire to remove African towns still existing in their midst. Conflicts between different tribes were not only obstacles to trade but also delicate problems in which the Maryland residents had to exercise caution not to provoke attack upon themselves.

One such controversy, raging for two years along the Cavally River, a route regularly traveled upcountry for rice and palm oil, was settled late in 1853 by Commodore Isaac Mayo, heading the African Squadron. A few months later, with the squadron still off the coast, the ex-Americans wanted to wage war with the Poor River people who had overrun some society territory. Only McGill's cool appraisal of the danger prevented the proposed sortie. This generally bellicose attitude became increasingly prevalent after Maryland in Liberia declared its independence. Quick to anger, the colonists paid little heed to their precarious existence. The lack of stable leaders who could dissuade them from rash action and the presence of men who did more inciting than pacifying was soon to bring the infant republic close to doom.[22]

The citizens had routinely tolerated interference with commerce by the surrounding indigenes since the colony was

---

21 "Governor Prout and His Message," *Maryland Colonization Journal,* n.s., VIII, no. 7 (Dec., 1855), 98–103; "Report of the Board of Managers of the Maryland State Colonization Society," *ibid.,* no. 9 (Feb., 1856), 135; IX, no. 8 (Jan., 1858), 119–20.

22 MSCS MSS, *Letters,* vol. XX, McGill to Hall, Harper, Sept. 10, 1853, Jan. 10, 1854.

founded in 1834. The interspersion of native towns through the settlement became more bothersome as immigrants arrived and additional territory was surveyed and inhabited. Although some African groups sold their plots to the society and others gradually moved farther from the Maryland community, many remained firmly planted and let the newcomers crowd close in on them. The ex-Americans became even more aware of the desirability of evicting nearby Africans as they prepared for self-government and negotiated land agreements with the Maryland board. The threatened owners, opposed to any change of habitat and mindful of rights granted them by the original deeds, finally appealed to John Latrobe to honor those agreements. On the eve of independence chiefs and headmen protested that the colonists wanted to take their land by force. They complained that they had already given up most of it and now wished to retain at least their towns. Hearing nothing from Latrobe, they gradually evacuated. They would not respond, however, to feelers regarding sale of the towns. The Cape Palmas tribe wished to retain them as a refuge should it be menaced by unfriendly bands. Governor Prout, while unhappy at his neighbors' obstinacy, at least understood their reasoning and made no move to force the issue.[23]

Within a short time conflict among surrounding tribes generated rebellion against established authority in the nation. The Poor River people and the Grahways disputed control of territory owned by the Maryland republic. This was an issue unresolved since the end of McGill's administration and although he had prevented war between the unhappy landowners and the usurpers, the battle raged between the Poor River people and the Grahways. The economic barriers resulting finally induced Prout to attempt reconciliation between the combatants. But to get the Poor River tribe to the palaver, Prout considered it necessary to take several men hostage. The opportunity presented itself when a delegation of three arrived in Harper bearing a

23 *Ibid.*, vol. XXI, Gov. SouBol, Semile Belle, and headmen to Latrobe, Cape Palmas, May 12, 1854; Prout to Hall, Harper, July 13, 1854; vol. XXII, Prout to Hall, Harper, Aug. 14, 1855.

bullock, the standard peace symbol. They were arrested and held, pending talks. The following day a large band of citizens, led by the militia, appeared at Prout's door and demanded his resignation. Alarmed that bloodshed might follow if he resisted, Prout stepped down.

In a later defense Prout contended that the mob was led by the settlement's chronic grumblers and others who had been filled with rum and wines by such leaders as Cassell and Drayton, and that the participants were armed with cudgels, pistols, and knives. Anthony Wood agreed that liquor had been used to sway colonists in the rebellion and deplored the fact that a majority of citizens gloried in violation of the constitution. He was particularly outraged that Boston Drayton, a Baptist minister, had openly encouraged mutiny.[24]

Joseph Gibson, the society's paid agent, siding with the rebellious colonists, charged that Prout's constant drunkenness had made him unpopular for many months before his removal from office. The immediate impetus, however, had come when the governor, in a state of intoxication, had imprisoned the peaceable Africans. Drayton, succeeding Prout, claimed that this drastic action had been taken only when the Chief Executive's policy put in jeopardy the lives of colonists out cultivating fields near the Poor River territory and threatened the nation's existence. He charged further that it was a common occurrence to see Prout, while governor, sprawled in the street drunk. Relating events surrounding the man's removal from office, Drayton stated that Prout, during his eighteen months' tenure, had lost the people's confidence by his administration of affairs. Two-thirds of the qualified voters had asked for his resignation and he complied. Drayton called it a "revolution of moral suasion." [25]

As lieutenant governor, Drayton ran the community from December, 1855, until June, 1856, when the regular biennial election was scheduled. By the constitution, the governorship

24 *Ibid.*, vol. XXII, Prout to Hall, Harper, Mar. 20, 1856; Anthony Wood to Hall, Harper, Mar. 24, 1856.
25 *Ibid.*, Gibson to Hall, Harper, Mar. 26, 1856; vol. XXIII, Drayton to Howard, Harper, Oct. 21, 1856.

and half the four Senate seats were to be contested at two-year intervals. Drayton decreed, however, that all Senate positions be refilled. Running at the head of a party known to favor county annexation, Drayton was elected governor and his supporters replaced all four Senate incumbents. Prout, living in retirement at Harper, considered it strange that there were no complaints about the unconstitutional procedure. He noted that even the deposed senators seemed ignorant of their prerogatives. The ex-governor conceded that a civil war or uprising would be fatal to the settlement altogether. The Africans had taken a great deal of interest in the strife and their soldiers were armed with guns and knives, apparently in anticipation of attack from the colonists.[26]

At home, Maryland colonizationists were aghast at the turn of events in their former possession. Admitting that the society no longer had the right to interfere with political concerns, Charles Howard chided the citizens for their hasty, moblike movements. He acknowledged that in some cases such measures might be justifiable but claimed that more often than not greater evils resulted from the illegal effort to redress grievances than from the ills themselves. Warning the inhabitants that rash and inconsiderate conduct would cut them off from the blessing of Providence, the society president urged further a return to strict adherence to the temperance principle.[27]

Privately, James Hall, at least, had ambivalent feelings respecting Prout's dismissal. Rejecting Demsey Fletcher's request for a shipment of alcoholic beverages, Hall advised him to give up drinking. Prout, the general agent remarked, had disgraced the colony sufficiently on this count and he was glad that the people had taken the matter in hand constitutionally or otherwise. To agent Gibson, however, Hall commented that while Prout's discharge was undoubtedly desirable, it was better to endure a drunken governor for years than once to allow the masses to defy the constitution. Hall urged Gibson thereafter to

26 *Ibid.*, vol. XXII, Prout to Hall, Harper, June 24, 1856.
27 MSCS MSS, *Records*, vol. IV, Howard to people of Maryland in Liberia, Baltimore, July 29, 1856 (read at meeting of the Board of Managers, Dec. 28, 1856).

defend the side of law and order. Hall's reply to Prout was an indignant protest that the ex-governor should be so bold as to blame the political chaos on drunkenness among the people when his own intemperance had been the concern of citizens, missionaries, naval officers, and nearly everyone else who had recently visited the tiny nation.[28]

In the year following Prout's deposition, 1856, the Maryland republic experienced general tranquillity. Farmers attended their fields with the usual nonchalance. Other citizens quietly engaged in their several occupations. The General Assembly gave some attention to gaining diplomatic recognition from Britain and France and recommended that the Chief Executive "purchase, build, or accept the donation of a vessel to be employed in the Revenue service." The object of the latter was to improve the nation's financial position, but, with no resources of its own for such a ship, the administration called upon society beneficence. Subsequent events were to render that action unnecessary. Governor Drayton reported the citizens determined to avoid any repetition of past unconstitutional conduct. As late as October, 1856, he voiced gratitude that the republic was at peace with surrounding tribes, although native war still raged upcountry.[29]

A few months later the peace of the nation was shattered by events which nearly brought its total destruction. The Cape Palmas tribe living within the settlement and the Grahway peoples inhabiting towns along the beach became the victims of the colonists' wrath. Annoyances and misunderstandings accumulating for more than twenty years became the basis for a declaration of war on these nearest Grebos.

In December, 1856, government officials in Harper received word that Africans in several neighboring towns planned an armed attack upon the settlement during the night. The community was put in a state of defense but no conflict ensued. Several days later the Cape Palmas king and headmen were

---

28 MSCS MSS, *Letter Press Books*, vol. I, Hall to Demsey Fletcher, Baltimore, May 17, 1856; vol. II, Hall to Gibson, Baltimore, Aug. 1, 1856; Hall to Prout, Baltimore, Aug. 1, 1856.

29 MSCS MSS, *Letters*, vol. XXIII, Drayton to Howard, Harper, Oct. 21, 1856.

summoned to confess their intentions. Acknowledging that they had been armed, the native leaders insisted that they themselves had expected to be attacked by the colonists; their military preparations had been only defensive in nature. Governor Drayton and his advisers nonetheless considered the Africans the potential aggressors.

During the following week the Cape Palmas people, seeking vengeance for past injuries, engaged in skirmishes with outlying tribal groups. Drayton attempted to intervene. Commissioners sent to mediate among the warring forces barely escaped with their lives, giving the governor reason to believe that the Palmas and Grahway blacks, by now allied against their African neighbors, were actually forming a broad front against the American-founded community.

On December 20 martial law was declared. In an emotional and almost unintelligible message, Drayton called for unity: "I invoke all good and patriotic citizens to promote the majesty of the republic, to aid the supremacy of the law, the dignity of the state, in the decisiveness by rendering obedience to seek a remedy for series of evils, . . . prepared for any emergency the appeal to arms if essential to testify our attachment to the state, to repulse and resent if needed savage insults, to our national pride." Two days later the Chief Executive, intending to dictate a treaty, demanded a conference with the Cape Palmas king and headmen. He offered to pardon all insults and outrages against the Marylanders over the years in exchange for the large African towns near Harper. When the delegation refused to concede, Drayton decided that "the Government had been trifled with long enough and I beleived the time was come when it was necessary for the Government to maintain its dignity among this heathenish and rebellious people; and if there was any strength in the Government, to bring its strong arm to bear in this direction—and quickly check this strong current of insubordination and conspiracy."

Accordingly, on the night of December 22 Drayton ordered bombardment of those towns close to Harper. The inhabitants fled without much fight but as they reached the outlying districts, they burned some colonist homes and the Mount Vaughan mission. Several individuals on each side were killed or wounded. The next few nights small African parties attacked unprotected sections of the community, robbing and burning deserted homes. On December 25, in alliance with nearly 200 Rocktown and Fishtown warriors, a sixty-man militia retaliated against the Grahways who lived on the beach below Cape Palmas. Four towns were burned to ashes and about thirty tribesmen killed. Loss was slight for the Maryland forces.

Drayton's military success in these two ventures convinced him that the aborigines had finally been taught to respect his authority. He noted that friendly tribes were coming in from all directions to express their amity and that hostile tribes were seeking peace because they could not cope with the community's arms. He seemed unconcerned that many colonist families were destitute and in need of philanthropy as a consequence of his folly.[30]

Word of hostilities between the government and Africans at Cape Palmas reached Monrovia on January 6, 1857. Samuel Ford McGill, familiar with the tension that had always existed between the colonists and bordering tribes and dubious that the settlement would long survive without foreign assistance, embarked the next day for Harper. Arriving there on the 10th, he found only 125 fit soldiers. Although all had muskets, one-fourth were not serviceable. There were only six cannon. The government had run out of some ammunition and owned but small quantities of other shot. There was no food surplus in the settlement and the treasury was empty. Once hostilities had broken out, the citizens themselves had run rampant through the farms of their more industrious neighbors, feasting upon or destroying agricultural products which, if carefully used, could have fed the entire population two or three months. The soldiers had slaughtered all unprotected stock on the cape, regardless of ownership, and women and children, with a few male escorts, daily raided outlying cassava fields belonging to the Cape Palmas people.

---

30 *Ibid.*, Gibson to Hall, Harper, Dec. 30, 1856; Drayton to Howard, Harper, Dec. 30, 1857 [*sic*]; "A Proclamation [to the citizens of the Republic of Maryland in Liberia]," Harper, Dec. 20, 1857 [*sic*].

Meanwhile, the homeless Africans, including 800 fighting men, had camped at Sheppard Lake, some four miles to the interior of the Maryland frontier. Though destitute and eager for revenge, they lacked gunpowder to attack their assailants, the colonists.

Peace moves had not progressed far for want of faith in the Drayton administration. As early as December 29 the Africans sent a neutral agent to Harper to arrange a reconciliation. The governor requested that headmen from both tribes confer with him about a treaty. Promised safe conduct, two chiefs appeared before Drayton on January 2. Rather than participating in a negotiated peace, they were presented a three-point ultimatum: (1) the Grahways, numbering about 3,000, were to transplant themselves to Bereby, some sixty miles from the republic; (2) the Cape Palmas people were to settle across the Cavally River; and (3) both removals were to be accomplished within one week. To insure compliance, the two kings were held hostage. Their insistence that they possessed no means of transporting their people from the cape vicinity, that they lacked provisions for the journey, and that they had no assurance that other tribes would allow them to settle at Bereby and along the Cavally River had no effect.

When the chieftains could get no compromise from Drayton, they appealed to McGill to intercede. He sought to dissuade the governor from aggressive measures but succeeded only in delaying a colonist assault. Finally, on January 19 an expedition of sixty immigrants and 200 Rocktown allies marched to the enemy's encampment on Sheppard Lake. In the ensuing battle the ex-Americans boarded three canoes in order to storm the barricade on one side of the lake, while the Rocktown supporters covered them from the beach. One canoe carrying twenty-six men and a cannon overturned, with complete loss of life and property. Only the Rocktown troops kept the remaining forces from being wiped out. In fact, the panic and confusion accompanying the Marylanders' retreat were such that the whole settlement could have easily been destroyed had the beleaguered Africans continued the battle. Altogether the colonists lost two cannon, all drums and musical instruments, three large canoes, and a quantity of ammunition, muskets, and bayonets.[31]

Undaunted by the loss of men, military equipment, and private property accompanying his efforts to force the Palmas and Grahway peoples from the cape vicinity, Drayton was determined to dislodge them from their position along Sheppard Lake. He estimated that his present troops were competent to hold off any offensive action, but he needed supplies and men if he were to storm the enemy stronghold again. He appealed to President Stephen A. Benson of the Liberian Republic for a loan of ammunition and muskets. Drayton also solicited volunteer corps from Monrovia and an occasional visit from the Liberian government's schooner while the unsettled state of affairs continued.[32]

At this point, Doctor James Hall, on the maiden voyage of the *Mary Caroline Stevens,* arrived in Monrovia. Hearing of events at Cape Palmas from Mrs. Russwurm, who had left about mid-January, Hall was sickened. Two days later, February 5, McGill returned from the Maryland community with news of the recent engagement at Sheppard Lake. He reported the state under martial law and with provisions to last but a few weeks. The triumphant Africans had hemmed in the settlement and were picking off any man so foolish as to leave Harper in search of food.

Drayton's appeal to the republic came at an inopportune time for it to render assistance. Just the year before the Monrovian government had been forced to conclude an African war at Sinoe, between Capes Mesurado and Palmas, leaving public finances at a low state. Realizing the Liberian legislature's inability to help the Marylanders, Hall offered it a society loan of up to $10,000 to be used in outfitting a military expedition. He stipulated, however, that the money was to be accepted entirely unconditionally, in no way contingent upon the merger of Harper with the Liberian Republic. This was perfectly agree-

---

31 *Ibid.,* McGill to Howard, Harper, Jan. 27, 1857.
32 *Ibid.,* Drayton to S. A. Benson, Harper, Jan. 26, 1857.

able to Benson, who claimed that the republic wanted unification only after mutual consent of the two states.

In a message to the legislature President Benson informed it of the tendered money and urged immediate action to assist the sister state whose history and purpose were so similar to their own. He reminded the lawmakers that they had come to the African continent to establish an asylum for the oppressed black race and to attempt the moral and intellectual improvement of the aborigines. Considering that the Maryland immigrants were the aggressors and had replied to African pleas for conciliation with the threat of their extermination, Benson's remarks were charitable indeed.

On February 6 the legislature authorized the president to form a voluntary militia for the war at Harper. Each recruit was to receive two months' pay in advance, a premium of one town lot, and a hundred acres of farm land in return for his services throughout the hostilities. Benson was permitted, further, to negotiate a $10,000 loan for the military campaign, upon condition that the government of Maryland in Liberia reimburse the republic. The lawmakers agreed to donate a quantity of such war materiel as buckshot, gunpowder, and muskets and to dispatch an armed government vessel to Harper for whatever beneficial purposes it could serve.[33]

In the next few days Monrovia bustled with preparations for the trip. More than a hundred volunteers were obtained. Hall gathered such supplies as food and clothing for the destitute colonists as well as such trade items as tobacco with which to secure rice and cassava from friendly Africans. The *Mary Caroline Stevens* sailed from Monrovia on February 11, anchoring at Cape Palmas on the 16th. Hall noted, erroneously, that it was the twenty-third anniversary of his first arrival there aboard the *Ann*.

---

33 *Ibid.*, Hall to Benson, Monrovia, Feb. 4, 1857; Benson to Hall, Monrovia, Feb. 6, 1857; Benson to Senate and House of Representatives, Executive Department, Monrovia, Feb. 4, 1857; act of the legislature of Republic of Liberia, [Monrovia], Feb. 7, 1857; Liberian Archives, *Minutes of the House, 1848–1859*, Feb. 4–7, 1857; *Minutes of the Senate, 1848—*, Feb. 4–6, 1857.

En route, Joseph J. Roberts, commander of the forces, drew up terms of cooperation with the Marylanders. Two basic propositions were that the Palmas government would be responsible for the expenses incurred by the republic in furnishing aid and that peace talks rather than military offensives were their major objective. Upon landing, he found that Drayton, although civil enough, would neither object nor consent to the proposals. The governor instead appointed seven commissioners, including Hall, to decide upon continuation of the war. This was additional evidence of Drayton's unfitness for office.

Hall concluded that his presence could be of value only in inducing the Africans to try bargaining again. He persuaded Drayton to release the two old chiefs and a young boy held since early January and sent with the boy a message to Yellow Will, an original party to the sale of Cape Palmas, that General Roberts could be trusted in any palaver. The usual dash was sent along to the king. Two hours after the released Africans left Harper, the sound of cannon from the Grebo camp announced their favorable reception of Hall's communication. Convinced that he had done everything within his power to restore peace, Hall left Cape Palmas on February 21. Three days after he reached Monrovia, the English man-of-war *Heckla* returned with Roberts and the troops and with word that the war had been settled. Measures had also been taken for the immediate union of the settlement with the republic as a county.[34]

The principal terms of the peace treaty between the government of Maryland in Liberia and the Cape Palmas and Grahway tribes, collectively known as the Grebo people, were as follows: (1) the Cape Palmas people were to settle at a new interior position along the Hoffman River; (2) the colonists would pay them $1,000 in trade articles for the towns formerly occupied on the cape; (3) the Palmas and Grahway tribes would pay for the burning of Mount Vaughan, return the cannon and drums lost in Sheppard Lake, and allow free trade throughout the territory; (4) the Palmas and Grahway Africans would not re-

---

34 MSCS MSS, *Letters*, vol. XXIII, Hall to Howard, Monrovia, Feb. 3, 1857; Hall to Howard, ship *M. C. Stevens*, Apr. 4, 1857.

taliate against other tribal groups involved in the recent war; and (5) the Grahway, Palmas, and Cavally River peoples would not plunder any shipwrecked vessel along the beach or engage in the slave trade. Other provisions covered peaceful arbitration of disputes among parties in the cape vicinity and promised safety to Cape Palmas people traversing colonist lands.[35]

County annexation was officially applied for after the Maryland colonists unanimously voted their consent and chose three commissioners to draw up conditions for the merger. The resulting petition contained the following proposals: (1) the state of Maryland in Liberia shall be known as the County of Cape Palmas; (2) the county shall have two senators and three representatives in the legislature; (3) stipulations entered into between the colony and the Maryland State Colonization Society in February, 1854, shall remain unimpaired; and (4) all contracts and claims now existing shall be equally binding as if no change had taken place in the government. The commissioners estimated the number of Americo-Liberian inhabitants at 900 and the aboriginal population at 60,000. Annual revenues were listed at $1,800, while current liabilities, mostly incurred during the recent war, were $3,000. Total government assets were placed at $10,000. Far from being a negotiated matter, the overture represented a complete capitulation to Monrovian control. At the same time that the commissioners, including Drayton, submitted their petition for county annexation, they dissolved their government and ceded the public domain and jurisdiction over all property to the republic.[36]

The Liberian legislature convened in an extra session on April 6 to consider the application from Harper. Upon Benson's initiative, the name recommended was County of Maryland instead of County of Cape Palmas. By act of April, 1857, Maryland County was made the fourth territorial division of the Liberian Republic. Although the legislature agreed that the Mary-

---

35 "Treaty of Peace between the Government of Maryland in Liberia and the Grebo People," *Maryland Colonization Journal*, n.s., VIII, no. 24 (May, 1857), 374–75.

36 "Petition for and Terms of County Annexation of Maryland in Liberia to the Republic," *ibid.*, pp. 375–77.

landers should have the two senators stipulated for each county by the Liberian Constitution, it would not alter that document in order to allow Cape Palmas to have more than one representative in the lower house. More delegates could be elected only as increased population in Maryland County enabled it to meet prerequisites for additional legislators. Accordingly, Anthony Wood and Thomas Fuller were elected senators and John Bowen, representative. President Benson reappointed Joseph Gibson superintendent of the Maryland State Colonization Society's property and chose Drayton to be the judge of the Quarterly Court. Most minor elected officials were retained. Monrovia assumed responsibility for all claims against the Cape Palmas government, including the $5,000 expense connected with the African war. Later it asked the Maryland board to release the republic from that loan. Aware that Maryland County would continue a financial drain upon the central government for some years to come, society officers voted to cancel the debt.[37]

37 MSCS MSS, *Letters,* vol. XXIII, Benson to Hall, Monrovia, July 4, 1857; vol. XXIV, Benson to Howard, Monrovia, Aug. 21, 1857; *Records,* vol. IV, meeting of the Board of Managers, Mar. 2, 1858; Liberian Archives, *Minutes of the House, 1848–1859,* Apr. 6–27, 1857; *Minutes of the Senate, 1848—,* Apr. 10–26, 1857.

X

Conclusion

Restoration of peace and incorporation within the Republic of Liberia had beneficial effects upon the Maryland settlers. The threat of complete annihilation by people formerly considered inferior in every respect impressed them sufficiently to override petty differences. The folly of Drayton's imprudent acts enchanced the memory of Russwurm, Prout, and Cassell, now deceased, who, for all their faults, had at least preserved friendly relations with neighboring tribes.

Though Palmas citizens still occasionally spoke contemptibly of the indigenes, turbulences which had so frequently in past years interrupted community life were now absent. The removal of the large African towns from the cape eliminated much of the day-by-day friction that had often ended in violence. Africans and colonists no longer had to traverse each other's property en route to their fields. Immigrant residences were now contiguous and the settlement more compact. Turning their attention to cultivation, citizens had more acreage planted in June, 1857, than at any earlier time in the colony's history.

The great need of the Maryland territory was immigrants, especially men. Repeatedly, the society's African agent, Joseph T. Gibson, asked for large expeditions of suitable males. These failed to materialize. The reason, of course, was the detrimental publicity accorded Cape Palmas by the African war. Whereas Maryland colonizationists had found it difficult to procure emigrants before 1857, thereafter they discovered it impossible. Even American Colonization Society efforts to populate that southern Liberian point were to no avail because prospective colonists had a choice of settlements. Cape Palmas, by virtue of its misfortunes, was considered the least desirable destination.[1]

After 1857 the history of the American-founded settlements upon the African west coast merged. Maryland colonizationists took only superficial interest in their former dependency once it was annexed and no longer a separate entity. Like most Americans of the day, they became immersed in events leading to the Civil War, which, as noted, ended the society's active existence. What efforts were made in later years to recruit emigrants and funds for colonization were done on behalf of the national movement, of which John Latrobe remained president.

Visitors to Cape Palmas made interesting comments upon its progress. Charles W. Thomas, serving as chaplain to the American African Squadron from 1856 to 1858, toured Maryland County after its annexation and was highly complimentary. The cultivation, cleanliness, and industry evident in the settlement surpassed that exhibited in Monrovia, he thought. But, remarking generally about Liberia, he concluded:

> The great obstacle to improvement among all the transplanted people on the coast, has been the idea, brought with them from America, that, when they reached Africa, they would become ladies and gentlemen, and so on, at once; and, oh delectable vision! all without work. Experience . . . has tried to enlighten them on this subject, and, *by hard knocks,* has succeeded in several instances; but there are some hopeless scholars left yet, who, intent upon realizing their dreams, are *going through the motions;* and

1 MSCS MSS, *Letters,* vol. XXIII, J. T. Gibson to James Hall, Harper, June 3, 1857; vol. XXIV, Gibson to Hall, Harper, Aug. 14, 1857, July 14, 1858; *Letter Press Books,* vol. II, Hall to Gibson, Baltimore, Oct. 31, 1857.

I verily believe that, often against the testimony of their stomachs and backs, many have almost persuaded themselves that they are all they expected to be—rich, grand, wise and great. But our hope is in the next generation; and that hope is not without some rational basis.[2]

Alexander M. Cowan, for many years traveling agent for the Kentucky Colonization Society, visited Liberia late in 1857 and touched at all points along the coast. Walking from one end of the Cape Palmas settlement to the other, Cowan saw everywhere evidence of the late war. He did not doubt that it had been wrong, destroying years of effort and bringing great suffering to the colonists. He was surprised, however, to find that citizens, despite their financial embarrassment, still felt above such work as carrying cordwood and paid African women to bring it to their doors. He attributed the general listlessness to the Maryland society's fostering care and charged that Liberia was still sustained by foreign labor. American Colonization Society funds and money expended by various American mission boards, he argued, supported colonists and filled the treasury with indirectly procured revenue. He was especially critical of the republic's discrimination against the nation's original inhabitants. Noting that laws clarified the relationship between Americo-Liberian and African, Cowan deplored the withholding of civil privileges from the latter and concluded that there was no feeling of common brotherhood toward him. In spite of his many criticisms, Cowan still had not the least doubt that Liberia provided the best home for America's blacks.[3]

The observations of these two visitors contained great truth. The Maryland settlement, numbering nearly a thousand souls in 1857, could not stand alone after twenty-odd years of tutelage and expense. It had produced not one genuine leader. Russwurm was an educated mulatto whose American background and Monrovian newspaper experience served him well while

2 Charles W. Thomas, *Adventures and Observations on the West Coast of Africa, and Its Islands* (New York: Derby and Jackson, 1860), pp. 183–86.
3 Alexander M. Cowan, *Liberia, as I Found It, in 1858* (Frankfort, Ky.: A. G. Hodges, 1858), pp. 113–84.

governor of Maryland in Liberia. Cassell had been chosen and trained specifically for a top colonial office but had not lived in Africa long enough even to qualify for the presidency of the Maryland republic in 1854. Prout, elected to that position, came the closest to being a product of the colony, but then he was deposed for drunkenness and inept administration. Drayton was a Baptist missionary come to the colony only in 1849.

The costs attending the Maryland scheme far surpassed visible results. By the end of 1857 the society had expended nearly a half-million dollars in recruiting emigrants and supporting the Cape Palmas community. Given every advantage money could buy, that spark of industry and enterprise necessary for greatness could not be kindled. Most colonists resisted all efforts to create a flourishing settlement of which their benefactors could be proud. The tendency of the ex-American slaves to look down upon the Africans and to enslave them was indicative of their slovenly ways and haughty spirit.

Although society officers maintained a cheerful countenance whenever the colonization subject was raised, they must have wondered at their past proceedings and decisions. In actuality, they should never have fostered independent state action, for it splintered the national movement without correspondingly greater success. To insist that the Washington-based society and the Maryland group were not rivals was nonsense. While the Marylanders staged some remarkable coups in obtaining emigrants—the Tubmans of Georgia being the best example—going it alone was far more detrimental to Maryland success than to parent society activity.

The founding of a separate colony more than 200 miles down the coast from Monrovia was also a mistake. It would have been difficult enough to accomplish the feat with the resources and experience of the American Colonization Society, but to break with that group and to boast of superior planning and methods distracted from the purer motives of colonization. As state action at home reduced the movement's potency, so the existence of two independent colonies in Africa was also divisive. Latrobe should have taken the advice he once offered George McGill—he should have worked at making the first settlement a success before attempting a second. Had a new colony remained imperative, then it should have been founded under parent board auspices.

Measurement of domestic colonization goals against achievements during the twenty-six active years of the Baltimore organization produces a second woeful tale. Although a basic purpose was to alter the state's racial composition and, specifically, to reduce the free Negro population, natural increase and refusal to emigrate spelled total failure. Whereas blacks in 1830 numbered 155,932, of which one-third were free, they totaled 167,131 in 1860 and slightly more than half possessed liberty.[4] Altogether, fewer than 1,200 Marylanders sailed to Liberia under society auspices between 1831 and 1857. The effort to make the state a white sanctuary or at least a free white and slave black society patently miscarried. The colonization movement proved too inconsequential to affect slavery either by removing the hated free black class or by strengthening the bonds of servitude.

Conclusions about colonizationist motives are more difficult to reach. The Maryland legislature whose financial aid was crucial was certainly animated by slave interests. It supported colonization for selfish, evil reasons. How many citizens upheld the cause for similar purposes can never be known. The Baltimore leadership, to the contrary, was genuinely humanitarian and liberal. Moses Sheppard, John Latrobe, and Charles Howard are three examples of society officials who had no slave connections, who deplored slavery in any form, and who considered the Negro capable of the same improvements accomplished by white men. There was a singular absence of racism in Latrobe's public statements and correspondence. Unlike many pre–Civil War polemicists, Latrobe worried about the effect of the white population upon the black once the inevitable emancipation came. It was for this reason that he advocated a Negro refuge.

If, as abolitionists charged, colonization patronage had ex-

---

4 U.S. Bureau of the Census, *Negro Population 1790–1915* (Washington: U.S. Government Printing Office, 1918), p. 57.

tended only as far as ridding Maryland of free blacks, there would never have been the continuing interest in Liberian conditions or the decision to found a new settlement at Cape Palmas. There would have been no effort to endow Maryland in Liberia with workable political and legal instruments. The cynic may claim that society officials abhorred unfavorable reports from Africa merely because these deterred prospective emigrants, but archival records disprove that notion.

Another element in the founding of American colonies along Africa's west coast was the expectation that western political and religious ideas would be thereby conveyed to the benighted "natives." Colonization was considered a means of spreading a superior American civilization. It was the thesis of the white man's burden all over again, but with a special twist—the burden was to be carried by black men. However justifiable this concept may have been, it at least attested to the belief in Negro equality. An assumption of Negro inferiority could not have inspired confidence that the Maryland colony or any other American-sponsored community would disseminate those political and moral principles accepted in the United States. Further, by placing immigrants in charge of society affairs from an early date and encouraging a progressive acceptance of colonial management, colonization leadership demonstrated its faith in Negro capability.

It was the intangible accomplishments of the enterprise that the ordinarily practical Baltimore business and professional men held up to skeptics. Their pride in the establishment of a Negro republic and their part in giving Maryland blacks an opportunity to return to their ancestral home somehow compensated for the unimpressive statistics. If the surface results of Maryland colonization were meager, the outbreak of the Civil War at least sustained supporters in their contention that free and slave populations could not coexist.

Bibliography

SOURCE MATERIALS

Ames, Herman V. *State Documents on Federal Relations*. Philadelphia: University of Pennsylvania, 1911.

Annual Reports of the Board of Managers to the Maryland State Colonization Society. 1835–1846; Feb., 1852; Jan., 1856; Jan., 1858. Baltimore: John D. Toy.

Baltimore Gazette and Daily Advertiser. 1831–1832.

Carey, John L. *Slavery in Maryland Briefly Considered*. Baltimore: John Murphy, 1845.

Constitution and Laws of Maryland in Liberia; with an Appendix of Precedents. 2nd ed. Baltimore: John D. Toy, 1847.

Cowan, Alexander M. *Liberia, as I Found It, in 1858*. Frankfort, Ky.: A. G. Hodges, 1858.

Douglass, Frederick. *My Bondage and My Freedom*. New York: Miller, Orton and Co., 1857.

Garrison, William Lloyd. *The Maryland Scheme of Expatriation Examined*. Boston: Garrison and Knapp, 1834.

Houghton Library. American Board of Commissioners for Foreign Missions Papers.

Jefferson, Thomas. *Writings*. Edited by Paul Leicester Ford. 10 vols. New York: G. P. Putnam's Sons, 1892–1899.

Latrobe, John H. B. *Maryland in Liberia. A History of the Colony Planted by the Maryland State Colonization Society under the Auspices of the State of Maryland, U.S., at Cape Palmas on the South-West Coast of Africa, 1833–1853.* Maryland Historical Society Fund Publication 21. Baltimore: John Murphy, 1885.

Liberia Herald. 1844–1858. Monrovia.

Liberian Archives. *Minutes of the House, 1848–1859.*

―――. *Minutes of the Senate, 1848―.*

Library of Congress. American Colonization Society Papers.

Maryland, Board of Managers for Removing the Free People of Color. *Colonization of the Free Colored Population of Maryland, and of Such Slaves as May Hereafter Become Free. Statement of Facts, for the Use of Those Who Have Not yet Reflected on This Important Subject.* 1832.

―――. *News from Africa. A Collection of Facts, Relating to the Colony in Liberia, for the Information of the Free People of Colour in Maryland.* 1832.

Maryland. *Journal of Proceedings of the House of Delegates.* December Session, 1827–December Session, 1833.

―――. *Journal of Proceedings of the Senate. Report on the Coloured Population,* Appendix. December Session, 1835.

―――. *Laws of Maryland.* 1828–1858.

―――. *Maryland Public Documents.* 1830–1858.

―――. *Report of the Committee upon the Coloured Population, to Which Was Referred an Order of This House, Directing Them to Enquire into the Expediency "of forcing all the Free People of Colour to leave this State within a certain period of time."* Annapolis: Committee on the Coloured Population, 1836.

―――. *Report on the Order Directing an Enquiry as to the Expediency of Repealing the Law of 1831–32, Relating to the Coloured Population.* Annapolis: Committee on the Coloured Population, 1836.

Maryland Colonization Journal. 1835–1858.

Maryland Gazette. 1832.

Maryland Historical Society. "African Colonization. Proceedings of a Meeting of the Friends of African Colonization, Held in the City of Baltimore, on the 17 October, 1827."

―――. *Broadsides,* "Constitution for the Government of the Maryland Auxiliary Society, for Colonizing the Free People of Color of the United States." [1817].

————. *Diary of John Latrobe, August 2, 1833–May 1, 1839.*

————. Maryland State Colonization Society Papers. 1831–1858.

Maryland Republican. 1836.

Maryland State Colonization Society. *Communications from the Board of Managers of the Maryland State Colonization Society, to the President and Members of the Convention Now Assembled in Baltimore, in Reference to Subject of Colonization.* Baltimore: John D. Toy, 1841.

————. *Proceedings against William Lloyd Garrison for a Libel.* Baltimore: William Wooddy, 1847.

National Archives. *African Squadron Letters.* Vols. IV and V (Jan. 5, 1829, to Apr. 25, 1836).

————. *African Squadron Letters: Cruise of Commodore Isaac Mayo, 1853 to June 1, 1855.*

————. *African Squadron Letters: Cruise of Matthew C. Perry, April 10, 1843 to April 29, 1845.*

Niles' Weekly (National) Register. 1830–1849.

Thomas, Charles W. *Adventures and Observations on the West Coast of Africa, and Its Islands.* New York: Derby and Jackson, 1860.

U.S. *Treaties and Other International Acts of the United States of America.* Vol. IV. Edited by Hunter Miller. 6 vols. Washington: U.S. Government Printing Office, 1934.

U.S. Bureau of the Census. *A Century of Population Growth from the First Census of the United States to the Twelfth, 1790–1900.* Washington: U.S. Government Printing Office, 1909.

————. *Fifth Census, 1830.* Washington: Duff Green, 1832.

————. *History and Statistics of the State of Maryland According to the Returns of the Seventh Census of the United States, 1850.* Washington: Gideon and Co., 1852.

————. *Negro Population 1790–1915.* Washington: U.S. Government Printing Office, 1918.

U.S. Catholic Historical Society. "The Mission to Liberia: Diary of the Rev. John Kelly." *Historical Records and Studies,* XIV (1920), 120–53.

SECONDARY WORKS

Baltimore: Past and Present. Baltimore: Richardson and Bennett, 1871.

Bane, Martin J. *The Catholic Story of Liberia.* New York: Declan X. McMullen Co., 1950.

The Biographical Cyclopedia of Representative Men of Maryland and District of Columbia. Baltimore: National Biographical Publishing Co., 1879.

Blake, John B. *Benjamin Waterhouse and the Introduction of Vaccination: A Reappraisal.* Philadelphia: University of Pennsylvania Press, 1957.

Brackett, Jeffrey R. *The Negro in Maryland. A Study of the Institution of Slavery.* Baltimore: Johns Hopkins Press, 1889.

Cordell, Eugene F. *The Medical Annals of Maryland, 1799–1899.* Baltimore: Medical and Chirurgical Faculty of the State of Maryland, 1903.

Craven, Avery O. *Soil Exhaustion as a Factor in the Agricultural History of Virginia and Maryland, 1606–1860.* Urbana: University of Illinois, 1926.

Dyer, Brainerd. "The Persistence of the Idea of Negro Colonization." *Pacific Historical Review,* XII (Mar., 1943), 53–65.

Eaton, Clement. *The Growth of Southern Civilization, 1790–1860.* New York: Harper and Brothers, 1961.

Fox, Early Lee. *The American Colonization Society, 1817–1840.* Johns Hopkins University Studies in Historical and Political Science. Baltimore: Johns Hopkins Press, 1919.

Fyfe, Christopher. *A History of Sierra Leone.* London: Oxford University Press, 1962.

Genovese, Eugene D. *The Political Economy of Slavery.* New York: Random House, 1965.

Glushakov, Abraham D. *A Pictorial History of Maryland Jewry.* Baltimore: Jewish Voice Publishing Co., 1955.

Gray, Lewis Cecil. *History of Agriculture in the Southern United States to 1860.* 2 vols. Washington: Carnegie Institution, 1933.

Hoyt, William D., Jr. "The Papers of the Maryland State Colonization Society." *Maryland Historical Magazine,* XXII (Sept., 1937), 247–71.

Huberich, Charles Henry. *The Political and Legislative History of Liberia.* 2 vols. New York: Central Book Co., 1947.

Koren, Henry J. *The Spiritans: A History of the Congregation of the Holy Ghost*. Pittsburgh: Duquesne University, 1958.

Laughon, Samuel W. "Administrative Problems in Maryland in Liberia—1836–1851." *Journal of Negro History*, XXVI, no. 3 (July, 1941), 325–64.

Scharf, J. Thomas. *History of Maryland*. 3 vols. Reprint. Hatboro, Pa.: Tradition Press, 1967.

Semmes, John Edward. *John H. B. Latrobe and His Times, 1803–1891*. Baltimore: Norman, Remington Co., 1917.

Sherwood, Henry Noble. "Early Negro Deportation Projects." *Mississippi Valley Historical Review*, II, no. 4 (Mar., 1916), 484–508.

Smith, Elbert B. *The Death of Slavery. The United States, 1837–65*. Chicago: University of Chicago Press, 1967.

Spencer, Richard Henry, ed. *Genealogical and Memorial Encyclopedia of the State of Maryland*. 2 vols. New York: American Historical Society, 1919.

Staudenraus, Philip J. *The African Colonization Movement, 1816–1865*. New York: Columbia University Press, 1961.

Tracy, Joseph. *History of the American Board of Commissioners for Foreign Missions*. 2nd ed. rev. New York: M. W. Dodd, 1842.

Wright, James M. *The Free Negro in Maryland, 1634–1860*. Studies in History, Economics & Public Law, vol. XCVII, no. 3. New York: Columbia University, 1921.

Index

The following abbreviations are used: MSCS for Maryland State Colonization Society; ACS for American Colonization Society

A NOTE ON THE AUTHOR

Penelope Campbell is associate professor of history and political science at Agnes Scott College in Decatur, Georgia. She earned her Ph.D. in 1967 from Ohio State University and was the recipient of a Ford Foundation grant in 1958 and a Fulbright grant in 1968. *Maryland in Africa* is her first book.